MARTIN BUBER

Israel and the World

ESSAYS IN A TIME OF CRISIS

SCHOCKEN BOOKS • NEW YORK

Second Edition

First SCHOCKEN PAPERBACK edition 1963

Fourth Printing, 1978

Library of Congress Catalog Card No. 48-9322

Manufactured in the United States of America

Preface

Israel and the World is a discussion of the encounter between the historic spirit of Israel and a world which regards it as foreign, incomprehensible, or irrelevant. Written over a period of about thirty years, the essays in this volume represent a dual attempt: first, to clarify the relation of certain aspects of Jewish thinking and Jewish living to contemporary intellectual movements, and second, to analyze (and refute) those trends within Jewish life which, surrendering to certain current ideologies, tend to weaken the teachings of Israel internally.

With one exception ("Imitatio Dei"), the essays here presented in a slightly abridged form were written to meet the needs of particular moments, and bear the mark of time. Nevertheless, I dare to hope that I have touched on fundamental issues, and that, taken together, the reader will find they form a natural whole.

Let me try to explain what I mean by tracing the history of some of the essays.

More than a quarter of a century ago, at a Zionist congress where I spoke in behalf of an understanding between Jews and Arabs, I made use of a recess in the proceedings to present a detailed argument as to why Zionism—if it is to preserve the significance of "Zion"—must be something different from the concepts of nationalism accepted in our own age (see "Nationalism" in this volume). Eleven years later, not long before Hitler came into power, I was invited to speak at an international meeting of Jewish youth at which "Israel and World Peace" was to be the topic for discussion. My address there supplemented my earlier speech in its most essential aspect by stating that just as Zion, if it is to be Zion, must be built "with justice," so world peace can be brought about only by our realizing peace wherever and to whatever extent it depends on ourselves (see "And If Not Now, When?"). Six years after this, when I had already settled in Palestine, I was to give my first public address to a large gathering in Jerusalem. There I had the privilege of placing this concept within the framework of the history of the Jewish spirit, the history of the relationship between Judaism and Christianity, and the history of anti-Semitism (see "The Spirit of Israel and the World of Today"). And when recently, after nine years of absence from Europe—and what years!—I spoke at a public meeting in London, arranged by the Council for Christians and Jews under the chairmanship of the dean of St. Paul's, I delivered virtually the same lecture with only a few modifications, for all that had happened in the interim had served to make it even more relevant.

To give another example: in 1928 a leading academic institution wanted me to speak on the nature of Jewish faith. In my lecture I pointed out the most essential fact, namely that, according to Jewish faith, the history of mankind as well as the life of the individual is a dialogue with God (see "The Faith of Judaism"). Two years later the Judenmissions-Gesellschaften deutscher Zunge wanted me to explain to them the nature of the Jewish soul. I fell in with this request also, and in this lecture I tried to elucidate one basic idea of my former paper, that of the Jewish striving for redemption (see "The Two Foci of the Jewish Soul"). Another five years later, under the Hitler regime, I gave a public address in Berlin and contrasted this Jewish faith with unleashed paganism (see "The Power of the Spirit"). No wonder that immediately after this lecture the German authorities forbade me to speak publicly; thus again I became conscious of the fact that though the power of the spirit is the hidden kernel of history—its visible husk remains the spirit's lack of power.

And one last example: in 1928 I spoke in Munich to a small group, among whom I particularly remember Thomas Mann. I talked to them about leadership as it appears in the Bible, a form of leadership that is in sharp contrast to what at that time was commonly acknowledged as leadership, and what even today many people, non-Jews as well as Jews, understand by this term (see "Biblical Leadership"). Ten years later, in my introductory lecture at the Hebrew University in Jerusalem, I again seized the opportunity to supplement the ideas I had expressed in Munich, by showing through the figure of Isaiah how the spiritual leader in the Bible stands in relation to the present and the future of his community, to its task and to the ruling trends of his times, which are antagonistic to this task (see "Plato and Isaiah"). Subsequently I was able to add to the contrast I had drawn between Isaiah and Plato, hence between Judaism and Hellenism, by voicing certain ideas on true and false prophets, that is, on conflicting tendencies within Israel, the difference between true and presuming leadership (see "False Prophets").

So it becomes clear that the essays included in this volume combine into a theory representing the teachings of Israel. My presentation aims to point to the reality of this historical moment: out of its distress one can find a way only by rediscovering the eternal, forgotten truth, one of whose rays has entered the teachings of Israel.

Jerusalem, February 1948

Two NEW LECTURES have been added to this edition. The first was delivered at the Jerusalem Ideological Conference of 1957 in answer to an address by David Ben Gurion. The second was presented in New York City in 1958 at a gathering of the American Friends of Ihud. It appears here as subsequently revised for the sake of greater accuracy and clarity. I have sought in both of these essays to elicit from our tradition, as presented in this book, those conclusions which are relevant to the present situation of the Jewish people. Like the earlier ones these more recent essays do not deal with theory. They deal with the more practical task of admonition and warning.

MARTIN BUBER

Jerusalem, May 1963

Table of Contents

III. LEARNING AND EDUCATION

IV. ISRAEL AND THE WORLD

V. NATIONALISM AND ZION

JEWISH RELIGIOSITY

The Faith of Judaism

1. The Way of Faith

My subject is not the religion but only the faith of Judaism. I do not wish to speak to you about cult, ritual, and moral-religious standards, but about faith, and faith taken in its strictest and most serious sense. Not the so-called faith which is a strange mingling of assumptions and cognitions, but that faith which means trust and loyalty. It follows that I do not start from a Jewish theology, but from the actual attitude of faithful Jews from the earliest days down till our own time. Even though I must of necessity use theological concepts when I speak of this realm of faith, I must not for a moment lose sight of the nontheological material from which I draw those concepts: the popular literature, and my own impressions of Jewish life in Eastern Europe—but there is nothing in the East something of which may not be found in the West, as well.

When I refer to this popular material, it often happens that people say to me, "You mean, I take it, hasidism?" That is a question which is natural enough, only it is not primarily hasidism which I have in mind. In hasidism I see merely a concentrated movement, the concentration of all those elements which are to be found in a less condensed form everywhere in Judaism, even in "rabbinic" Judaism. Only, in rabbinic Judaism this movement is not visible in the structure of the community, but holds sway over the inaccessible structure of the personal life. What I am trying to formulate may be called the theologoumena of a popular religion.

It is impossible to trace any one of these theologoumena back to any one epoch; my intention is to present the unity to be found in the changing forms. Religious truths are generally of a dynamic kind; they are truths which cannot be understood on the basis of a cross-section of history, but only when they are seen in the whole line of history, in their unfolding, in the dynamic of their changing forms. The most important testimony to the truth of this conception comes from the way in which these truths clarify and fulfil themselves, and from their struggle for purity. The truth of the history of religion is the growth of the image of God, the *way* of faith. Though my subject does not impose the historical form on me, it is still of the *way* of the Jewish faith that I have to speak.

2. *The Dialogical Situation*

The question has often been raised whether a Jewish dogmatics does or does not exist. The emphasis should rather fall on the question of the relative power of dogma in Judaism. There is no need to prove that there are dogmas, in view of the incorporation of the thirteen articles of faith of Maimonides into the liturgy. But dogma remains of secondary importance. In the religious life of Judaism, primary importance is not given to dogma, but to the remembrance and the expectation of a concrete situation: the encounter of God and men. Dogma can only arise in a situation where detachment is the prevailing attitude to the concrete, lived moment—a state of detachment which easily becomes misunderstood in dogmatics as being superior to the lived moment itself. Whatever is enunciated *in abstracto* in the third person about the divine, on the thither side of the confrontation of I and Thou, is only a projection onto the conceptual construct plane which, though indispensable, proves itself again and again to be unessential.

It is from this point of view that we must regard the problem of so-called monotheism. Israel's experience of the Thou in the direct relationship, the purely singular experience, is so overwhelmingly strong that any notion of a plurality of principles simply cannot arise. Over against this stands "the heathen," the man who *does not recognize* God in his manifestations. Or rather: a man is a heathen to the extent to which he does not recognize God in his manifestations.

The fundamental attitude of the Jews is characterized by the idea of the *yihud,* the "unification," a word which has been repeatedly misunderstood. *Yihud* involves the continually renewed confirmation of the unity of the Divine in the manifold nature of His manifestations, understood in a quite practical way. Again and again this recognition, acknowledgment, and reacknowledgment of the divine unity is brought about through human perception and verification [*Bewaehrung*] in the face of the monstrous contradictions of life, and especially in the face of that primal contradiction which shows itself in multitudinous ways, and which we call the duality of good and evil. But the unification is brought about not to spite these contradictions, but in spirit of love and reconciliation; not by the mere profession of the unification, but by the fulfilment of the profession. Therefore, the unification is contained in no pantheistic theorem, but in the reality of the impossible, in translating the Image into actuality, in the *imitatio Dei*. The mystery behind this fact is fulfilled in martyrdom, in the death with the cry of unity on one's lips, the "Hear, O Israel" which at this point becomes testimony in the most vital sense.

A wise man of the Middle Ages said, "My God, where can I find you, but where can I not find you?" The Eastern European Jewish beggar of today softly and unfalteringly whispers his *Gotenyu* in the trembling and dread of his harshest hour; the pet name is untranslatable, naive, but in its saying it becomes rich in meanings. In both there is the same recognition, the same reacknowledgment of the One.

It is the dialogical situation in which the human being stands that here finds its sublime or childlike expression.

Judaism regards speech as an event which grasps beyond the existence of mankind and the world. In contradiction to the static of the idea of Logos, the Word appears here in its complete dynamic as "that which happens." God's act of creation is speech; but the same is true of each lived moment. The world is given to the human beings who perceive it, and the life of man is itself a giving and receiving. The events that occur to human beings are the great and small, untranslatable but unmistakable signs of their being addressed; what they do and fail to do can be an answer or a failure to answer. Thus the whole history of the world, the hidden, real world history, is a dialogue between God and his creature; a dialogue in which man is a true, legitimate partner, who is entitled and empowered to speak his own independent word out of his own being.

I am far from wishing to contend that the conception and experience of the dialogical situation are confined to Judaism. But I am certain that no other community of human beings has entered with such strength and fervor into this experience as have the Jews.

3. The Human Action

What is presupposed when one is serious about the lived dialogue, regarding the moment as word and answer, is, of course, that one is serious about the appointment of Man to the earth.

In the strongest contrast to the Iranian conception with all its later ramifications, the Jewish conception is that the happenings of this world take place not in the sphere between two principles, light and darkness, or good and evil, but in the sphere between God and men, these mortal, brittle human beings who yet are able to face God and withstand his word.

The so-called evil is fully and as a primary element included in the power of God, who "forms the light, and creates darkness"

(Isa. 45:7). The divine sway is not answered by anything which is evil in itself, but by the individual human beings, through whom alone the so-called evil, the directionless power, can become real evil. Human choice is not a psychological phenomenon but utter reality, which is taken up into the mystery of the One who is. Man is truly free to choose God or to reject him, and to do so not in a relationship of faith which is empty of the content of this world, but in one which contains the full content of the everyday. The "Fall" did not happen once and for all and become an inevitable fate, but it continually happens here and now in all its reality. In spite of all past history, in spite of all his inheritance, every man stands in the naked situation of Adam: to each, the decision is given. It is true that this does not imply that further events are deducible from that decision; it only implies that the human being's choice is that side of reality which concerns him as one called upon to act.

It is only when reality is turned into logic and A and non-A dare no longer dwell together, that we get determinism and indeterminism, a doctrine of predestination and a doctrine of freedom, each excluding the other. According to the logical conception of truth only one of two contraries can be true, but in the reality of life as one lives it they are inseparable. The person who makes a decision knows that his deciding is no self-delusion; the person who has acted knows that he was and is in the hand of God. The unity of the contraries is the mystery at the innermost core of the dialogue.

I said above that "evil" is to be taken only as a primary element; humanly speaking, as passion. Passion is only evil when it remains in the directionless state, when it refuses to be subject to direction, when it will not accept the direction that leads toward God—there is no other direction. In Judaism there recurs again and again in many forms the insight that passion, "the Evil Urge," is simply the elemental force which is the sole origin of the great human works, the holy included. The verse in the Scripture which says that at the end of the last day of creation God allowed himself to see his work "that it was very good" has been taken by tradition to refer to the so-called Evil Urge. Of all the works of creation, it is passion which is the very good, without which man cannot serve God, or truly live. The words, "And thou shalt love the Lord thy God with all thine heart" (Deut. 6:5) are interpreted, "With both thy Urges," with the evil, undirected, elemental, urge, as well as the good, because directed, urge. It is of this so-called Evil Urge that God says to man, "You have made it evil."

Consequently, "inertia" is the root of all evil. The act of decision implies that man is not allowing himself any longer to be carried along on the undirected swirl of passion, but that his whole power is included in the move in the direction for which he has decided—and man can decide only for the direction of God. The evil, then, is only the "shell," the wrapping, the crust of the good, a shell that requires active piercing.

Some time ago a Catholic theologian saw in this conception a "Jewish activism" to which grace is unknown. But it is not so. We are not less serious about grace because we are serious about the human power of deciding, and through decision the soul finds a way which will lead it to grace. Man is here given no complete power; rather, what is stressed is the ordered perspective of human action, an action which we may not limit in advance. It must experience limitation as well as grace in the very process of acting.

The great question which is more and more deeply agitating our age is this: How can we act? Is our action valid in the sight of God, or is its very foundation broken and unwarranted? The question is answered as far as Judaism is concerned by our being serious about the conception that man has been appointed to this world as an originator of events, as a real partner in the real dialogue with God.

This answer implies a refusal to have anything to do with all separate ethics, any concept of ethics as a separate sphere of life, a form of ethics which is all too familiar in the spiritual history of the West. Ethical life has entered into religious life, and cannot be extracted from it. There is no responsibility unless there is One to whom one is responsible, for there is no reply where there is no appeal. In the last resort, "religious life" means concreteness itself, the whole concreteness of life *without reduction,* grasped dialogically, included in the dialogue.

Thus, man has a real start in the dialogue over and over again. However mysteriously, something has been allotted to man, and that something is the beginning. Man cannot finish, and yet he must begin, in the most serious, actual way. This was once stated by a hasid in a somewhat paradoxical interpretation of the first verse of Genesis: " 'In the beginning'—that means: for the sake of the beginning; for the sake of beginning did God create heaven and earth." For the sake of man's beginning; that there might be one who would and should begin to move in the direction of God.

At the end of the tractate of the Mishnah which deals with the Day of Atonement there occurs a great saying, which must be understood in the same way as the hasid understood the words of Genesis. Here Rabbi Akiba is speaking to Israel: "Happy are ye, O Israel. Before whom do ye cleanse yourselves, and who is it who makes you clean? Your Father who is in Heaven." Here both the reality and the insufficiency of man's action are clearly expressed, the reality of man's action and his dependence upon grace. And, pregnant with meaning, the saying ends with words whose origin is a daring scriptural exegesis: "The Lord is the waters of immersion of Israel."

4. *The Turning*

This "beginning" by process of man manifests itself most strongly in the act of the turning. It is usual to call it "repentance," but to do so is a misleading attempt to psychologize; it is better to take the word in its original, literal meaning. For what it refers to is not something which happens in the secret recesses of the soul, showing itself outwardly only in its "consequences" and "effects"; it is something which happens in the immediacy of the reality between man and God. The turning is as little a "psychic" event as is a man's birth or death; it comes upon the whole person, is carried out by the whole person, and does not take place as a man's self-intercourse, but as the plain reality of primal mutuality.

The turning is a human fact, but it is also a world-embracing power. We are told that when God contemplated creating the world, and sat tracing it on a stone, in much the same way as a master-builder draws his ground plan, he saw that the world would have no stability. He then created the turning, and the world had stability. For from that time on, whenever the world was lost in the abyss of its own self, far away from God, the gates of deliverance were open to it.

The turning is the greatest form of "beginning." When God tells man: "Open me the gate of the turning as narrow as the point of a needle, and I shall open it so wide that carriages can enter it"; or when God tells Israel: "Turn to me, and I shall create you anew," the meaning of human beginning becomes clear as never before. By turning, man arises anew as God's child.

When we consider that the turning means something so mighty, we can understand the legend that Adam learned the power to turn from Cain. We can understand the saying which is reminiscent of a New Testament text, but which is quite independent of it, "In the place where those who have turned stand, the perfectly righteous cannot stand." *

Again we see that there is no separate sphere of ethics in Judaism. This, the highest "ethical" moment, is fully received

* Talmud, Berakhot 34 b.

into the dialogical life existing between God and man. The turning is not a return to an earlier "sinless" state; it is the revolution of the whole being—in whose process man is projected onto the way of God. This, ἡ ὁδὸς τοῦ θεοῦ, however, does not merely indicate a way which God enjoins man to follow; it indicates that he, God himself, walks in the person of his *Shekhinah,* his "indwelling," through the history of the world; he takes the way, the fate of the world upon himself. The man who turns finds himself standing in the traces of the living God.

When we remember this, we understand the full, pregnant meaning of the word with which first the Baptist, then Jesus, then the disciples begin their preaching, the word which is falsely rendered by the Greek μετανοεῖτε referring to a spiritual *process,* but which in the original Hebrew or Aramaic idiom cannot have been anything else than that cry of the prophets of old: "Turn ye!" And when we remember this, we can also understand how the following sentence is linked to that beginning of the sermon: "For ἡ βασιλεία τῶν οὐρανῶν is at hand," which, according to the Hebrew or Aramaic usage of the time cannot have meant the "Kingdom of Heaven" in the sense of "another world"; *shamayim,* Heaven, was at that time one of the paraphrases for the name of God; *malkhut shamayim,* ἡ βασιλεία τῶν οὐρανῶν, does not mean the Kingdom of Heaven, but the Kingdom of God, which wills to fulfil itself in the whole of creation, and wills thus to complete creation. The Kingdom of God is at the hand of man, it wills him to grasp and realize it, not through any theurgical act of "violence," but through the turning of the whole being; and not as if he were capable of accomplishing anything through so doing but because the world was created for the sake of his "beginning."

5. *Against Gnosis and Magic*

The two spiritual powers of gnosis and magic, masquerading under the cloak of religion, threaten more than any other powers the insight into the religious reality, into man's dialogical situation. They do not attack religion from the outside; they penetrate into religion, and once inside it, pretend to be its essence. Because Judaism has always had to hold them at bay and to keep separate from them, its struggle has been largely internal. This struggle has often been misunderstood as a fight against myth. But only an abstract-theological monotheism can do without myth, and may even see it as its enemy; living monotheism needs myth, as all religious life needs it, as the specific form in which its central events can be kept safe and lastingly remembered and incorporated.

Israel first confronted gnosis and magic in its two great neighboring cultures: gnosis, the perception of the knowable mystery, in the Babylonian teaching about the stars whose power holds all earthly destinies in custody, which was later to reach its full development in the Iranian doctrine concerning the world-soul imprisoned in the cosmos; and magic, the perception of the domitable mystery, in the Egyptian doctrine that death can be conquered and everlasting salvation attained by the performance of prescribed formulas and gestures.

The tribes of Jacob could only become Israel by disentangling themselves from both gnosis and magic. He who imagines that he knows and holds the mystery fast can no longer face it as his "Thou"; and he who thinks that he can conjure it and utilize it, is unfit for the venture of true mutuality.

The gnostic temptation is answered by "the Instruction," the Torah, with the truly fundamental cry: "The secret things belong unto the Lord our God; but the things that are revealed belong unto us and to our children for ever, that we may do all the words of this instruction" (Deut. 29:28). Revelation does not deal with the mystery of God, but with the life of man. And it deals with the life of man as that which can and should be lived in the face of the mystery of God, and turning toward that mystery, even more, the life of man *is* so lived, when it is his true life.

The magical temptation is confronted with the word of God from out of the burning bush. Moses expected the people in their distress to ask him what was the name of the god as whose messenger he spoke (not, what was the name of the "God of their Fathers"!—[cf. Exod. 3:13]). For according to the usage common to primitive peoples, once they seized the secret of the name, they could conjure the god, and thus coerce him to manifest himself to them and save them. But when Moses voices his scruple as to what reply he should give to the people, God answers him by revealing the sense of the name, for he says explicitly in the first person that which is hidden in the name in the third. Not "I am that I am" as alleged by the metaphysicians—God does not make theological statements—but the answer which his creatures need, and which benefits them: "I shall be there as I there shall be" (Exod. 3:14). That is: you need not conjure me, for I am here, I am with you; but you cannot conjure me, for I am with you time and again in the form in which I choose to be with you time and again; I myself do not anticipate any of my manifestations; you cannot learn to meet me; you meet me, when *you* meet me: "It is not in heaven; that thou shouldst say: 'Who shall go up for us to heaven, and bring it unto us, and make us to hear it that we may do it . . .' Yea, the word is very nigh unto thee, in thy mouth, and in thy heart, that thou mayest do it" (cf. Deut. 30:14).

It is also in the light of its own inner battle against the infiltration of gnosis and magic that the dynamic of later Judaism must be understood, and especially that vexatious Talmud. We can only grasp some of its apparently abstract discussions when we keep in mind this constant double threat to the religious reality, the threat from gnosis taking the form of the late-Iranian teaching of the double principles and the intermediary substances, and the threat from magic taking the form of the Hellenistic practice of theurgy. Both of these amalgamated inside Judaism and became the Kabbalah, that uncannily powerful undertaking by the

Jew to wrest himself free of the concreteness of the dialogical situation.

The Kabbalah was overcome because it was taken just as it was into the primal Jewish conception of the dialogical life. This overcoming of the Kabbalah is the significant work of hasidism. Hasidism caused all intermediary substances to fade before the relationship between God's transcendence, to be named only "the Unlimited," the suspension of all limited being, and his immanence, his "indwelling." The mystery of this relationship is, however, no longer knowable, but is applied directly to the pulsating heart of the human person as the *yihud,* the unification which man must profess and verify [*bewaehren*] in every moment of his life, and in his relationship to all the things of the world. On the other hand, hasidism drains theurgy of its poison, not by attempting to deny the influence of humanity on deity, but by proclaiming that, far above and beyond all formulas and gestures, above all exercises, penances, preparations, and premeditated actions, the hallowing of the whole of the everyday is the one true bearer of the human influence. Thus it dissolves the technique of theurgy, and leaves no "practicable," specific means behind, no means which are valid once and for all and applicable everywhere. In this way hasidism renews the insight into the mutuality where the whole of life is put unreservedly at stake; the insight into the dialogical relationship of the undivided human being to the undivided God in the fulness of this earthly present, with its unforeseeable, ever changing and ever new situations; the insight into that differentiation between "secret" and "revelation," and the union of both in that unknowable but ever to be experienced "I shall be there"; the insight into the reality of the divine-human meeting.

Gnosis misunderstands that meeting; magic offends it. The meaning of revelation is that it is to be prepared; hasidism interprets that revelation is to be prepared in the whole reality of human life.

6. *The Triad of World Time*

The insight which Judaism has with regard to the dialogical situation, or rather the fact that it is completely imbued with the dialogical situation, gives Judaism its indestructible knowledge of the threefold chord in the triad of time: creation, revelation, redemption.

Within early Christianity the Gospel according to John was the first to try to substitute a duad for the triad by weaving revelation and redemption into one. The light which shone in darkness and was not received by the darkness, the light enlightening the whole man, which comes into the world—that light is at the same time revelation and redemption; by his coming into the world God reveals himself, and the soul is redeemed. The Old Testament shrinks into a prologue to the New Testament.

Marcion went further: he tried to substitute a monad for the duad by banishing creation from religious reality; he tore God the Creator apart from God the Redeemer, and declared that the former was not worthy of being adored. The "alien" God, who reveals himself in redeeming the world, redeems the soul from the cosmos and simultaneously from the cosmos' builder, who becomes the merely "righteous"—not "good"—God of the Jews, the demiurge, the lawgiver, the sham god of this aeon. The Old Testament was rejected as being anti-God.

Marcion's work has not been accepted by the Church, which has indeed fought a great battle against it. The extent to which Marcion's influence has persisted in Christian thought, however, is shown by Adolf von Harnack's Marcionizing thesis, which is only one of many evidences. In his thesis Harnack stamps the "preservation" of the Old Testament in Protestantism as a canonical document as "the consequence of religious and ecclesiastical paralysis." But more would be gained with the victory of this thesis than the separation of two books, and the profanation of one for Christendom: man would be cut off from his origin, the world would lose its history of creation, and with that its creaturely character; or creation would itself become the Fall. Existence would be divided not only cosmologically, but in the last resort it would be divided religiously beyond possibility of redress into a "world" of matter and moral law, and an overworld of spirit and love. Here the Iranian teaching of dual principles reaches its Western completion, and the duality of man, estranged from his natural, vitally trustful faith, finds its theological sanction. No longer does redemption crown the work of creation; redemption vanquishes creation. The world *as such* can no longer become the Kingdom of God. "The Unknown" who is worshipped at this point is the spirit of *reduction*.

For the Western peoples such an issue would only have meant a threat of disintegration; for Judaism it would have meant certain dissolution. What saved Judaism is not, as the Marcionites imagine, the fact that it failed to experience "the tragedy," the contradiction in the world's process, deeply enough; but rather that it experienced that "tragedy" in the dialogical situation, which means that it experienced *the contradiction as theophany*. This very world, this very contradiction, unabridged, unmitigated, unsmoothed, unsimplified, unreduced, this world shall be—not overcome—but consummated. It shall be consummated in the Kingdom, for it is that world, and no other, with all its contrariety, in which the Kingdom is a latency such that every reduction would only hinder its consummation, while every unification of contraries would prepare it. It is a redemption not from the evil, but of the evil, as the power which God created for his service and for the performance of his work.

If it is true that the whole world, all the world process, the whole time of the world, unsubtracted, stands in the dialogical situation; if it is true that the history of the world is a real dialogue between God and his creature—then the triad, as which that history is perceived, becomes not a man-made device for his own orientation, but actual reality itself. What comes to us out of the abyss of origin and into the sphere of our uncomprehending grasp and our stammering narrative, is God's cry of creation into the void. Silence still lies brooding before him, but soon things begin to rise and give answer—their very coming into existence is answer. When God blesses his creatures and gives them their appointed work, revelation has begun; for revelation is nothing else than the relation between giving and receiving, which means that it is also the relation between desiring to give and failing to receive. Revelation lasts until the turning creature answers and his answer is accepted by God's redeeming grace. Then the unity emerges, formed out of the very elements of contrariety, to establish amidst all the undiminished multiplicity and manifoldness the communion of creatures in the name of God and before his face.

Just as God's cry of creation does not call to the soul, but to the wholeness of things, as revelation does not empower and require the soul, but all of the human being—so it is not the soul, but the whole of the world, which is meant to be redeemed in the redemption. Man stands created, a whole body, ensouled by his relation to the created, enspirited by his relation to the Creator. It is to the whole man, in this unity of body, soul, and spirit, that the Lord of Revelation comes and upon whom he lays his message. So it is not only with his thought and his feelings, but with the sole of his foot and the tip of his finger as well, that he may receive the sign-language of the reality taking place. The redemption must take place in the whole corporeal life. God the Creator wills to consummate nothing less than the whole of his creation; God the Revealer wills to actualize nothing less than the whole of his revelation; God the Redeemer wills to draw into his arms nothing less than the all in need of redemption.

The Two Foci of the Jewish Soul

[AN ADDRESS DELIVERED IN 1930]

You have asked me to speak to you about the soul of Judaism. I have complied with this request, although I am against the cause for which you hold your conference, and I am against it not "just as a Jew," but also truly as a Jew, that is, as one who waits for the Kingdom of God, the Kingdom of Unification, and who regards all such "missions" as yours as springing from a misunderstanding of the nature of that kingdom, and as a hindrance to its coming. If in spite of this I have accepted your invitation, it is because I believe that when one is invited to share one's knowledge, one should not ask, "Why have you invited me?" but should share what one knows as well as one can—and that is my intention.

There is however one essential branch of Judaism about which I do not feel myself called upon to speak before you, and that is "the Law." My point of view with regard to this subject diverges from the traditional one; it is not a-nomistic, but neither is it entirely nomistic. For that reason I ought attempt neither to represent tradition, nor to substitute my own personal standpoint for the information you have desired of me. Besides, the problem of the Law does not seem to me to belong at all to the subject with which I have to deal. It would be a different matter were it my duty to present the teaching of Judaism. For the teaching of Judaism comes from Sinai; it is Moses' teaching. But the *soul* of Judaism is pre-Sinaitic; it is the soul which approached Sinai, and there received what it did receive; it is older than Moses; it is patriarchal, Abraham's soul, or more truly, since it concerns the *product* of a primordial age, it is Jacob's soul. The Law put on the soul and the soul can never again be understood outside of the Law; yet the soul itself is not of the Law. If one wishes to speak of the soul of Judaism, one must consider all the transformation it underwent through the ages till this very day; but one must never forget that in every one of its stages the soul has remained the same, and gone on in the same way.

This qualification, however, only makes the task more difficult. "I should wish to show you Judaism from the inside," wrote Franz Rosenzweig in 1916 to a Christian friend of Jewish descent, "in the same 'hymnal' way as you can show Christianity to me, the outsider; but the very reasons which make it possible for you to do so make it impossible for me. The soul of Christianity may be found in its outward expressions; Judaism wears a hard protective outer shell and one can speak about its soul only if one is within Judaism." * If, therefore, I still venture here to speak about the soul of Judaism from the outside, it is only because I do not intend to give an account of that soul, but only some indication of its fundamental attitude.

It is not necessary for me to labor the point that this fundamental attitude is nothing else than the attitude of faith, viewed from its human side. "Faith," however, should not be taken in the sense given to it in the Epistle to the Hebrews, as faith that God exists. That has never been doubted by Jacob's soul. In proclaiming its faith, its *emunah,* the soul only proclaimed that it put its trust in the everlasting God, *that he would be present* to the soul, as had been the experience of the patriarchs, and that it was entrusting itself to him, who was present. The German romantic philosopher Franz Baader did justice to the depth of Israel's faith relationship when he defined faith as "a pledge of faith,† that is, as a tying of oneself, a betrothing of oneself, an entering into a covenant."

The fealty of the Jew is the substance of his soul. The living

* Franz Rosenzweig, "Judentum und Christentum," appendix to *Briefe,* Berlin 1935.

† Baader assumes that the German *Glaube* (faith) is derived from *geloben* (to pledge).

God to whom he has pledged himself appears in infinite manifestations in the infinite variety of things and events; and this acts both as an incentive and as a steadying influence upon those who owe him allegiance. In the abundance of his manifestations they can ever and again recognize the One to whom they have entrusted themselves and pledged their faith. The crucial word which God himself spoke of this rediscovery of his presence was spoken to Moses from the midst of the burning bush: "I shall be there as I there shall be" (Exod. 3:14). He is ever present to his creature, but always in the form peculiar to that moment, so that the spirit of man cannot foretell in the garment of what existence and what situation God will manifest himself. It is for man to recognize him in each of his garments. I cannot straightaway call any man a pagan; I know only of the pagan in man. But insofar as there is any paganism, it does not consist in not discerning God, but in not recognizing him as ever the same; the Jewish in man, on the contrary, seems to me to be the ever renewed rediscernment of God.

I shall therefore speak to you about the Jewish soul by making a few references to its fundamental attitude; I shall regard it as being the concretion of this human element in a national form, and consider it as the nation-shaped instrument of such a fealty and rediscernment.

I see the soul of Judaism as elliptically turning round two centers.

One center of the Jewish soul is the primeval experience that God is wholly raised above man, that he is beyond the grasp of man, and yet that he is present in an immediate relationship with these human beings who are absolutely incommensurable with him, and that he faces them. To know both these things at the same time, so that they cannot be separated, constitutes the living core of every believing Jewish soul; to know both, "God in heaven," that is, in complete hiddenness, and man "on earth," that is, in the fragmentation of the world of his senses and his understanding; God in the perfection and incomprehensibility of his being, and man in the abysmal contradiction of this strange existence from birth to death—and between both, immediacy!

The pious Jews of pre-Christian times called their God "Father"; and when the naively pious Jew in Eastern Europe uses that name today, he does not repeat something which he has learned, but he expresses a realization which he has come upon himself of the fatherhood of God and the sonship of man. It is not as though these men did not know that God is also utterly distant; it is rather that they know at the same time that however far away God is, he is never unrelated to them, and that even the man who is farthest away from God cannot cut himself off from the mutual relationship. In spite of the complete distance between God and man, they know that when God created man he set the mark of his image upon man's brow, and embedded it in man's nature, and that however faint God's mark may become, it can never be entirely wiped out.

According to hasidic legend, when the Baal Shem conjured up the demon Sammael, he showed him this mark on the forehead of his disciples, and when the master bade the conquered demon begone, the latter prayed, "Sons of the living God, permit me to remain a little while to look at the mark of the image of God on your faces." God's real commandment to men is to realize this image.

"Fear of God," accordingly, never means to the Jews that they ought to be afraid of God, but that, trembling, they ought to be aware of his incomprehensibility. The fear of God is the creaturely knowledge of the darkness to which none of our spiritual powers can reach, and out of which God reveals himself. Therefore, "the fear of God" is rightly called "the beginning of knowledge" (Ps. 111:10). It is the dark gate through which man must pass if he is to enter into the love of God. He who wishes to avoid passing through this gate, he who begins to provide himself with a comprehensible God, constructed thus and not otherwise, runs the risk of having to despair of God in view of the actualities of history and life, or of falling into inner falsehood. Only through the fear of God does man enter so deep into the love of God that he cannot again be cast out of it.

But fear of God is just a gate; it is not a house in which one can comfortably settle down—he who should want to live in it in adoration would neglect the performance of the essential commandment. God is incomprehensible, but he can be known through a bond of mutual relationship. God cannot be fathomed by knowledge, but he can be imitated. The life of man who is unlike God can yet be an *imitatio Dei*. "The likeness" is not closed to the "unlike." This is exactly what is meant when the Scripture instructs man to walk in God's way and in his footsteps. Man cannot by his own strength complete any way or any piece of the way, but he can enter on the path, he can take that first step, and again and again that first step. Man cannot "be like unto God," but with all the inadequacy of each of his days, he can follow God at all times, using the capacity he has on that particular day—and if he has used the capacity of that day to the full, he has done enough. This is not a mere act of faith; it is an entering into the life that has to be lived on that day with all the active fulness of a created person. This activity is within man's capacity: uncurtailed and not to be curtailed, the capacity is present through all the generations. God concedes the might to abridge this central property of decision to no primordial "Fall," however far-reaching in its effects, for the intention of God the Creator is mightier than the sin of man. The Jew knows from his knowledge of creation and of creatureliness that there may be burdens inherited from prehistoric and historic times, but that there is no overpowering original sin which could prevent the late-comer from deciding as freely as did Adam; as freely as Adam let God's hand go the late-comer can clasp it. We are dependent on grace; but we do not do God's will when we take it upon ourselves to begin with grace instead of beginning with ourselves. Only our beginning, our having begun, poor as it is, leads us to grace. God made no tools for himself, he needs none; he created for himself a partner in the dialogue of time and one who is capable of holding converse.

In this dialogue God speaks to every man through the life which he gives him again and again. Therefore man can only answer God with the whole of life—with the way in which he lives this given life. The Jewish teaching of the wholeness of life is the other side of the Jewish teaching of the unity of God. Because God bestows not only spirit on man, but the whole of his existence, from its "lowest" to its "highest" levels as well, man can fulfil the obligations of his partnership with God by no spiritual attitude, by no worship, on no sacred upper story; the whole of life is required, every one of its areas and every one of its circumstances. There is no true human share of holiness without the hallowing of the everyday. Whilst Judaism unfolds itself through the history of its faith, and so long as it does unfold itself through that history, it holds out against that "religion" which is an attempt to assign a circumscribed part to God, in order to satisfy him who bespeaks and lays claim to the whole. But this unfolding of Judaism is really an unfolding, and not a metamorphosis.

To clarify our meaning we take the sacrificial cultus as an example. One of the two fundamental elements in biblical animal sacrifice is the sacralization of the natural life: he who slaughters an animal consecrates a part of it to God, and so doing hallows his eating of it. The second fundamental element is the sacramentalization of the complete surrender of life; to this element belong those types of sacrifice in which the person who offers the sacrifice puts his hands on the head of the animal in order to identify himself with it; in doing so he gives physical expression to the thought that he is bringing himself to be sacrificed in the person of the animal. He who performs these sacrifices without having this intention in his soul makes the cult meaningless, yes, absurd; it was against him that the prophets directed their fight against the sacrificial service which had been emptied of its core. In the Judaism of the Diaspora prayer takes the place of sacrifice; but prayer is also offered for the reinstatement of the cult, that is for the return of the holy unity of body and spirit. And in that consummation of Diaspora Judaism which we call hasidic piety, both fundamental elements unite into a new conception which fulfils the original meaning of the cult. When the purified and sanctified man in purity and holiness takes food into himself, eating becomes a sacrifice, the table an altar, and man consecrates himself to the Deity. At that point there is no longer a gulf between the natural and the sacral; at that point there is no longer the need for a substitute; at that point the natural event itself becomes a sacrament.

The Holy strives to include within itself the whole of life. The Law differentiates between the holy and the profane, but the Law desires to lead the way toward the messianic removal of the differentiation, to the all-sanctification. Hasidic piety no longer recognizes anything as simply and irreparably profane: "the profane" is for hasidism only a designation for the not yet sanctified, for that which is to be sanctified. Everything physical, all drives and urges and desires, everything creaturely, is material for sanctification. From the very same passionate powers which, undirected, give rise to evil, when they are turned toward God, the good arises. One does not serve God with the spirit only, but with the whole of his nature, without any subtractions. There is not one realm of the spirit and another of nature; there is only the growing realm of God. God is not spirit, but what we call spirit and what we call nature hail equally from the God who is beyond and equally conditioned by both, and whose kingdom reaches its fulness in the complete unity of spirit and nature.

The second focus of the Jewish soul is the basic consciousness that God's redeeming power is at work everywhere and at all times, but that a state of redemption exists nowhere and never. The Jew experiences as a person what every openhearted human being experiences as a person: the experience, in the hour when he is most utterly forsaken, of a breath from above, the nearness, the touch, the mysterious intimacy of light out of darkness; and the Jew, as part of the world, experiences, perhaps more intensely than any other part, the world's lack of redemption. He feels this lack of redemption against his skin, he tastes it on his tongue, the burden of the unredeemed world lies on him. Because of this almost physical knowledge of his, he *cannot* concede that the redemption has taken place; he knows that it has not. It is true that he can discover prefigurations of redemption in past history, but he always discovers only that mysterious intimacy of light out of darkness which is at work everywhere and at all times; no redemption which is different in kind, none which by its nature would be unique, which would be conclusive for future ages, and which had but to be consummated. Most of all, only through a denial of his own meaning and his own mission would it be possible for him to acknowledge that in a world which still remains unredeemed an anticipation of the redemption had been effected by which the human soul—or rather merely the souls of men who in a specific sense are believers—had been redeemed.

With a strength which original grace has given him, and which none of his historic trials has ever wrested from him, the Jew resists the radical division of soul and world which forms the basis of this conception; he resists the conception of a divine splitting of existence; he resists most passionately the awful notion of a *massa perditionis*. The God in whom he believes has not created the totality in order to let it split apart into one blessed and one damned half. God's eternity is not to be conceived by man; but—and this we Jews know until the moment of our death—there can be no eternity in which *everything* will not be accepted into God's atonement, when God has drawn time back into eternity. Should there however be a stage in the redemption of the world in which redemption is first fulfilled in one *part* of the world, we would derive no claim to redemption from our faith, much less from any other source. "If You do not yet wish to redeem Israel, at any rate redeem the goyim," the rabbi of Koznitz used to pray.

It is possible to argue against me, that there has been after all another eschatalogy in Judaism than that which I have indicated, that the apocalyptic stands beside the prophetic eschatology. It is actually important to make clear to oneself where the difference between the two lies. The prophetic belief about the end of time is in all essentials autochthonous; the apocalyptic belief is in all essentials built up of elements from Iranian dualism. Accordingly, the prophetic promises a consummation of creation, the apocalyptic its abrogation and supersession by another world, completely different in nature; the prophetic allows "the evil" to find the direction that leads toward God, and to enter into the good; the apocalyptic sees good and evil severed forever at the end of days, the good redeemed, the evil unredeemable for all eternity; the prophetic believes that the earth shall be hallowed, the apocalyptic despairs of an earth which it considers to be hopelessly doomed; the prophetic allows God's creative original will to be fulfilled completely; the apocalyptic allows the unfaithful creature power over the Creator, in that the creatures' actions force God to abandon nature. There was a time when it must have seemed uncertain whether the current apocalyptic teaching might not be victorious over the traditional prophetic messianism; if that had happened, it is to be assumed that Judaism would not have outlived its central faith—explicitly or imperceptibly it would have merged with Christianity, which is so strongly influenced by that dualism. During an epoch in which the prophetic was lacking, the Tannaites, early talmudic masters, helped prophetic messianism to triumph over the apocalyptic conception, and in doing so saved Judaism.

Still another important difference separates the two forms of Jewish belief about the end of days. The apocalyptists wished to predict an unalterable immovable future event; they were following Iranian conceptions in this point as well. For, according to the Iranians, history is divided into equal cycles of thousands of years, and the end of the world, the final victory of good over evil, can be predetermined with mathematical accuracy.

Not so the prophets of Israel: They prophesy "for the sake of those who turn." * That is, they do not warn against something which will happen in any case, but against that which will happen if those who are called upon to turn do not.

The Book of Jonah is a clear example of what is meant by prophecy. After Jonah has tried in vain to flee from the task God has given him, he is sent to Nineveh to prophesy its downfall. But Nineveh turns—and God changes its destiny. Jonah is vexed that the word for whose sake the Lord had broken his resistance had been rendered void; if one is forced to prophesy, one's prophecy must stand. But God is of a different opinion; he will employ no soothsayers, but messengers to the souls of men—the souls that are able to decide which way to go, and whose decision is allowed to contribute to the forging of the world's fate. Those who turn co-operate in the redemption of the world.

Man's partnership in the great dialogue finds its highest form of reality at this point. It is not as though any definite act of man could draw grace down from heaven; yet grace answers deed in unpredictable ways, grace unattainable, yet not self-withholding. It is not as though man has to do this or that "to hasten" the redemption of the world—"he that believeth shall not make haste" (Isa. 28:16); yet those who turn co-operate in the redemption of the world. The extent and nature of the participation assigned to the creature remains secret. "Does that mean that God cannot redeem his world without the help of his creatures?" "It means that God does not will to be able to do it." "Has God need of man for his work?" "He wills to have need of man."

He who speaks of activism in this connection misunderstands

* Talmud, Berakhot 34 b.

the mystery. The act is no outward gesture. "The ram's horn," runs an haggadic saying, "which God will blow on that day will have been made from the right horn of the ram which once took Isaac's place as a sacrifice." The "servant" whom God made "a polished shaft" to hide apparently unused in his quiver (Isa. 49:2), the man who is condemned to live in hiding—or rather, not one man, but the type of men to whom this happens generation after generation—the man who is hidden in the shadow of God's hand, who does not "cause his voice to be heard in the street" (Isa. 42:2), he who in darkness suffers for God's sake (*ibid.*)—he it is who has been given as a light for the tribes of the world, that God's "salvation may be unto the end of the earth" (Isa. 49:6).

The mystery of the act, of the human part in preparing the redemption, passes through the darkness of the ages as a mystery of concealment, as a concealment within the person's relation to himself as well, until one day it will come into the open. To the question why according to tradition the Messiah was born on the anniversary of the day of the destruction of Jerusalem, a hasidic rabbi answered: "The power cannot rise, unless it has dwelt in the great concealment.... In the shell of oblivion grows the power of remembrance. That is the power of redemption. On the day of the Destruction the power will be lying at the bottom of the depths and growing. That is why on this day we sit on the ground; that is why on this day we visit the graves; that is why on this day was born the Messiah."

Though robbed of their real names, these two foci of the Jewish soul continue to exist for the "secularized" Jew too, insofar as he has not lost his soul. They are, first, the immediate relationship to the Existent One, and second, the power of atonement at work in an unatoned world. In other words, first, the *non-incarnation* of God who reveals himself to the "flesh" and is present to it in a mutual relationship, and second, the unbroken continuity of human history, which turns toward fulfilment and decision. These two centers constitute the ultimate division between Judaism and Christianity.

We "unify" God, when living and dying we profess his unity; we do not unite ourselves with him. The God in whom we believe, to whom we are pledged, does not unite with human substance on earth. But the very fact that we do not imagine that we can unite with him enables us the more ardently to demand "that the world shall be perfected under the kingship of the Mighty One."

We feel salvation happening; and we feel the unsaved world. No savior with whom a new redeemed history began has appeared to us at any definite point in history. Because we have not been stilled by anything which has happened, we are wholly directed toward the coming of that which is to come.

Thus, though divided from you, we have been attached to you. As Franz Rosenzweig wrote in the letter which I have already quoted: "You who live in an *ecclesia triumphans* need a silent servant to cry to you whenever you believe you *have partaken* of God in bread and wine, 'Lord, remember the last things.' "

What have you and we in common? If we take the question literally, a book and an expectation.

To you the book is a forecourt; to us it is the sanctuary. But in this place we can dwell together, and together listen to the voice that speaks here. That means that we can work together to evoke the buried speech of that voice; together we can redeem the imprisoned living word.

Your expectation is directed toward a second coming, ours to a coming which has not been anticipated by a first. To you the phrasing of world history is determined by one absolute midpoint, the year nought; to us it is an unbroken flow of tones following each other without a pause from their origin to their consummation. But we can wait for the advent of the One together, and there are moments when we may prepare the way before him together.

Pre-messianically our destinies are divided. Now to the Christian the Jew is the incomprehensibly obdurate man, who declines to see what has happened; and to the Jew the Christian is the incomprehensibly daring man, who affirms in an unredeemed world that its redemption has been accomplished. This is a gulf which no human power can bridge. But it does not prevent the common watch for a unity to come to us from God, which, soaring above all of your imagination and all of ours, affirms and denies, denies and affirms what you hold and what we hold, and which replaces all the creedal truths of earth by the ontological truth of heaven which is one.

It behooves both you and us to hold inviolably fast to our own true faith, that is to our own deepest relationship to truth. It behooves both of us to show a religious respect for the true faith of the other. This is not what is called "tolerance," our task is not to tolerate each other's waywardness but to acknowledge the real relationship in which both stand to the truth. Whenever we both, Christian and Jew, care more for God himself than for our images of God, we are united in the feeling that our Father's house is differently constructed than our human models take it to be.

The Prejudices of Youth

[FROM A SPEECH DELIVERED IN 1937]

YOUNG PEOPLE are apt to think that prejudices are something peculiar to age, and that they themselves are unbiased and free from all prejudice. But this is not so. Prejudices are judgments formed previous to experience, which provides the only possible basis for judgment. We should therefore be tempted to assume that since old people have sufficient experience, they must have no prejudices. Unfortunately, however, the judgments which spring from the soil of experience very often petrify and prevent the individual from having new and stirring experiences which might beget new and honest judgments.

What of youth? In spite of their hunger for experience, young people nowadays seem to fend off "getting experience." At the very outset they passionately take sides in an issue. They make their choice vehemently and passionately, seize on something and clutch it to themselves as though it were not petrified matter but molten stuff which they want to keep from hardening. Just because they want to nurse the glow, they resist comparing judgments made at an earlier time with new and different experiences. They do not want to have experiences which might contradict or lay their emotional concepts open to question. They wish to experience only what will confirm them in their "position."

Prejudices are not necessarily bad. There are some which strengthen the individual and still leave him with an open mind, so that while he takes a very definite stand, he is not shut off from the world. But there are prejudices which lock a man out of the world, and keep him from admitting anything new. Such a man is already "taken." The one thing which has become clearer and clearer to me in the course of my life is that keeping an open mind is of the utmost importance. The right kind of openness is the most precious human possession. I said, the right kind of openness. One can take a certain stand and hold to it passionately but one must remain open to the whole world, see what there is to see, experience what experience offers, and include all of experience in the effectuation of whatever cause one has decided for. Though constantly changing, our stand will yet remain true to itself, but deepened by an insight which grows more and more true to reality. We need to take a firm stand, but we also need to feel that we have not thus put our feet in shackles. Wherever we stand, we should stand free and unbiased and grow aware of the world.

History

The prejudice youth in general and our younger generation in particular have against history is an excellent illustration of how prejudices may be good and bad at the same time. Young people like to assume that the world begins with them. "What the old folks have done is nothing but patchwork. We'll do it differently." There is something fine and fruitful about this point of view. In order to accomplish anything, youth must have faith in itself. But the very same prejudice can become a dangerous stumbling block to a generation which in consequence of this prejudice rejects the effects of past history, and the forces that have produced this generation. This prejudice prevents the living stream of tradition from entering their souls. When this occurs, they are diverted from the eternal values they were to represent and incarnate in this era in their own particular way. Their urge to realization is severed from the primal reality of being itself. True, every new generation is a link in the great chain, and every new ring must be white-hot in the passion of its new existence before it can be welded to the chain as a new link. But both: the passion for a new beginning and the ability to join as a link in the chain, must go together. Youth must have the essential knowledge that the generations which produced them are within them, and that whatever new thing they accomplish draws its real significance from that fact.

Spirit

The prejudices I am discussing with you are common to the whole contemporary younger generation. But when they appear among our people, every one of them is especially grave and ominous, because in our case everything is different, more weighty, more dangerous, more pregnant with consequences. The reason for this is that we are the least stable of all peoples.

That is why I am deeply distressed to find a great number of our young people sharing a prejudice against spirituality—even though I quite understand how this came about. It is not difficult to comprehend why many now guard themselves against having faith or confidence in the spirit. For during the past decades the race of man has not, by and large, fared well at the hands of the spirit. For the spirit was not simply silent; it spoke falsely at junctures when it should have had an important voice in history, when it should have told the truth about what was being done or not being done to those who were making or seemed to be making history. On frequent occasions the spirit consented to be a tool when it should have acted on its own in the capacity of judge and censor. Then again, it has repeatedly retired to a magnificent isolated kingdom of its own, poised high above the world in the realm of circling ideas. Whenever the spirit has done so, it has sacrificed the very factor which makes it legitimate, particularly in crises: its readiness to expose itself to reality, to prove and express itself in reality.

But should the spirit resign, simply because it has wronged our era? The situation reminds me of the old story of the king and the evil spirit.* One day it came to pass that the king was dethroned and driven into the wilderness. On the throne sat a demon who wore the royal robes and was so like the king in appearance and behavior that no one doubted it was the king himself. But no matter what shape the devil assumes he cannot stop being a devil, and the subjects found it harder and harder and more and more painful to witness the doings of their king. At last they rebelled and refused to obey him at all. But it did not occur to any of them that a person who did such things could not possibly be the king, and that they should set out and search for the true king who, during all this time, was in the wilderness and had nowhere to lay his head.

It is of course not easy to think of the right thing to do in a situation of this kind; but that is how it is with the spirit, too. The actions attributed to the spirit were performed by a counterfeit spirit, which looked like the true spirit and managed to deceive a good many people. The practical application of the tale is not to deny the spirit, but to turn from the false to the true king. If he cannot be found—set forth into the wilderness and search for him.

That is the gist of the prejudice against the spirit. Others may sometimes try to get along without the spirit and still not run the danger of losing their life. But if we Jews undertook to imitate them, we should lose ourselves. If we stop believing in the power of the spirit, and helping it, we destroy the foundation of our existence and our right to existence: we sacrifice our vocation and our future.

* I am not giving this story of Solomon and Asmodeus in the well-known version of the Haggadah, but in the way my grandmother told me when I was a child.

Truth

The prejudice against truth follows on the heels of the prejudice against spirit. It is connected with a theory which won more and more converts in the course of the last quarter of a century, the theory that truth is relative. Applied to everyday life, this theory implies that there is no definitive truth for mankind, but only a special something for every individual which he regards as the truth, but which is wholly determined by his own psychic constitution and by the social environment in which he grew up. According to this theory, a man is conditioned by various external and internal circumstances, and these conditionally enter into his concept of the truth, and what he terms true. This theory is both right and wrong. It would be quite absurd to regard the individual as a vessel which is to hold one general truth. The individual can most certainly think, and know, and express himself only on the basis of his own particular being. Certainly, we are dependent in manifold ways both on the social stratum in which we move, and on the psychic strata within ourselves. But the strangest thing about us human beings is that our life is interspersed with volcanic hours in which all is topsy-turvy and an outburst takes place. We suddenly find it intolerable to be hedged about by the conditional; we break out and reach into the darkness with both hands in search of unconditional truth, of a truth which is not conditioned by our character and environment. We court this truth; we struggle for it. Certainly, even then we do not own it, certainly, we cannot rid ourselves of the conditional which is our destiny. And yet something is changed. Something unconditional has invaded our conditional state and pervaded it. Something which we were unable to think up to this point has become both thinkable and sayable, and this "something" belongs to that series of unpredictable things which renew the world. That which leads to decisions and alters directions is the outburst of the individual in the encounter with truth. It is the soul's continual rebirth both in individual man and in mankind. Our era, and our youth along with it, has become estranged from this fundamental fact of our life. The doubt that unconditional truth can be attained causes our era and our youth to exploit the theory of relative truth, i.e., to tend to label "truth" anything which serves one's own purposes, but not even to dream of searching for truth—a search many reject as ludicrous. Last of all, our era is happy to utilize mankind's ancient superstition that there is such a thing as truth.

But what is the real situation? Is there a truth we can possess? Can we appropriate it? There certainly is none we can pick up and put in our pocket. But the individual can have an honest and uncompromising attitude toward the truth; he can have a legitimate relationship to truth and hold and uphold it all his life. A man may serve Truth for seven years and yet another seven and still not win her, but his relationship has become more genuine and true, more and more truth itself. He cannot achieve this relationship to truth without breaking through his conditionality. He cannot shed it altogether; that is never within his power, but he can, at least, sense something of unconditionality—he can breathe its air. From that time on, this *"something of"* will quicken his relationship to the truth. Human truth becomes real when one tries to translate one's relationship to truth into the reality of one's life. And human truth can be communicated only if one throws one's self into the process and answers for it with one's self.

Responsibility

With this I have touched on another subject of the utmost importance: the life of personal responsibility. Another prejudice of youth is directed precisely against such responsibility. This prejudice too is based on a medley of right and wrong, on the just criticism of a form of individualism which regarded the individual as the meaning and goal of the whole, and the disastrously unjust reluctance to recognize the insight that true community among men cannot come into being until each individual accepts full responsibility for the other; particularly, that a crisis in the community, such as that of today, can only be overcome if the individual charges himself with a share in the situation, and discharges it as a personal responsibility. Contemporary man, and unfortunately young men as well as old, evades this demand for steadfastness, escaping into membership in a "collective," for which he needs decide only once and which, from that moment on, relieves him of all further worry about responsibility. Now, so he thinks, he can unconcernedly co-operate toward a common end without having to ask himself whether this or that means to the desired end is really worthy and adequate, or whether an end which was desecrated because it was attained by such means has anything still in common with the end which it was the original hope to achieve. By this I do not mean to say that our younger generation should not work in collectives and in and for groups. On the contrary! Membership in a group need not constitute escape from more and more new and different responsibilities; it can be the place for the truest and most serious responsibility, and its constant test. When the membership is of such a nature, the responsible human being can prove himself more wholly and profoundly there than anywhere else. The individual—and this holds for young and old alike—must be able to belong to his group with passionately active and passionately combative love. At the same time, however, he must refuse to let the power of any slogan coined within the group prevent him from standing up for what is right, for worthy and adequate rather than unworthy and inadequate means. He must have the courage to stand up for true realization and against mere empty accomplishment, and to pledge his entire existence not only to fight the world without in behalf of the just demand of his group, but to fight within the group against false interpretations and applications of that demand, with the whole of his responsible personality.

Spontaneity

The collective is not the only factor which threatens the individual with the loss of personality. His most intimate province, the real content of his personal relationships has become subject to question. I am referring to the prejudice against spontaneity which is cropping up everywhere in the life patterns of the younger generation. This too originated in a well-founded protest against the modern forms of the overestimation of the personal sphere of feeling and the sentimentalizing of life. But with these something of inestimable value has been given up: the unreserved spontaneity between men. A certain impersonality occupies the space between man and man, often begetting a strange distrust even in kindred spirits, an attitude of assumed superiority in a critical appraisal and dismissal of one's fellow which creates a sense of distance in nearness. It has become very rare for one person to open up spontaneously to another. He holds back, observes, calculates, and criticizes. The other no longer is a personal world like myself, a world which I can understand and affirm from the vantage of my own; he is a sum of qualities which are more or less useful to me; he is an aggregate of forces which I regard as excellent or poor prospects for my exploitation. Nothing is substantially changed if the cause in regard to which I weighed his usability is not a personal but a common cause. Even if it is a common cause, let me point out that this impersonal analysis of a comrade makes barren the soil on which the community is based, and destroys the secret of its organic life, which can prosper only when a spontaneous relationship between each and every member can unfold unimpeded. When the innermost possession, personal love itself, is treated as a means to further the mechanism of life, and made subject to it, then what is innermost must die too.

Faith

All the prejudices which I have brought to your attention are, in one way or another, connected with the ultimate or rather with the penultimate prejudice, that against faith. For this, too, there is reason and even some justification in the fact that the religious institutions and procedures which are supposed to be objective expressions of the reality of faith are so often and in so many different ways contrary to true faith and to the truth of faith. They have become stumbling blocks in the path of the true believer; they have placed themselves in opposition to his humble life, and on the side of whatever happens to be powerful and accepted as valid in this world. This error, which is in the foreground of our time, has affected the souls of the generations which grew up in a time of crisis; it has invalidated their faith. Here again, the right has been abandoned along with the wrong. Real faith does not mean professing what we hold true in a ready-made formula. On the contrary: it means holding ourselves open to the unconditional mystery which we encounter in every sphere of our life and which cannot be comprised in any formula. It means that, from the very roots of our being, we should always be prepared to live with this mystery as one being lives with another. Real faith means the ability to endure life in the face of this mystery. The forms in which the mystery approaches us are nothing but our personal experiences. At times it is very difficult to live with the mystery, and to be constant to it in the midst of these ever new, unforeseen, surprising, precipitating and overpowering experiences. But there is something which can help us and there are helpers. There is the living transmission of those who have really lived with the mystery, and above all those who are of our kind and who had our tidings. They help us through the pure strength with which they experienced the mystery, faced it, and engaged their lives to it. For to believe means to engage oneself. I know only too well that all of this past reaches us in the rigid and often conventional form of mechanical religion. But it can be loosened up, and then the way will again open to the vital force of that which has been lived and transmitted to us, back to the life in our Bible. We too can hear the voice ring forth from the black letters.

God

But this brings us to the last and most extreme prejudice, which hides behind the prejudice against faith, the prejudice against God.

There is a story, that during the reign of the emperor Tiberius, people on a ship passing close to Epirus heard a mournful voice from one of the islands which bade the helmsman carry to another coast the tidings that great Pan had died. Men of all eras have heard tidings of the death of gods. But it was reserved for our era to have a philosopher feel called upon to announce that God himself had died. Whether or not we know it, what we really mean when we say that a god is dead is that the images of God vanish, and that therefore an image which up to now was regarded and worshipped as God, can no longer be so regarded and so worshipped. For what we call gods are nothing but images of God and must suffer the fate of such images. But Nietzsche manifestly wished to say something different, and that something different is terribly wrong in a way characteristic of our time. For it means confusing an image, confusing one of the many images of God that are born and perish, with the real God whose reality men could never shake with any one of these images, no matter what forms they might honestly invent for the objects of their particular adoration. Time after time, the images must be broken, the iconoclasts must have their way. For the iconoclast is the soul of man which rebels against having an image that can no longer be believed in, elevated above the heads of man as a thing that demands to be worshipped. In their longing for a god, men try again and again to set up a greater, a more genuine and more just image, which is intended to be more glorious than the last and only proves the more unsatisfactory. The commandment, "Thou shalt not make unto thee an image," means at the same time, "Thou canst not make an image." This does not, of course, refer merely to sculptured or painted images, but to our fantasy, to all the power of our imagination as well. But man is forced time and again to make images, and forced to destroy them when he realizes that he has not succeeded.

The images topple, but the voice is never silenced. "Ye heard the voice of words but ye saw no form" (Deut. 4:12). The voice speaks in the guise of everything that happens, in the guise of all world events; it speaks to the men of all generations, makes demands upon them, and summons them to accept their responsibility. I have pointed out that it is of the utmost importance not to lose one's openness. But to be open means not to shut out the voice—call it what you will. It does not matter what you call it. All that matters is that you hear it.

Judaism

Now, how can you overcome all these unjustified prejudices, which prevent you from hearing the voice? We have seen that every one of them springs from a protest against something distorted, corrupt and decadent, which swells into a revolt which ignores what is original and true and thus rejects the right with the wrong. Therefore right must be distinguished from the wrong. A line must be drawn to separate the false from the genuine and the full reality of the genuine must be sought out and recognized so that it may serve as the material with which to build our lives.

Up to this point I have not spoken expressly of Judaism, but I have had it in mind, and all my general statements have had reference to Judaism in particular. As regards its actual form,

Judaism also is a mixture of the false and the genuine, but as regards its genuine character, we find a great unity of everything genuine and original and pure which we need to overcome our unjustified prejudices; the meaningfulness of history, the sovereignty of spirit, the verifiability of truth, the power of decision ensuing from personal responsibility, the spontaneity between men and—finally—faith as the engagement of one's entire life to the Lord of the one voice, who wishes to be recognized in each of his manifestations. All this is the original tidings of Judaism, and the openness of Jewish people, of Jewish youth, should consist in trying to understand these tidings by tracing them back to their origins. In order to find the great helping power which will aid you to overcome unjustifiable prejudices, you must first strip yourselves of these prejudices wherever they keep you from experiencing the reality and the genuine content of true, eternal Judaism.

The Love of God and the Idea of Deity

[ON HERMANN COHEN]

I.

IN THOSE scribbled lines which seem to cry from his very soul, which Pascal wrote after two ecstatic hours, and which he carried about with him until his death, sewn into the lining of his doublet, we find under the heading *Fire* the note: "God of Abraham, God of Isaac, God of Jacob—not of the philosophers and scholars."

These words represent Pascal's change of heart. He turned, not from a state of being where there is no God to one where there is a God, but from the God of the philosophers to the God of Abraham. Overwhelmed by faith, he no longer knew what to do with the God of the philosophers; that is, with the God who occupies a definite position in a definite system of thought. The God of Abraham, the God in whom Abraham had believed and whom Abraham had loved ("The entire religion of the Jews," remarks Pascal, "consisted only of the love of God"), is not susceptible of introduction into a system of thought precisely because he is God. He is beyond each and every one of those systems, absolutely and by virtue of his nature. What the philosophers describe by the name of God cannot be more than an idea. But God, "the God of Abraham," is not an idea; all ideas are absorbed in him. Nor is that all. If I think even of a state of being in which all ideas are absorbed, and think some philosophic thought about it as an idea—then I am no longer referring to the God of Abraham. The "passion" peculiar to philosophers is, according to a hint dropped by Pascal, pride. They offer humanity their own system in place of God.

"What!" cries Pascal, "the philosophers recognized God and desired not merely that men should love him, but that they should reach their level and then stop!" It is precisely because the philosophers replace him by the image of images, the idea, that they remove themselves and remove the rest of us furthest from him. There is no alternative. One must choose. Pascal chose, during one of those revolutionary moments, when his sickbed prayer was answered: "To be apart from the world, divested of all things, lonely in your Presence, in order to respond to your justice with all the motions of my heart."

Pascal himself, to be sure, was not a philosopher but a mathematician, and it is easier for a mathematician to turn his back on the God of the philosophers than for a philosopher. For the philosopher, if he were really to wish to turn his back on that God, would be compelled to renounce the attempt to include God in his system in any conceptual form. Instead of including God as one theme among others, that is, as the highest theme of all, his philosophy both wholly and in part would be compelled to point toward God, without actually dealing with him. This means that the philosopher would be compelled to recognize and admit the fact that his idea of the Absolute was dissolving at the point where the Absolute *lives;* that it was dissolving at the point where the Absolute is loved; because at that point the Absolute is no longer the "Absolute" about which one may philosophize, but God.

2.

Those who wish clearly to grasp the nature of the endless and hopeless struggle which lay in wait for the philosopher of the critical period should read the very long notes in Kant's unfinished posthumous works, written over a period of seven years during his old age. They reveal a scene of incomparable existential tragedy. Kant calls the principle constituting the transition to the completion of the transcendental philosophy by the name of the "Principle of Transcendental Theology"; here his concern is with the questions, "What is God?" and "Is there a God?"

Kant explains: "The function of transcendental philosophy is still unresolved: Is there a God?" As long as there was no reply to that question, the task of his philosophy was still unfulfilled; at the end of his days, when his spiritual powers were waning, it was "still unresolved." He toiled on at this problem, constantly increasing his efforts, from time to time weaving the answer, yet time and again unraveling the woof. He reached an extreme formulation: "To think Him and to believe in Him is an identical act." Furthermore, "the thought of Him is at one and the same time the belief in Him and his personality." But this faith does not result in God's becoming existent for the philosophy of the philosopher. "God is not an entity outside of me, but merely a thought within me." Or, as Kant says on another occasion, "Merely a moral relation within me."

Nevertheless, He possesses a certain kind of "reality." "God is only an idea of reason, but one possessing the greatest practical internal and external reality." Yet it is obvious that this kind of reality is not adequate to make the thought about God identical with the "belief in Him and his personality." Transcendental philosophy, whose task was to ascertain whether there is a God, finally found itself compelled to state: "It is preposterous to ask whether there is a God."

The contradiction goes even deeper when Kant treats belief from this point of view. He incidentally outlines a fundamental distinction between "to believe God" and "to believe in God." "To believe God" certainly means that God should be the ideational content of one's faith. This is a deduction from the fact that "to believe in God" means in the terminology of Kant, as he himself expressly states, to believe in a living God. To believe in God means, therefore, to stand in a personal relationship to that

God; a relationship in which it is possible to stand only toward a living entity.

This distinction becomes still clearer through Kant's addendum: to believe "not in an entity which is only an idol and is not a personality." It follows that a God who is not a living personality is an idol. Kant comes that close at this point to the "reality" of faith. But he does not permit its validity to stand. His system compels him decisively to restrict what he has said. The same page of manuscript contains the following passage: "The idea of God as a living God is nothing but the inescapable fate of man." But if the idea of God is only that, then it is totally impossible to "believe in God" legitimately; that is, it is impossible to stand in a personal relationship with him. Man, declares the philosopher, is compelled to believe in him the moment he thinks God. But the philosopher is compelled to withdraw the character of truth from this faith, and together with it the character of reality (any reality, that is, which is more than merely psychological). Here, apparently of necessity, that which was decisive for Pascal, as it was for Abraham, is missing; namely, the love of God.

3.

But a philosopher who has been overwhelmed by faith "must" speak of love. Hermann Cohen, the last in the series of great disciples of Kant, is a shining example of a philosopher who has been overwhelmed by faith.

Belief in God was an important point in Cohen's system of thought as early as in his youth, when it interested him as a psychological phenomenon. His explanations of "the origin of the mythology of gods" and of the "poetic act" involved in "god-creating fantasy," contained in his study on "Mythological Conceptions concerning God and Soul" which appeared in 1886 in Steinthal's periodical, *Zeitschrift fuer Voelkerpsychologie,* was an expression of this interest. Faith was there treated as relative to psychological distinction; but in the course of the development of Cohen's philosophical system, faith's status as an independent concept, distinct from knowledge, was to become questionable.

In his "Ethics of Pure Will" (1904), Cohen writes: "God must not become the content of belief, if that belief is to mean something distinct from knowledge." Of the two kinds of belief which Kant distinguishes in his posthumous work, namely, "to believe God" (that is, to introduce the idea of God into a system of knowledge), and "to believe in a living God" (that is, to have a vital relationship to him as a living entity), Cohen rejects the second even more strongly than Kant. In this way he overcomes the "great equivocality" of the word "belief." Whereas Kant saw in the idea of God only the "fate" of the human species, Cohen wishes to "separate the concept of life" from that of God. He finds support for his argument in Maimonides (though he limited the extent of that support three years later, saying that Maimonides had been careful to distinguish between the concept of life when applied to God and the same concept when applied to man; a distinction on the part of Maimonides which entirely differs from Cohen's distinction).

God is an idea for Cohen, as he was for Kant. "We call God an idea," says Cohen, "meaning the center of all ideas, the idea of truth." God is not a personality; as such he only appears "within the confines of myth." And he is no existence at all, neither a natural existence nor a spiritual, "just as in general the idea cannot be linked with the concept of existence." The concept of God is introduced into the structure of ethical thought, because, as the idea of truth, it is instrumental in establishing the unity of nature and morality. This view of God as an idea Cohen regards as "the true religiosity," which can evolve only when every relation involving belief in a living God is shown to be problematical, and nullified. God's only place is within a system of thought. The system defends itself with wonderful vigor against the living God who is bound to undermine its perfection, and even its absolute authority. Cohen, the thinker, defends himself against the belief which, rising out of an ancient heritage, threatened to overwhelm him. He defended himself with success; the success of the system-creator. Cohen has constructed the last home for the God of the philosopher.

And yet Cohen has been overwhelmed by faith in more exemplary fashion than any other of the contemporary philosophers, although his labors to incorporate God into a system were in no way hindered. On the contrary: from that moment his labors turned into a remarkable wrestle with his own experience.

Cohen objectified the results of his succumbing to faith by merging it in his system of concepts. Nowhere in his writings does he directly state it; but the evidence is striking. When was it that the decisive change occurred?

4.

The answer lies in the change that crept into Cohen's way of thinking about the love of God. It was only at a late period that Cohen, who concurrently with the development of his system was treating in a series of essays with the heritage of the Jewish faith, gave an adequate place to the cornerstone of that faith, the love of God, the sole means by which the Jewish faith realized its full and unique value. Only three years after the "Ethics," in his important research into "Religion and Morality," whose formulations, even keener than those of the "Ethics," interdict "interest in the so-called person of God and the so-called living God," declaring that the prophets of Israel "combatted" the direct relation between man and God, do we find a new note about the love of God. "The more that the knowledge of God is simultaneously felt to be love of God, the more passionate becomes the battle for faith, the struggle for the knowledge of God and for the love of God." It is evident that at this point Cohen is beginning to approach the vital character of faith. Yet the love of God still remains something abstract and not given to investigation.

Once again, three years later, Cohen's short essay on "The Love of Religion" begins with the curious sentence, "The love of God is the love of religion," and its first section ends with the no less curious sentence, "The love of God is therefore the knowledge of morality." If we carefully consider the two uses of the word "is," we are able to distinguish a purpose: which is to classify something as yet unclassified but nevertheless obtruding as central; to classify it by a process of identification with something else already comprehended, and thus put it in its place; but that identification does not prove successful. All that is necessary to see this clearly is to compare the above-cited sentences with any one of the biblical verses which enjoin or praise the love of God, which are the origin of that concept. What Cohen is enjoining and praising at this point is something essentially and qualitatively different from the love of religion and the knowledge of morality, although it includes both. Yet in Cohen's revision of his Berlin lectures of 1913–14, published in 1915 under the title, "The Concept of Religion in the System of Philosophy," he gives expression to a love which does away once and for all with that curious "is."

"If I love God," says Cohen (and this use of his of "I" touches the heart of the reader, like every genuine "I" in the work of every genuine philosopher), "then I no longer think him . . ." (and that "no longer" is almost direct testimony) ". . . only the sponsor of earthly morals. . . ." But what? But the avenger of the poor in world history. "It is that avenger of the poor whom I love." And later, to the same effect: "I love in God the father of mankind." At this point "father" means the "shield and aid of the poor," for, "Man is revealed to me in the poor man."

How long a way have we come from the "love of religion"! Yet the new element in Cohen is expressed with even greater clarity and energy: "Therefore shall the love of God exceed all knowledge . . . A man's consciousness is completely filled when he loves God. Therefore, this knowledge, which absorbs all others, is no longer merely knowledge, but love." And it is extremely logical that the biblical commandment to love God is cited and interpreted at this point in the same connection: "I cannot love God without devoting my whole heart (insofar as it lives for the sake of my fellow men), without devoting my entire soul (insofar as it is responsive to all the spiritual trends in the world around me), without devoting all my force to this God (insofar as he has a correlation with man)."

At this point I wish to introduce a concept related, admittedly, not to these sentences of Cohen's, but to another that has a connection with them. Cohen speaks of the paradox "that I have to love man." "Worm that I am," he continues, "consumed by passions, cast as bait for egoism, I must nevertheless love man. If I am able to do so, and so far as I am able to do so, I shall be able to love God." Strong words these, powerful words, yet the lives of many important persons contravert the last sentence. The teaching of the Bible overcomes the paradox in a precisely contrary fashion. The Bible knows that it is impossible to command the love of man. I am incapable of feeling love toward every man, though God himself command me. The Bible does not directly enjoin the love of man, but by using the dative puts it rather in the form of an *act* of love (Lev. 19:18, 34). I must act lovingly toward my *rea,* my "companion" (usually translated "my neighbor"), that is, toward every man with whom I deal in the course of my life, including the *ger,* the "stranger" or "sojourner"; I must bestow the favors of love on him, I must treat him with love as one who is "like unto me." (I must love "to him"; a construction only found in these two verses in the Bible.) I must love him naturally, not merely with superficial gestures but with an essential relationship. It lies within my power to will it, and so I can accept the commandment. It is not my will which gives me the emotion of love toward my "neighbor"—it is my behavior which arouses love within me.

On the other hand, the Torah commands one to love God (Deut. 6:5; 10:12; 11:1); only in that connection does it enjoin heartfelt love of the sojourner who is one's "neighbor" (Deut. 10:19)—because God loves the sojourner. If I love God, in the course of loving him I come to love the one whom God loves, too. I can love God as God from the moment I know him; and Israel, to whom the commandment is addressed, does know him. Thus I can accept the injunction to love my fellow man.

Cohen is, to be sure, actually referring to something else. For now he raises the question whether he should take offense at God's being "only an idea." "Why should I not be able," he replies, "to love ideas? What is man after all but a social idea, and yet I can love him as an individual only through and by virtue of that fact. Therefore, strictly considered, I can only love the social idea of man."

To me, it seems otherwise. Only if and because I love this or that specific man can I elevate my relation to the social idea of man into that emotional relationship involving my whole being which I am entitled to call by the name of love. And what of God? Franz Rosenzweig warned us that Cohen's idea of God should not be taken to mean that God is "only an idea" in Cohen's eyes. The warning is pertinent: Rosenzweig is right to emphasize that an idea for Cohen is not "only an idea." Yet, at the same time, we must not ignore that other "only," whose meaning is quite different indeed in Cohen's phrase, "a God who is only an idea." Let us, if we will, describe our relation to the idea of the beautiful and the idea of the good by the name of love—though in my opinion all this has content and value for the soul only in being rendered concrete and made real. But to love God differs from that relationship in essential quality. He who loves God loves him precisely insofar as he is not "only an idea," and can love him *because* he is not "only an idea." And I permit myself to say that though Cohen indeed thought of God as an idea, Cohen too loved him as—God.

5.

In the great work prepared after "Concept of Religion" and posthumously published under the title of "Religion of Reason, from the Sources of Judaism," Cohen returns to this problem with even greater prominence: "How can one love an idea?"—and replies, "How can one love anything save an idea?" He substantiates his reply by saying, "For even in the love of the senses one loves only the idealized person, only the idea of the person." Yet even if it were correct that in the love of "the senses" (or more correctly, in the love which comprehends sensuality) one loves only the idealized person, that does not at all mean that nothing more than the idea of the person is loved; even the idealized person remains a person, and has not been transformed into an idea. It is only because the person whom I idealize actually exists that I can love the idealization. Even though for Dante it was *la gloriosa donna della mia mente,* yet the decisive fact is that first he saw the real Beatrice, who set the "spirit of life" trembling in him. But does not the motive force which enables and empowers us to idealize a beloved person arise from the deepest substance of that beloved person? Is not the true idealization in the deepest sense a *discovery* of the essential self placed by God in the person whom I love?

"The love of men for God," says Cohen, "is the love of the moral ideal. I can love only the ideal, and I can comprehend the ideal in no other way save by loving it." Even on this level, the very highest for the philosopher who is overwhelmed by faith, he declares what the love of God is, and not what it includes. But man's love for God *is not* love of the moral ideal; it only includes that love. He who loves God only as the moral ideal is bound soon to reach the point of despair at the conduct of the world where, hour after hour, all the principles of his moral idealism are apparently contradicted. Job despairs because God and the moral ideal seem diverse to him. But He who answered

Job out of the tempest is more exalted even than the ideal sphere. He is not the archetype of the ideal, but he contains the archetype. He issues forth the ideal, but does not exhaust himself in the issuing. The unity of God is not the Good; it is the Supergood. God desires that men should follow his revelation, yet at the same time he wishes to be accepted and loved in his deepest concealment. He who loves God loves the ideal and loves God more than the ideal. He knows himself to be loved by God, not by the ideal, not by an idea, but by him exactly whom ideality cannot grasp, namely, by that *absolute personality* we call God. Can this be taken to mean that God "is" a personality? The absolute character of his personality, that paradox of paradoxes, prohibits any such statement. It only means that God loves as a personality and that he wishes to be loved like a personality. And if he was not a person in himself, he, so to speak, became one in creating Man, in order to love man and be loved by him—in order to love me and be loved by me. For, even supposing that ideas can also be loved, the fact remains that people are the only ones who love. Even the philosopher who has been overwhelmed by faith, though he afterward continue to hug his system even more closely than before, and to interpret the love between God and man as the love between an idea and a person—even he, nevertheless, testifies to the existence of a love between God and man that is basically reciprocal. That philosophy too, which, in order to preserve the Being (*esse; Sein*) of God, deprives him of existence (*existentia; Dasein*), indicates however unintentionally the bridge standing indestructibly on the two pillars, one imperishable and the other ever crumbling, God and man.

6.

Cohen once said of Kant, "What is characteristic of his theology is the nonpersonal, spiritualized principle of God, the sublimation of God into an idea." And he adds, "And nothing less than this is the deepest basis of the Jewish idea of God." As far as Kant is concerned, Cohen was correct in this judgment. But throughout Kant's posthumous work we can see emerging every now and then resistance to this sublimation of God into an idea; a sublimation which later even more prominently prevents the linking in Cohen of the idea with the concept of existence.

"Under the concept of God," writes Kant, "Transcendental Philosophy refers to a substance possessing the greatest existence," but he also qualifies God as "the ideal of a substance which we create ourselves." Elsewhere, he writes once again: "The concept of such a being is not that of a substance, that is, of a thing existing independent of other things in my thinking." What we have in these notes, which sometimes appear chaotic, are the records of a suit at law, the last phase which the thought of the idea of God assumes for its thinker, of a suit between the two elements, "idea" and "God," which are contained in the idea of God; a suit which time and again reverts to the same point, until death cuts it short. Cohen set out to put the idea into a sequence so logical as to make it impossible for any impulse to opposition to develop. Even when overwhelmed by faith, Cohen continued the struggle to preserve this sequence. In so doing, he was of the opinion that "the deepest basis of the Jewish idea of God" was on his side. Yet this deepest basis of the Jewish idea of God can be achieved only by plunging into that phrase by which God identified himself to Moses, "I shall be there." * It gives exact expression to the personal "existence" of God (not to his abstract "being"), and expression even to his living presence, which most directly of all his attributes touches the man to whom he manifests himself. The speaker's self-designation as the God of Abraham, God of Isaac, and God of Jacob (Exod. 3:15) is indissolubly united with that manifestation of "I shall be there," and he cannot be reduced to a God of the philosophers.

---

* Exod. 3:14, part of the phrase commonly translated: "I am that I am."

But the man who says, "I love in God the father of mankind" has essentially already renounced the God of the philosophers in his innermost heart, even though he may not confess it to himself. Cohen did not consciously choose between the God of the philosophers and the God of Abraham, rather believing to the last that he could succeed in identifying the two. Yet his inmost heart, that force from which, too, thought derives its vitality, had chosen and decided for him. The identification had failed, and of necessity had to fail. For the idea of God, that masterpiece of man's construction, is only the image of images, the most lofty of all the images by which man imagines the imageless God. It is essentially repugnant to man to recognize this fact, and remain satisfied. For when man learns to love God, he senses an actuality which rises above the idea. Even if he makes the philosopher's great effort to sustain the object of his love as an object of his philosophic thought, the love itself bears witness to the existence of the Beloved.

Imitatio Dei

They imitate God's mercy.

—ARISTEIDES OF ATHENS, ON THE JEWS

1.

IN PLATO'S *Theaetetus* Socrates declares that evil can never vanish from our world. Evil is needed as the opposite of good, and as it has no place with the gods it must dwell with men; this being so, we had better make haste to flee hence. The way of this flight is, however, to become as like God as we can; and that means to become just and pious through knowledge.

It is probably correct to trace this doctrine to the Pythagorean school, to which the phrase "follow after God" is ascribed by the Greek anthologist Stabaeus and of whose founder Jamblichus said that the whole of his and of his disciples' lives was directed toward this "following after God." Plato too repeatedly uses the conception of "following after," as for instance when he says in the *Phaedrus* that only the soul which best follows after God and assimilates to him shall see true being.

We can only fully understand what is meant here by "following after God" and "becoming his likeness" when we recall the Pythagorean conception of metempsychosis as developed by Plato. The soul is a fallen godlike being, which as a punishment for its guilt has been enclosed in the tomb of the body and must migrate through the bodies of animals and men; when the souls purify themselves in the course of their transmigrations and win back their likeness to God, they free themselves from the compulsion to re-enter the corporeal life and enter anew the world of the gods. God is, then, the model of the soul that purifies itself in order to return home.

God—but what kind of god is this? When these philosophers from Pythagoras to Plato say "God," or "the god," what do they mean and whom do they mean? In order to imitate God one must know him—who is he? "Zeus, the great leader in heaven," says Plato in the section of the *Phaedrus* from which I have already quoted. But who is Zeus?

When we put this question to ourselves, the first thing that comes to mind is the gold and ivory statue by Phidias of Zeus with the olive wreath on his head, the goddess of victory standing in his right hand, in his left the many-metalled scepter surmounted by an eagle, and on his mantle animal figures and flowers; the statue which, as Pausanias tells us, the god himself ratified by a roar of thunder in answer to Phidias' prayer.

But whence did Phidias take his conception? Tradition has him answer this question by saying that he kept to the model given in the famous verses of the Iliad (I. 527) in which the sovereign is depicted with his dark brows raising and lowering and the ambrosial locks falling in waves down his immortal head. When one thinks of all the tales in this same Iliad in which Zeus behaves like a raving prehistoric giant rather than like the majestic Olympian, one feels the full power that artistic selection exercised in classical statuary. And one further understands from this that Zeus is the wishful creation of the Greek longing for perfection, accomplished by the elimination of everything inadequate. The imagination, in its struggle to achieve the final shape, tears away from him his original demonic character, such as has survived in the snake-bodied Zeus Ktesios, and, by sloughing off all which does not conform to the desired picture, makes the pure image stand forth clearly. Even before this happened, it is true, the longing for the ideal, finding no fulfilment in plastic forms, expressed itself in the sublime phrase of Aeschylus' *Heliades,* a phrase that utterly dissolves all form and shape: "Zeus is all, and that which rules over all"; and from here the way leads irresistibly on to that complete dissolution of the person, even of the substance itself, which we find in the prayer which Euripides in his *Trojan Women* put into the mouth of the queen of the Trojans, "Whoever you are, O Zeus, you who are hard to espy—necessity of nature or spirit of man, to you I cry!" But sculpture, the truest taskmaster of the Greek idea, defies its destiny, and troubled by what the tragic poets have done, makes the form conclusively visible, and with that imitable. Only then can the Platonic mimesis arise out of the Pythagorean "following after." However "insensuous" Platonism, especially later Platonism, thought to make its god, it cannot pry him loose from the sensuous world of Phidias, wherein form and shape are brought to perfection. The exemplary character of the god, the god in his character as a model to be imitated, remains founded on his figurative character, his character as a plastic representation of the desired. The Greek can only imitate the wish that he himself has given a visible form.

2.

"Be ye therefore followers of God, as most dear children; and walk in love, as Christ also hath loved us," says the Epistle to the Ephesians (V. 1f.) ascribed to the apostle Paul. The imitation of God is for Christianity identical with the imitation of its Founder, who represents to it the Deity in the image of a human being and a human life: so the Gospel of John (XIV. 9) has the Founder himself say: "He that seeth me seeth the Father also." These words, taken together with the repeated call, "Follow me," give the inner meaning of that tendency which is called *imitatio Christi*. It arose in the early days of Christianity, to reach its height more than a thousand years later; it did not however find its mature literary expression until the fifteenth century, and since then its influence has continued only in isolated and solitary lives.

One instance may suffice to illustrate the beginning and one the climax of this tendency. Polycarp, bishop of Smyrna in the first half of the second century, was a man without any outstanding intellectual gifts, but his strength of character and trustworthiness made him appear so important that the great Ignatius wrote to him that the age needed him to reach to God. In his Letter to the Philippians (VIII. 2) Polycarp urges them to be imitators of the patience of Jesus, or rather of his readiness to suffer. The written tradition was not the sole source of Polycarp's knowledge of this quality of Jesus and the deeds that had flowed from it, which he now desired the Philippians to imitate; he had received the knowledge in his youth by mixing with people who had been eyewitnesses of how his Master lived and died.* This knowledge did not merely transform itself in him into a demand on the Philippians—it determined his own living and dying. Of his conduct before his martyrdom we are told † that when the populace in the amphitheater clamored for him to be thrown to the lions, he neither fled nor gave himself up, but proceeded to a farm and waited there "to be betrayed," as he had been told that Jesus did. It is thus not surprising that in describing his death one of his fellow Christians counted him among "the witnesses and imitators." ‡

This tendency reached its consummation in Francis of Assisi. "The imitation of Christ's life of poverty" is the watchword of his order. In the introductory section to the first rule he wrote down for his order, he states that its aim is to follow in the footsteps of Jesus. From the time of his conversion he devoted his own person entirely to this aim, sympathetically participating in the acts and sufferings of Jesus in an utterly immediate way. But the account of his life given in legend shows clearly what had grown out of the tendency to imitation during these thousand years and more. Legend describes the similarity in the appear-

* Irenaeus' account in Eusebius, *Church History,* V. 20.

† *Martyrdom of Polycarp,* I. 2.

‡ Eusebius, *Church History,* IV. 15.

ance of Francis of Assisi and Jesus; it pursues the similarity through great things and small, often to the point of discovering "correspondences" that border on the trivial, finally to culminate in the miracle-stories connected with the stigmatization, in which the imitation of Jesus is bodily expressed. In ways such as these, legend made Francis the *signaculum similitudinis vitae Christi.** In place of the ethico-religious urge to imitate Jesus, we have here a miraculous metamorphosis, a mystical state of "conformatancy" with Jesus is achieved which indeed in individual cases almost verges on the magical; in place of the *Christo conformiter vivere* of Bonaventura, a hundred years later we have the register of the miraculous *conformitates* of Bartholomew of Pisa, whose book *Liber conformitatum* Luther introduced as "the Barefooted Monks' Eulenspiegel and Alcoran."

The core of all Christian imitation is however after all a memory, a remembrance handed down from one generation to the next; the core is in no way damaged by the accretion of myth deposited in the course of the process of transmission. Moreover, it is a question of the remembrance of a life, a human life. This double fact—life and remembrance—makes Christian imitation a complete contrast to Greek imitation. In spite of Plato's indignant remark† about the men of Crete who "follow" Zeus in his more questionable habits, it never occurred to the Greeks to incorporate what their myths told them about their supreme deity into the ideal form which they imitated; indeed, everything mythical had to fall away that the form might become a model; and this was possible, just because the Greeks were not linked to Zeus by a memory. For the Christian that one human life which established him a Christian is the standard and pattern; he does not imitate an image, he imitates a life-history.

This, to be sure, raises a great question all the more insistently: How far can this imitation of a human life be said to be an imi-

* Ubertinus de Casali, *Arbor vitae crucifixae.*

† *Laws,* 636 D.

tation of God? The Church answers this question with the dogma of the Incarnation. Other voices answer us from out of the early Christian communities. The clearest among these seems to be that of Ignatius of Antioch to whom reference has already been made. He writes in his Epistle to the Philadelphians (VII. 2): "Be ye followers of Jesus Christ, as he was a follower of his Father." This reminds one strangely of Paul's words in the First Epistle to the Corinthians (XI. 1): "Be ye followers of me, even as I also am of Christ." The imitation is made easier and possible by intermediary links. We need only transfer ourselves from mediacy to immediacy, from the imitation of Jesus to his imitation of our Father, and we are standing on Jewish soil.

3.

The imitation of God, and of the real God, not of the wishful creation; the imitation, not of a mediator in human form, but of God himself—this is the central paradox of Judaism.

A paradox, for how should man be able to imitate God, the invisible, incomprehensible, unformed, not-to-be-formed? One can only imitate that of which one has an idea—no matter whether it be an idea springing from the imagination or from memory; but as soon as one forms an idea of God, it is no longer he whom one conceives, and an imitation founded on this conception would be no imitation of him.

On what can the imitation of God be based?

The answer given in the Jewish teaching, insofar as we can draw it from the words of the Haggadah, is this: The Jewish teaching is founded on the fact that we are destined to be like Him.

The Midrash * interprets the saying of Moses, "Ye are this day as the stars of heaven for multitude" (Deut. 1:10), by taking the word *rov,* here translated "multitude," in the sense of "Lord,"

* Deut. Rabbah on 1:10.

"Master," and reads, "Today are ye like the stars, but in the time to come ye are destined to be like your Lord." And the Midrash* completes another passage of Deuteronomy (4:4) in still stronger language: "But ye that did cleave unto the Lord your God are alive every one of you this day," is interpreted as: "In this world Israel cleaves unto the Lord, but in the time to come they will be like him."

But has then the world to come, "the world of fulfilment," become so divided from the present world, the world of want, that no bridge of thought can any longer lead from here across to there? It is plainly impossible for us to comprehend that we should be like God; and it is really most comprehensible to us that we are unlike him, in just the way in which such a figurine kneaded out of "the dust of the earth" must be unlike the Creator of all things. How can human effort even in part fill the abyss between that "being like" and this unlikeness?

The teaching, however, does not remain content with the bare promise.

Rabbi Aha was a contemporary of the Emperor Julian; he was that astounding man who at weddings used to set the bride on his shoulder in order that he might thus dance the holy dance with her, and at his death it was said that the stars shone by day. It was this Rabbi Aha who commented on the verse of Psalm 100, "Know ye that the Lord He is God; it is He that hath made us, and we are His" by saying: "He hath made us, and toward him we perfect our souls." †

We perfect our souls "toward" God. "Being like" God is then not something which is unconnected with our earthly life; it is the goal of our life, provided that our life is really a perfecting of our soul "toward" God. And this being so, we may well add that the perfection of a soul is called its being like God, which yet does not mean any equality, but means that this soul has trans-

* Pesikta Rabbati, ed. Friedmann 46 b.

† Gen. Rabbah on 49:29.

lated into reality that likeness to God which was granted it. We perfect our souls "toward" God; this means that each of us who does this makes perfect *his* likeness to God, his *yehida,* his soul, his "only one," his uniqueness *as* God's image.

"For in the image of God made He man." It is on this that the imitation of God is founded. We are destined to be like him, this means we are destined to bring to perfection out of ourselves, in actual life, the image in which we were created, and which we carry in us, that we may—no longer in this life—experience its consummation.

Judaism, which more than any other religion has grasped the seriousness for actual life of the fact that God created man, has also most unequivocally recognized the importance for the life of man of that phrase "in His image." To this fact the saying of Rabbi Akiba bears witness, that saying which we are still far from understanding in all its profundity: "Beloved is man, in that he was created in the image of God. But it was a special act of love that *made it known* to him that he was created in the image of God." * The fact that it has been revealed to us that we are made in his image gives us the incentive to unfold this image, and in doing so to imitate God.

God said, "Let us make man in our own image, after our likeness"; but of the creative act itself it is said, "And God created man in His own image"; the image alone is mentioned here, without the likeness. How are we to understand that? A haggadic interpretation answers our question thus: "In His image alone and not also after His likeness, because the likeness lies in the hand of man." † The "likeness" is the process of becoming like.

The Fall of the first human being consisted in his wanting to reach the likeness intended for him in his creation by other means than by perfecting "the image."

---

* Sayings of the Fathers III, 18.

† Yalkut Reubeni on Gen. 1:27.

"The fundamental reason for the creation of man," says a hasidic book,* "is that he is to make himself as much like his Creator as he can." The book further cites the beautiful saying of Rabbi Hizkiah, the son of Rabbi Hiyya: "Happy are the pious prophets who liken what is formed to him who forms and what is planted to him who plants," † and explains it in the following manner: "They make themselves like their Creator by unifying all their limbs to resemble his unity, and driving all share of evil out of themselves that they may be perfect with the Lord their God . . . That is why God said, 'Let us make man in our image and after our likeness'—out of his love for man he created him in his own image, so that man should be able to make himself like his Creator."

Again the question which we seemed to have mastered rises up before us: How can we imitate God? True, his image has been placed in us, has been outlined in us, and therefore we can be sure that the goal exists, and that it is possible to walk "in the way." But what is "the way"? Have we to fasten our attention on our soul alone, on its hidden image, which we have been commanded to unfold? Or have we a model of what we should unfold and perfect our image into? Is God our model? And yet again: How can he, the unimaginable, be that?

Again the answer is given us by one of the masters of the Talmud, by one who lived after the death of Hadrian and who was a still more astounding man than Rabbi Aha—Abba Shaul. He was a giant in stature, by profession a baker in the house of the Patriarch; he devoted himself beyond everything else to the fulfilment of the religious duty to bury the dead, and he could tell of strange observations he made in this work; he was withal a man of prayer, and interpreted, obviously from very personal experience, the sentence of the Psalm (10:17)—"Lord, Thou hast heard the desire of the humble: Thou wilt strengthen their

* Beer Mayyim Hayyim on Gen. 1:26.

† Midrash Tehillim on 1:1.

heart, Thou wilt cause their ear to attend"—by saying that the granting of the prayer became manifest in the strengthening of the heart. It was he who used to comment on the word of God, "Ye shall be holy; for I the Lord your God am holy," by explaining: "It behooves the royal retinue to imitate the King." * But another of his sayings leads us even deeper into what he conceives *imitatio Dei* to be. He begins with a verse of the song which Moses and all Israel sang when they had passed through the sea: *Zeh eli veanvehu,* which has been rendered: "This is my God, and I will glorify Him." But Abba Shaul takes the contested word *veanvehu* in a different sense: "I will become like unto Him," or "I will make myself like unto Him." † Rashi ‡ explains the reason for this interpretation thus: Abba Shaul resolved the word *veanvehu* into its two component parts, *ani vehu,* and accordingly understood it as "I and He," and said: "I will become like unto Him," or as Rashi expresses it, "I will form myself after Him, I will cleave to his ways." And in fact, Abba Shaul continues: "As He is merciful and gracious, so be thou merciful and gracious."

To imitate God means then to cleave to his ways, to walk in his ways. By these are meant not the ways which God has commanded man as man to walk in, they are really God's own ways. But, yet again, the old question comes back in a new form: How can we walk in his ways? They are past finding out, and we are told that they are not like our ways!

Abba Shaul already indicates the answer in his last words; it is amplified in two explanatory comments on the words of Deuteronomy, which Schechter once called "Israel's book of *imitatio dei.*" It says: " 'To love the Lord your God, to walk in all His ways.' What are the ways of God? Those which He himself proclaimed to Moses: 'God, merciful, gracious, long-suffer-

---

* Sifra on Lev. 19:2.

† Palestinian Talmud, Peah 15 b.

‡ In his comment on Shabbat 133 b.

ing, abundant in lovingkindness and faithfulness.' " * Another saying † is still more explicit: "After the Lord your God shall ye walk" (Deut. 13:5); how should man be able to walk in the footsteps of the Divine Presence? Is it not written (Deut. 4:24): "The Lord thy God is a devouring fire"? But the meaning is: Follow after the *middot,* the "attributes," still better, the modes in which God works as far as these are made known to man. As he clothed the nakedness of the first human beings, as he visited the sick Abraham in the grove at Mamre (where according to tradition Abraham suffered the pangs of circumcision), as he comforted Isaac with his blessing after Abraham's death, until the last act of God in the Pentateuch, when he himself buried Moses—all these are enacted *middot,* visible patterns for man, and the *mitzvot,* the commandments, are *middot* made human. "My handicraft," as the Midrash has God say to Abraham, "is to do good—you have taken up my handicraft." ‡

The secret of God which stood over Job's tent (Job 29:4), before it grew fearfully into his suffering and questioning, can only be fathomed by suffering, not by questioning, and man is equally forbidden to question and to imitate these secret ways of God. But God's handicraft, his revealed way of working, has been opened before us and set up for us as a pattern.

Thus it was not vouchsafed to Moses to see God's "face," but he learned his "ways," which God himself proclaimed, when he passed by before him; and this proclamation God calls the proclamation of his "Name."

But where are the revealed ways of God's working revealed?

Just at the beginning of the wandering through the desert; just at the height of Job's trial; just in the midst of the terror of the other, the incomprehensible, ununderstandable works; just from out of the secret. God does not show mercy and grace alone to us;

* Sifre on Deut. 11:22.

† Talmud, Sotah 14 a.

‡ Gen. Rabbah on 23:19.

it is terrible when his hand falls on us, and what then happens to us does not somehow find a place *beside* mercy and grace, it does not belong to the same category as these: the ultimate does not belong here to the attribute of righteousness—it is beyond all attributes. It is indeed the secret, and it is not for us to enquire into it. But just in this quality of God's is his "handiwork" manifested to us. Only when the secret no longer stands over our tent, but breaks it, do we learn to know God's intercourse with us. And we learn to imitate God.

In the Midst of History

[A THEOLOGICAL NOTE]

AMONG THE various methods of looking at history, not only that of the past, but also that which is happening around us, two are particularly significant in that they consider history from a religious point of view, including it in the universal reality of faith. While this feature is common to both methods of regarding history, they are opposite in all other respects. The one method dominates and is domineering; even those historians whose outlook is completely secular live on its abundance, though they are for the most part not conscious of this. It carries with it the great seal which stamps that which is to be accepted as history. The other is a Cinderella with whom only a few childlike spirits hold converse. At times even a theologian may catch a glimpse of it, and be filled with wonder. But he will find it very easy to forget it. We may call these two methods of looking at history the way of looking at it from above and the way of looking at it from below.

The survey of history "from above" has always been widespread among nations; that of surveying history "from below" is peculiar to Israel. Christendom is the historical meeting place of these two methods of surveying history.

To the survey "from above" history represents God acting through man. Since God is all-powerful, the historical development which comes about through human agency takes place because he endows men with power. These men who "make history" fight for power, maintain and exert it. Their power is delegated to them by God; it is "power of attorney."

To the survey "from below" history is an action which takes

place between God and man—a dialogue of action. In creating his creature, God, who is Omnipotence, gave it freedom of action, by virtue of which it can turn to or from him, and act for or against him. Whatever happens between God and the participant in the dialogue whom he himself has appointed and made independent, is history. Whether a man is powerful or powerless makes no difference in the role he plays in the dialogue of history.

The survey "from above" sees history as a series of successes, every one of which is sponsored by God himself. The fact that a man is successful proves that he is empowered and blessed. Whoever is not successful has visibly been rejected by God. History is a series of seizures of power by the empowered and of their exploitations of victory. The defeated, the unempowered, are nothing but foils. Victory indicates a decision on the part of God, indicates the presence of God. Successes are revelations.

To the survey of history "from below" success is not a mark of ultimate distinction. A man may arrive at power because he has no inhibitions which prevent him from doing away with a fellow creature; but does this really make Hamlet's stepfather more historically worth while than Hamlet?

If history is a dialogue between Deity and mankind, then it may frequently occur that he who cannot fight his way through gives the more legitimate answer, and secretly receives an unemphatic, persistently unrecognized confirmation. And even though God may indeed use powerful men to accomplish the work with which he addresses mankind, the arrows he leaves in his quiver in all their shining strength are in no wise inferior to those he shoots. They are hidden in darkness, yet are not they too doing the work of God—his work that is secret and consists of other and different kinds of actions from those done in public and acclaimed by the world? One man exerts power, and another suffers from this exertion of power. But perhaps he is suffering for the sake of God? Is there not a suffering which God *loves?* Are we not told that the Divine Presence, wandering through history, suffers the darkness and sorrow of the *galut,* of the state of being "cast forth"? God's way through history is not surveyable, like the petty paths of history writers. Not only omnipotence but also all-suffering is God's.

The survey of history "from above" regards authoritative power as something instituted by God. It is true that time and again, from the time of Babylon on to the Western Middle Ages and their aftermath, stress has been laid on the fact that he who rules is not only in God's grace, but also has responsibilities toward him, that grace is not presented to him unconditionally and irrevocably. But how bold are the colors in which grace has been painted, and how pale the wash which depicts the responsibilities! How much more seriously history takes the one than the other! The historical concepts of Greece and of the post-Hellenic era do indeed include the idea of *hybris,* of the arrogant pride which may goad the mighty on to cross the forbidden bounds and cause his downfall. But the cases mentioned are all of notorious collapse, of ultimate failure, while all the *hybris* which did not become apparent in history was never censured.

The survey of history "from below" also regards authoritative power as having been instituted by God, but at the same time believes that that power is exposed to its own problematics. Here "responsibility" is not interpreted as an easy, fluent concept, but as an utterly serious and terrifying actuality. The power God lends a man gives God a claim upon the recipient, which he must satisfy with all he does and does not do. Power is, moreover, authorized by God only to the extent to which man uses it in full awareness of his responsibility. Power is not given, it is only invested. It is a loan which can be revoked if it is not administered according to what is stipulated in the contract. And even if it is not actually revoked, irresponsible power becomes confused and works against itself. The spirit of power that had been lent by the All-powerful turns into that "evil spirit from the Lord" (I Sam. 16:14) which corroded the life of Saul in his later years. Even those potentates who, in Isaiah, are called "the rod of the anger" of God (Isa. 10:5) are broken like rods when they presume to exceed their function of tools (Isa. 10:13 *et seq.*). Where history does not manifest the punishment, as in the case of Sennacherib, legend steps into the picture and tells, for instance, how Nebuchadnezzar was deprived of human understanding and ate grass with the beasts of the field. God carries on his dialogue with the creature to whom he has given power and it must render an account to him stating whether it has used this power in obedience to the given command. But he also carries on a dialogue with that other creature, that which suffers from the abuse of power. God hears its cry and himself renders an account in lieu of the wielder of power. God does not remain fixed "above" like a sun which illuminates the serene brows of the mighty. When Sarah "afflicts" Hagar, her handmaid, He comes down in the shape of a messenger, meets her on her own plane as she flees through the wilderness, and bids her submit to her mistress' "affliction" (Gen. 16:9). This means that she is told not to try to evade the "affliction" which God has "heard," but to suffer it willingly, in the certainty that his promise to her will be fulfilled. Thus, God is not a power, static in a region "above," from whom irresponsible potentates receive continual instalments of authority. When they act contrary to the pact, when they afflict a creature entrusted to their power, and this creature sinks to the ground, then God is no longer up above, but down below, on the ground beside the afflicted. For he is "nigh unto them that are of a broken heart" (Ps. 34:19).

Does this imply that we, of Israel, in our survey "from below" have at all times the potentiality of recognizing the "objective" meaning of the history that is taking place around us, and of making it intelligible to others? Can we judge and distinguish between what is according to, and what is contrary to, the will of God? That is certainly not what it means.

If history is a dialogue between Deity and mankind, we can understand its meaning only when we are the ones who are addressed, and only to the degree to which we render ourselves receptive. We are, then, flatly denied the capacity to judge current history and arrive at the conclusion that "This or that is its true meaning," or "This is what God intends, and that is contrary to God's will." But what we are permitted to know of history comes to this: "This, in one way or another, is history's challenge to me; this is its claim on me; and so this is its meaning as far as I am concerned."

This meaning, however, is not "subjective" in the sense that it originates in my emotion or cerebration, and then is transferred to objective happenings. Rather, it is the meaning I perceive, experience, and hear in reality. The meaning of history is not an idea which I can formulate independent of my personal life. It is only with my personal life that I am able to catch the meaning of history for it is a dialogical meaning.

Whenever Rabbi Levi Yitzhak of Berditchev read the Passover Haggadah and came to the passage about the fourth of the four sons, the one who "does not know how to ask," he always said: "The one who does not know how to ask—is me, Levi Yitzhak of Berditchev. I do not know how to ask you, Lord of the world, and even if I did know it I could never manage to do it. How could I ever venture to ask you why everything happens as it does, why we are driven from one exile to another, why our enemies are allowed to torture us! But in the Haggadah, the father of him who does not know how to ask is told: 'It is for you to open and begin.' This goes back to the Scriptures, where it is written: 'And thou shalt tell thy son' [Exod. 13:8]. And am I not your son, Lord of the world? I do not beg you to reveal to me the secrets of your way—for I could not endure them. But I implore you to reveal to me with great clearness and profundity what this, which is happening at the moment, means to me, what demands it makes upon me, and what you, Lord of the world, wish to tell me through it. Ah, I do not long to know why I suffer, but only if it is for your sake that I am to suffer."

BIBLICAL LIFE

What Are We to Do About the Ten Commandments?

[REPLY TO A CIRCULAR QUESTION]

YOU WANT to know what I think should be done about the Ten Commandments in order to give them a sanction and validity they no longer possess.

In my opinion the historical and present status of the Decalogue derives from a twofold fact.

1) The Ten Commandments are not part of an impersonal codex governing an association of men. They were uttered by an *I* and addressed to a *Thou.* They begin with the *I* and every one of them addresses the *Thou* in person. An *I* "commands" and a *Thou*—every *Thou* who hears this *Thou*—"is commanded."

2) In the Decalogue, the word of Him who issues commands is equipped with no executive power effective on the plane of predictable causality. The word does not enforce its own hearing. Whoever does not wish to respond to the Thou addressed to him can apparently go about his business unimpeded. Though He who speaks the word has power (and the Decalogue presupposes that he had sufficient power to create the heavens and the earth) he has renounced this power of his sufficiently to let every individual actually decide for himself whether he wants to open or close his ears to the voice, and that means whether he wants to choose or reject the I of "I am." He who rejects Him is not struck down by lightning; he who elects Him does not find hidden treasures. Everything seems to remain just as it was. Obviously God does not wish to dispense either medals or prison sentences.

This, then, is the situation in which "faith" finds itself. According to all criteria of predictable causality, the hearing of what there is to hear does not pay. Faith is not a mere business enterprise which involves risk balanced by the possibility of incalculable gain; it is the venture pure and simple, a venture which transcends the law of probability. This holds especially for those hardened believers whose idea about death and what comes after death is that it will all be revealed in due time, but cannot be anticipated by the imagination—not even by "religious" imagination.

Now human society, and by that I mean the living community at any definite period, as far as we can recognize the existence of a common will in its institutions, has at all times had an interest in fostering and keeping the Ten Commandments. It was, to be sure, less interested in those commandments which refer to the relationship to God, but it certainly wants the rest to be kept, because it would not be conducive to the welfare of society if murder, for example, ceased to be a crime and became a vice. To a certain extent this holds even for the prohibition against adultery, at least as long as society believes that it cannot get along without marriage, and indeed it never has gotten along without it, not even in its "primitive" stages of polyandry and polygamy. And as long as society cares about maintaining the connection between generations and transmitting forms and contents in a well-regulated manner, it must respect the command to honor one's parents. The Soviet Union has proven that even a society built up to achieve communistic goals must care about honoring that commandment.

It is understandable that society does not want to base so vital a matter on so insecure a foundation as faith—on wanting or not wanting to hear. So, society has always endeavored to transfer those commands and prohibitions it considered important from the sphere of *"religion"* to that of *"morals,"* to translate them from the language which uses the personal imperative to the impersonal formulation of "musts." Society wishes these commandments to be upheld by public opinion, which can to a certain extent be controlled, rather than by the will of God whose effectiveness cannot be predicted or counted on. But since even the security of opinion is not entirely dependable, the commands and prohibitions are once more transferred, this time to the sphere of "law," i.e., they are translated into the language of if-formulations: "If someone should do this or that, then such and such a thing shall be done to him." And the purpose of the threat of "such and such a thing" is not to limit the freedom of action of the law-breaker, but to punish him. God scorned to regulate the relation between what a man does and what, as a result of his doing, is done to him, by exact mathematical rules, but that is exactly what society attempts. To be sure, society certainly *has* the personnel to carry out its rulings, a personnel which, at least in principle, has well-defined work to perform: the courts, the police, jailers and hangmen. Oddly enough, however, the result is still far from satisfactory. Statistics, for example, do not show that the death penalty has had the effect of diminishing the number of murders.

For the sake of clarity, I have oversimplified the situation. In history, all these processes are far more circumstantial and interconnected. All this is not reprehensible just so long as the "translation" does not claim to be a translation. Plagiarism is legitimate here, but citation is not. Provided society does not insist that the moral and legal forms into which it has transformed the Ten Commandments, that that product which is an I-and-Thou deprived of the I and the Thou, is still the Ten Commandments, its activities are unobjectionable; it is as a matter of fact impossible to imagine how society could exist without them. But nothing of its vast machinery has anything to do with the situation of the human being who in the midst of a personal experience hears and feels himself addressed by the word "thou." "Thou shalt not take the name of the Lord thy God in vain" (Exod. 20:7), or "Thou shalt not bear false witness against thy neighbor" (Exod.

20:13). The vast machinery of society has nothing to do with the situation which prevails between the all-powerful Speaker who avoids exerting his power and him who is spoken to; and it has nothing to do with the daring, catastrophic, redeeming situation of faith. But if society were to have the temerity to pretend that its voiceless morals and its faceless law are really the Word—adapted to the times and extricated from the husk of superstitions and outmoded ideas—something would take place which has not yet happened in the history of mankind. And then it would, perhaps, be too late for society to discover that there is One who rejects jailers and hangmen as executors of his will.

Now, provided you have not given me up as someone who is simply behind the times, but ask me more insistently than before what should be done with the Ten Commandments, I shall reply: Do what I am trying to do myself: to lead up to them. Not to a scroll, not even to the stone tablets on which "the finger of God" (Exod. 31:18) once wrote the commandments, after they had been uttered; but to the Spoken Word.

The Man of Today and the Jewish Bible

Biblia, books, is the name of a book, of a Book composed of many books. It is really one book, for one basic theme unites all the stories and songs, sayings and prophecies contained within it. The theme of the Bible is the encounter between a group of people and the Lord of the world in the course of history, the sequence of events occurring on earth. Either openly or by implication, the stories are reports of encounters. The songs lament the denial of the grace of encounter, plead that it may be repeated, or give thanks because it has been vouchsafed. The prophecies summon man who has gone astray to turn, to return to the region where the encounter took place, promising him that the torn bond shall once more be made whole. If this book transmits cries of doubt, it is the doubt which is the destiny of man who after having tasted nearness must experience distance and learn from distance what it alone can teach. When we find love songs in the Bible, we must understand that the love of God for his world is revealed through the depths of love human beings can feel for one another.

Since this book came into being, it has confronted generation after generation. Each generation must struggle with the Bible in its turn, and come to terms with it. The generations are by no means always ready to listen to what the book has to say, and to obey it; they are often vexed and defiant; nevertheless, the preoccupation with this book is part of their life and they face it in the realm of reality. Even when generations negated the Book, the very negation confirmed the Book's claim upon them; they bore witness to the Book in the very act of denying it.

The picture changes when we shift to the man of today, and by this, I mean the "intellectual" man of our time, the man who holds it important for intellectual values to exist, and admits, yes, even himself declares that their reality is bound up with our own power to realize them. But if we were to question him and probe down to truth—and we do not usually probe that far down—he would have to own that this feeling of his about the obligations of the spirit is in itself only intellectual. It is the signature of our time that the spirit imposes no obligations. We proclaim the rights of the spirit, we formulate its laws, but they enter only into books and discussions, not into our lives. They float in mid-air above our heads, rather than walk the earth in our midst. Everything except everyday life belongs to the realm of the spirit. Instead of union, a false relationship obtains between the spirit and everyday life. This relationship may shape up as spurious idealism, toward which we may lift our gaze without incurring any obligation to recover from the exigencies of earth; or it may present itself as spurious realism, which regards the spirit as only a function of life and transforms its unconditionality into a number of conditional characters: psychological, sociological, and others. It is true that some contemporaries realize all the corroding consequences of this separation of two interdependent entities, a corrosion which is bound to penetrate into deeper and deeper strata, until the spirit is debased into a willing and complacent servant of whatever powers happen to rule the world. The men of whom I am speaking have pondered over how this corrosion can be halted, and have appealed to religion as the only power which is still capable of bringing about a new union between spirit and world. But what goes by the name of religion nowadays will never bring about such a union. For nowadays "religion" itself is part of the detached spirit. It is one of the subdivisions—one which is in high favor, to be sure—

of the structure erected over and above life, one of the rooms on the top floor, with a very special atmosphere of its own. But this sort of religion is not an entity which includes all of life and, in this its present status, can never become one. It has lost its unity and so it cannot lead man to inner unity. It has adapted to this twofold character of human existence. To exert an influence on contemporary man, religion itself would have to return to reality. And religion was always real only when it was free of fear, when it shouldered the load of concreteness instead of rejecting it as something belonging to another realm, when it made the spirit incarnate, and sanctified everyday life.

The so-called Old Testament constitutes the greatest document of such reality. Two traits—which are however interrelated—set it apart from the other great books of the world religions. One trait is that in the "Old Testament" both events and words are placed in the midst of the people, of history, of the world. What happens does not happen in a vacuum existing between God and the individual. The Word travels by way of the individual to the people, so that they may hear and translate it into reality. What happens is not superior to the history of the people; it is nothing but the secret of the people's history made manifest. But that very fact places the people acted upon in opposition to the nations which represent—in their own eyes—an end in themselves, to groups concerned only with their own welfare, to the "breath of world history." This people is called upon to weld its members into a community that may serve as a model for the so many and so different peoples. The historical continuity of "seed" and "earth" is bound up with the "blessing" (Gen. 12ff.), and the blessing with the mission. The Holy permeates history without divesting it of its rights.

The second trait is that in the Bible the law is designed to cover the natural course of man's life. Eating meat is connected with animal sacrifice; matrimonial purity is sanctified month after month; man is accepted as he is with all his urges and passions and included in holiness, lest his passions grow into a mania. The desire to own land is not condemned, and renunciation is not demanded, but the true Lord of the land is God, and man is nothing but a "sojourner" in his midst. The Landlord makes a harmonious balance of property ownership, lest inequality arise, grow, and break the bond between the members of the community. Holiness penetrates nature without violating it. The living spirit wishes to spiritualize and quicken life; it wishes spirit and life to find the way to one another; it wishes spirit to take shape as life, and life to be clarified through spirit. The spirit wishes creation to attain perfection through itself. The function of this Book is to bear witness to the spirit's will to perfection and to the command to serve the spirit in its search for union with life. If we accept the Old Testament as merely "religious writing," as a subdivision of the detached spirit, it will fail us, and we must needs fail it. If we seize upon it as the expression of a reality which comprises all of life, we really grasp it, and it grasps hold of us. But contemporary man is scarcely capable of this grasp any longer. If he "takes any interest" at all in the Scriptures, it is an abstract, purely "religious" interest, and more often not even that, but an interest connected with the history of religion or civilization, or an aesthetic interest, or the like—at any rate it is an interest that springs from the detached spirit with its numerous autonomous domains. Man of today is not like the generations of old, who stood before the biblical word in order to hearken to or to take offense at it. He no longer confronts his life with the Word; he locks life away in one of many unholy compartments, and then he feels relieved. Thus he paralyzes the power which, of all powers, is best able to save him.

Before demonstrating in greater detail and by way of examples what power the Jewish Bible has to guide the life of the man of today, I must broach the basic question which the thoughtful reader is asking himself at this point: Even if this man of today —even if we were able to approach this whole book with our whole selves, would we not still lack the indispensable prerequisite to its true reception? Would we be able to believe it? Could we believe it? Can we do more than believe that people once did believe as this book reports and claims?

The man of today has no access to a sure and solid faith, nor can it be made accessible to him. If he examines himself seriously, he knows this and may not delude himself further. But he is not denied the possibility of holding himself open to faith. If he is really serious, he too can open up to this book and let its rays strike him where they will. He can give himself up and submit to the test without preconceived notions and without reservations. He can absorb the Bible with all his strength, and wait to see what will happen to him, whether he will not discover within himself a new and unbiased approach to this or that element in the book. But to this end, he must read the Jewish Bible as though it were something entirely unfamiliar, as though it had not been set before him ready-made, at school and after in the light of "religious" and "scientific" certainties; as though he has not been confronted all his life with sham concepts and sham statements which cited the Bible as their authority. He must face the book with a new attitude as something new. He must yield to it, withhold nothing of his being, and let whatever will occur between himself and it. He does not know which of its sayings and images will overwhelm him and mold him, from where the spirit will ferment and enter into him, to incorporate itself anew in his body. But he holds himself open. He does not believe anything a priori; he does not disbelieve anything a priori. He reads aloud the words written in the book in front of him; he hears the word he utters and it reaches him. Nothing is prejudged. The current of time flows on, and the contemporary character of this man becomes itself a receiving vessel.

In order to understand the situation fully, we must picture to ourselves the complete chasm between the Scriptures and the man of today.

The Jewish Bible has always approached and still does every generation with the claim that it must be recognized as a document of the true history of the world, that is to say, of the history according to which the world has an origin and a goal. The Jewish Bible demands that the individual fit his own life into this true history, so that "I" may find my own origin in the origin of the world, and my own goal in the goal of the world. But the Jewish Bible does not set a past event as a midpoint between origin and goal. It interposes a movable, circling midpoint which cannot be pinned to any set time, for it is the moment when I, the reader, the hearer, the man, catch through the words of the Bible the voice which from earliest beginnings has been speaking in the direction of the goal. The midpoint is this mortal and yet immortal moment of mine. Creation is the origin, redemption the goal. But revelation is not a fixed, dated point poised between the two. The revelation at Sinai is not this midpoint itself, but the perceiving of it, and such perception is possible at any time. That is why a psalm or a prophecy is no less "Torah," i.e., instruction, than the story of the exodus from Egypt. The history of this people—accepting and refusing at once—points to the history of all mankind, but the secret dialogue expressed in the psalms and prophecies points to my own secret.

The Jewish Bible is the historical document of a world swinging between creation and redemption, which, in the course of its history, experiences revelation, a revelation which *I* experience *if I am there.* Thus, we can understand that the resistance of the man of today is that of his innermost being.

The man of today has two approaches to history. He may contemplate it as a freethinker, and participate in and accept the shifting events, the varying success of the struggles for power, as a promiscuous agglomeration of happenings. To him history will seem a medley of the actions and deaths of peoples, of grasping and losing, triumph and misery, a meaningless hodge-podge to which the mind of man, time and again, gives an unreliable and unsubstantial semblance of meaning. Or he may view history dogmatically, derive laws from past sequences of events and calculate future sequences, as though the "main lines" were already traced on some roll which need merely unroll; as though history were not the vital living, growing, of time, constantly moving from decision to decision, of time into which my time and my decisions stream full force. He regards history as a stark, ever-present, inescapable space.

Both these approaches are a misinterpretation of historic destiny, which is neither chance nor fatality. According to the biblical insight historic destiny is the secret correlation inhering in the current moment. When we are aware of origin and goal, there is no meaningless drift; we are carried along by a meaning we could never think up for ourselves, a meaning we are to live—not to formulate. And that living takes place in the awful and splendid moment of decision—your moment and mine no less than Alexander's and Caesar's. And yet your moment is not yours but rather the moment of your encounter.

The man of today knows of no beginning. As far as he is concerned, history ripples toward him from some prehistorical cosmic age. He knows of no end; history sweeps him on into a posthistorical cosmic age. What a violent and foolish episode this time between the prehistorical and the posthistorical has become! Man no longer recognizes an origin or a goal because he no longer wants to recognize the midpoint. Creation and redemption are true only on the premise that revelation is a present experience. Man of today resists the Scriptures because he cannot endure revelation. To endure revelation is to endure this moment full of possible decisions, to respond to and to be responsible for every moment. Man of today resists the Scriptures because he does not want any longer to accept responsibility. He thinks he is venturing a great deal, yet he industriously evades the one real venture, that of responsibility.

Insight into the reality of the Bible begins with drawing a distinction between creation, revelation, and redemption.* Christianity withdrew from such insight—and thus from the grounds of the "Old Testament"—in its earliest theology which fused the essentials of revelation and the essentials of redemption in the Christ. It was entirely logical for Marcion to dispute the value of a creation which from this point of view was bound to seem nothing but a premise, and to brand it as the blunder of another, inferior god. With that act, the essence of time which was closely allied to the essence of our spirit was abandoned, time which distinguishes between past, present, and future—structures which in the Bible reach their most concrete expression in the three structures of creation, revelation, and redemption. The only gate which leads to the Bible as a reality is the faithful distinction between the three, not as hypostases or manifestations of God, but as stages, actions, and events in the course of his intercourse with the world, and thus also as the main directions of his movement toward the world. But such distinction must not be exaggerated to mean separation. From the point of view of the Bible, revelation is, as it were, focused in the "middle," creation in the "beginning," and redemption in the "end." But the living truth is that they actually coincide, that "God every day renews the work of the Beginning," but also every day anticipates the work of the end. Certainly both creation and redemption are true only on the premise that revelation is a present experience. But if I did not feel creation as well as redemption happening to myself, I could never understand what creation and redemption are.

* Franz Rosenzweig, in his *Stern der Erloesung,* has the great merit of having shown this to our era in a new light.

This fact must be the starting point for the recurring question, if and how the chasm between man of today and the Scriptures can be bridged. We have already answered the question whether the man of today can believe, by saying that while he is denied the certainty of faith, he has the power to hold himself open to faith. But is not the strangeness of biblical concepts a stumbling stone to his readiness to do so? Has he not lost the reality of creation in his concept of "evolution," that of revelation in the theory of the "unconscious," and that of redemption in the setting up of social or national goals?

We must wholly understand the very substantial quality of this strangeness, before we can even attempt to show that there is still an approach or rather *the* approach.

And again we must begin with the center.

What meaning are we intended to find in the words that God came down in fire, to the sound of thunder and horn, to the mountain which smoked like a furnace, and spoke to his people? It can mean, I think, one of three things. Either it is figurative language used to express a "spiritual" process; or if biblical history does not recall actual events, but is metaphor and allegory, then it is no longer biblical, and deserves no better fate than to be surrendered to the approach of modern man, the historical, aesthetic, and the like approaches. Or it is the report of a "supernatural" event, one that severs the intelligible sequence of happenings we term natural by interposing something unintelligible. If that were the case, man of today in deciding to accept the Bible would have to make a sacrifice of intellect which would cut his life irreparably in two, provided he does not want to lapse into the habitual, lazy acceptance of something he does not really believe. In other words, what he is willing to accept would not be the Bible in its totality including all of life, but only religion abstracted from life.

But there is a third possibility: it could be the verbal trace of a natural event, i.e., of an event which took place in the world of the senses common to all men, and fitted into connections which the senses can perceive. But the assemblage that experienced this event experienced it as revelation vouchsafed to them by God, and preserved it as such in the memory of generations, an enthusiastic, spontaneously formative memory. Experience undergone in this way is not self-delusion on the part of the assemblage; it is what they see, what they recognize and perceive with their reason, for natural events are the carriers of revelation, and revelation occurs when he who witnesses the event and sustains it experiences the revelation it contains. This means that he listens to that which the voice, sounding forth from this event, wishes to communicate to him, its witness, to his constitution, to his life, to his sense of duty. It is only when this is true that man of today can find the approach to biblical reality. I, at any rate, believe that it is true.

Sometimes we have a personal experience related to those recorded as revelations and capable of opening the way for them. We may unexpectedly grow aware of a certain apperception within ourselves, which was lacking but a moment ago, and whose origin we are unable to discover. The attempt to derive such apperception from the famous unconscious stems from the widespread superstition that the soul can do everything by itself, and it fundamentally means nothing but this: what you have just experienced always was in you. Such notions build up a temporary construction which is useful for psychological orientation, but collapses when I try to stand upon it. But what occurred to me was "otherness," was the touch of the other. Nietzsche says it more honestly, "You take, you do not ask who it is that gives." But I think that as we take, it is of the utmost importance to know that someone is giving. He who takes what is given him, and does not experience it as a gift, is not really receiving; and so the gift turns into theft. But when we do experience the giving, we find out that revelation exists. And we set foot on the path which will reveal our life and the life of the world as a sign communication. This path is the approach. It is on this path that we shall meet with the major experience that is of the same kind as our minor experience.

The perception of revelation is the basis for perceiving creation and redemption. I begin to realize that in inquiring about my own origin and goal I am inquiring about something other than myself, and something other than the world. But in this very realization I begin to recognize the origin and goal of the world.

What meaning are we intended to find in the statement that God created the world in six days? Certainly not that he created it in six ages, and that "create" must mean "come into being"—the interpretation of those who try to contrive an approach to the Bible by forcing it into harmony with current scientific views. But just as inadequate for our purposes is the mystic interpretation, according to which the acts of creation are not acts, but emanations. It is in keeping with the nature of mysticism to resist the idea that, for our sake, God assumed the lowly form of an acting person. But divest the Bible of the acting character of God, and it loses its significance, and the concepts of a Platonic or Heraclitean system—concepts born from the observation of reality—are far preferable to the homunculus-like principles of emanation in such an interpretation. What meaning, then, are we intended to find? Here there can be no question of verbal traces of an event, because there was none to witness it. Is then access barred to everyone who cannot believe that the biblical story of creation is the pure "word of God"? The saying of our sages (Babylonian Talmud, Berakhot 31b) to the effect that the Torah speaks the language of men hides a deeper seriousness than is commonly assumed. We must construe it to mean that what is unutterable *can* only be uttered, as it is here expressed, in the language of men. The biblical story of creation is a legitimate stammering account. Man cannot but stammer when he lines up what he knows of the universe into a chronological series of commands and "works" from the divine workshop. But this stammering of his was the only means of doing justice to the task of stating the mystery of how time springs from eternity, and world comes from that which is not world. Compared to this, every attempt to explain cosmogony "scientifically," to supply a logical foundation for the origin of all things, is bound to fail.

If then, the man of today can find the approach to the reality of revelation in the fact that it is our life which is being addressed, how can he find the approach to the reality of creation? His own individual life will not lead him straight to creation as it does to revelation, which he can find so readily because—as we have seen—every moment we live can in itself be its midpoint. Nevertheless the reality of creation can be found, because every man knows that he is an individual and unique. Suppose it were possible for a man to make a psycho-physical inventory of his own person, to break down his character into a sum of qualities; and now suppose it were possible for him to trace each separate quality and the concurrence of all back to the most primitive living creatures, and in this way make an uninterrupted genetic analysis of his individuality by determining its derivation and reference—then his form, his face, unprecedented, comparable to none, unique, his voice never heard before, his gestures never seen before, his body informed with spirit, would still exist as the untouched residue, underived and underivable, an entity which is simply present and nothing more. If after all this futile effort, such a man had the strength to repeat the question, whence, he would in the final analysis discover himself simply as something that was created. Because every man is unique, another first man enters the world whenever a child is born. By being alive, everyone groping like a child back to the origin of his own self, we may experience the fact that there is an origin, that there is creation.

And now to the third, the last, and the most difficult problem:

How are we to understand the concept that "in the end of days" everything in the world will be resolved, that the world will be so perfectly redeemed that, as it is written, there will be "a new heaven and a new earth"? Here again, two opposite interpretations must be avoided. We must not regard the tidings in the light of another world to come. They mean that this, our world, will be purified to the state of the Kingdom, that creation will be made perfect, but not that our world will be annulled for the sake of another world. But neither do the tidings refer to a more righteous order, but to "righteousness," not to mankind grown more peaceful, but to "peace."

Here too, the voice we hear stammers legitimately. The prophet, who is overwhelmed by the divine word, can only speak in the words of men. He can speak only as one who is able to grasp from what and whence he is to be redeemed, but not for what and whither. And the man of today? Must not this he hears be strangest to him, exactly because it is closest to his fathomless yearning? He dreams of change, but does not know transformation. He hopes that if not tomorrow, then the next day things will be better, but the idea that truth will come means nothing to him. He is familiar with the idea of development and the overcoming of obstacles, but he can realize neither that a power wishes to redeem him and the world from contradiction, nor that because of the existence of this power it is demanded of him that he turn with the whole of his being. How can we mediate between this man and the biblical message? Where is the bridge?

This is the most difficult of all. The lived moment leads directly to the knowledge of revelation, and thinking about birth leads indirectly to the knowledge of creation. But in his personal life probably not one of us will taste the essence of redemption before his last hour. And yet here too, there is an approach. It is dark and silent and cannot be indicated by any means, save by my asking you to recall your own dark and silent hours. I mean those hours in the lowest depths when our soul hovers over the frail trap door which, at the very next instant, may send us down into destruction, madness, and "suicide" at our own verdict. Indeed, we are astonished that it has not opened up until now. But suddenly we feel a touch as of a hand. It reaches down to us, it wishes to be grasped—and yet what incredible courage is needed to take the hand, to let it draw us up out of the darkness! This is redemption. We must realize the true nature of the experience proffered us: It is that our "redeemer liveth" (Job 19:18), that he wishes to redeem us—but only by our own acceptance of his redemption with the turning of our whole being.

Approach, I said. For all this still does not constitute a rootedness in biblical reality. But it is the approach to it. It is a beginning.

Plato and Isaiah

[FROM AN INTRODUCTORY LECTURE DELIVERED AT THE HEBREW UNIVERSITY IN JERUSALEM]

PLATO WAS about seventy-five years old when the assassination of the prince Dion, master of Syracuse, his friend and disciple, put an end to the enterprise of founding a republic in accordance with the concepts of the philosopher. It was at this time that Plato wrote his famous letter to his friends in Sicily, in which he rendered an account of his lifelong ambition to change the structure of the state (which for him included the structure of society), of his attempts to translate this purpose into reality, and of how he failed in these attempts. He wrote them that, having observed that all states were poorly governed, he had formed the opinion that man would not be free from this evil until one of two things happened: either true philosophers were charged with the function of government, or the potentates who ruled states lived and acted in harmony with the precepts of philosophy. Plato had formulated this thesis—though somewhat differently—about twenty years earlier as the central passage of his *Republic*. This central position which he gave this passage indicates that in the final analysis he believed that individuals, above all, leaders, were of prime importance rather than any particular institutions—such institutions as the book deals with. According to Plato, there are two ways of obtaining the right persons as leaders: either the philosopher himself must come to power, or he must educate those who rule to conduct their lives as philosophers.

In his memorable tractate *Zum ewigen Frieden,* Kant opposed this thesis of Plato's without mentioning him by name. The rebuttal is part of a passage which appeared only in the second edition and which Kant designated as a "secret article" of his outline on international law. He wrote: "Because the wielding of power inevitably destroys the free judgment of reason, it is not to be expected that kings should philosophize or philosophers be kings, nor even to be desired. But one thing is indispensable to both philosophers and kings, because the possession of sovereign power inevitably corrupts the free judgment of reason, and that is that kings or kingly nations, i.e., nations which govern themselves on the basis of laws of equality, should not dispense with or silence the class of philosophers, but let them express themselves in public." Previously, Kant emphasized that this was not meant to suggest that the state should prefer its power to be represented by the principles of the philosopher rather than the dicta of the jurist, but merely that the philosopher should be heard. This line of thought is a clear indication not only of resignation, but also of disappointment in the spirit [*Geist*] itself, for Kant had been forced to relinquish faith in the spirit's ability to rise to power and, at the same time, remain pure. We may safely assume that Kant's disillusionment is motivated by his knowledge of the course of Church history which in the more than two thousand years intervening between Plato and Kant came to be the spirit's actual history of power.

Plato believed both in the spirit and in power, and he also believed in the spirit's call to the assumption of power. The power he saw was decadent, but he thought it could be regenerated and purified by the spirit. The young Plato's own epochal and grave encounter with "history" took place when the city-state of Athens condemned and executed his teacher Socrates because he had disobeyed the authority of power, and obeyed the Voice. And yet, among all those who concerned themselves with the state, Socrates alone knew how to educate the young for a true life dedicated to the community; like the seer Tiresias in Hades, he was the only one spiritually alive amid a swarm of hovering shades. Plato regarded himself as Socrates' heir and deputy. He knew himself to be called to renew the sacred law and to found the just, law-abiding state. And he knew that for this reason he had a right to power. But while the spirit is ready to accept power at the hands of God or man, it is not willing to seize it. In the *Republic,* Socrates is asked whether the philosophic man would, if he is as Socrates describes him, be at all apt to concern himself with affairs of state. To this question Socrates replies that the philosophic man, in his own state, would certainly concern himself with such matters, but the state which he conceives and which is suitable to him would have to be one other than his native land, "unless there is some divine intervention." But even prior to this passage, he speaks of the man who is blessed with spirit and yet confronts a furious mob, confronts them without confederates who could help maintain justice, and feels like one who suddenly finds himself surrounded by wild beasts. Such a man, he goes on to say, will henceforth keep silence, attend to his own work, become a spectator, and live out his life without doing any wrong to the end of his days. But when Socrates' listeners interpose that such a man will thus have accomplished a great work by the time he dies, he contradicts them, saying: "But not the greatest, since he has not found the state which befits him." That is the gist of Plato's resignation. He was called to Syracuse and went there time after time, even though there too he suffered one disappointment after another. He went because he was called and because there is always the possibility that the divine voice may be speaking in the voice of man. According to Dion's words, there was a possibility that then, if ever, the hope to link the philosophers and the rulers of great states to each other could be fulfilled. Plato decided to "try." He reports that he was ashamed not to go to Syracuse, lest he should seem to himself to be nothing but "words." "Manifest," is the word he once used to Dion, we must manifest ourselves by truly being what we profess in words. He had used the word "must," not "should." He went and failed, returned home, went once more and still another time, and failed again. When he came home after the third failure, he was almost seventy. Not until then did the man Plato had educated come into power. But before he was able to master the confusion of the people, he was murdered by one who had been his fellow student at Plato's Academy.

Plato held that mankind could recover from its ills only if either the philosophers—"whom we termed useless"—became kings, or the kings became philosophers. He himself hoped first for the one and then for the other of these alternatives to occur as the result of "divine intervention." But he was not elevated to a basileus in Greece and the prince whom he had educated to be a philosopher did not master the chaos in Sicily. One might possibly say that the peace which Timoleon of Corinth established in Sicily after the death of this prince was achieved under the touch of Plato's spirit, and that Alexander, who later united all of Greece under his rule, had certainly not studied philosophy with Plato's most renowned disciple without benefit to himself, but neither in the one case nor the other was Plato's ideal of the state actually realized. Plato did not regenerate the decadent Athenian democracy, and he did not found the republic he had projected in theory.

But does this glorious failure prove that the spirit is always helpless in the face of history?

Plato is the most sublime instance of that spirit which proceeds in its intercourse with reality from its own possession of truth. According to Plato, the perfect soul is one which remembers its vision of perfection. Before its life on earth, the soul had beheld the idea of the good. In the world of ideas, it had beheld the shape of pure justice and now, with the spirit's growth, the soul recollects what it had beheld in the past. The soul is not content to know this idea and to teach others to know it. The soul wishes to infuse the idea of justice with the breath of life and establish it in the human world in the living form of a just state. The spirit is in possession of truth; it offers truth to reality; truth becomes reality through the spirit. That is the fundamental basis of Plato's doctrine. But this doctrine was not carried out. The spirit did not succeed in giving reality the truth it wished to give. Was reality alone responsible? Was not the spirit itself responsible as well? Was not its very relationship to the truth responsible? These are questions which necessarily occur to us in connection with Plato's failure.

But the spirit can fail in another and very different way.

"In the year that King Uzziah died" (Isa. 6:1) Isaiah had a vision of the heavenly sanctuary in which the Lord chose him as his prophet. The entire incident points to the fact that King Uzziah was still alive. The king had been suffering from leprosy for a long time. It is well known that in biblical times leprosy was not regarded merely as one ailment among others, but as the physical symptom of a disturbance in man's relationship to God. Rumor had it that the king had been afflicted because he had presumed to perform sacral functions in the sanctuary of Jerusalem which exceeded his rights as a merely political lieutenant of God. Moreover, Isaiah feels that Uzziah's leprosy was more than a personal affliction, that it symbolized the uncleanliness of the entire people, and Isaiah's own uncleanliness as well. They all have "unclean lips" (Isa. 6:5). Like lepers they must all cover "their upper lip" (Lev. 13:45) lest by breath or word their uncleanliness go forth and pollute the world. All of them have been disobedient and faithless to the true King, to the King whose glory Isaiah's eyes now behold in his heavenly sanctuary. Here God is called *ha-Melekh* and this is the first time in the Scriptures that he is designated so nakedly, so plainly, as the King of Israel. *He* is the King. The leper whom the people call "king" is only his faithless lieutenant. And now the true King sends Isaiah with a message to the entire people, at the same time telling him that his message will fail; he will fail, for the message will be misunderstood, misinterpreted and misused, and thus confirm the people—save for a small "remnant"—in their faithlessness, and harden their hearts. At the very outset of his way, Isaiah, the carrier of the spirit, is told that he must fail. He will not suffer disappointment like Plato, for in his case failure is an integral part of the way he must take.

Isaiah does not share Plato's belief that the spirit is a possession of man. The man of spirit—such is the tradition from time immemorial—is one whom the spirit invades and seizes, whom the spirit uses as its garment, not one who houses the spirit. Spirit is an event, it is something which happens to man. The storm of the spirit sweeps man where it will, and then storms on into the world.

Neither does Isaiah share Plato's belief that power is man's possession. Power is vouchsafed man to enable him to discharge his duties as God's lieutenant. If he abuses this power, it destroys him, and in place of the spirit which came to prepare him for the use of power (I Sam. 16:14), an "evil spirit" comes upon him. The man in power is responsible to one who interrogates him in silence, and to whom he is answerable, or all is over with him.

Isaiah does not believe that spiritual man has the vocation to power. He knows himself to be a man of spirit and without power. Being a prophet means being powerless, and powerless confronting the powerful and reminding them of their responsibility, as Isaiah reminded Ahaz "in the highway of the fuller's field" (Isa. 7:3). To stand powerless before the power he calls to account is part of the prophet's destiny. He himself is not out for power, and the special sociological significance of his office is based on that very fact.

Plato believed that his soul was perfect. Isaiah did not. Isaiah regarded and acknowledged himself as unclean. He felt how the uncleanliness which tainted his breath and his words was burned from his lips so that those lips might speak the message of God.

Isaiah beheld the throne and the majesty of Him who entrusted him with the message. He did not see the just state which Plato beheld in his mind's eye as something recollected. Isaiah knew and said that men are commanded to be just to one another. He knew and said that the unjust are destroyed by their own injustice. And he knew and said that there would come a dominion of justice and that a just man would rule as the faithful lieutenant of God. But he knew nothing and said nothing of the inner structure of that dominion. He had no idea; he had only a message. He had no institution to establish; he had only to proclaim. His proclamation was in the nature of criticism and demands.

His criticism and demands are directed toward making the people and their prince recognize the reality of the invisible sovereignty. When Isaiah uses the word *ha-Melekh* it is not in the sense of a theological metaphor, but in that of a political constitutional concept. But this sovereignty of God which he propounded is the opposite of the sovereignty of priests, which is commonly termed theocracy and which has very properly been described as "*the* most unfree form of society," for it is "unfree through the abuse of the Highest knowable to man." * None but the powerless can speak the true King's will with regard to the state, and remind both the people and the government of their *common* responsibility toward this will. The powerless man can do so because he breaks through the illusions of current history and recognizes potential crises.

That is why his criticism and demands are directed toward society, toward the life men live together. A people which seriously calls God himself its King must become a true people, a community all the members of which are governed by hon-

---

* Lorenz v. Stein, *System der Staatswissenschaft* (Stuttgart, 1856), II, 384.

esty without compulsion, kindness without hypocrisy, and the brotherliness of those who are passionately devoted to their divine Leader. When social inequality, when distinction between the free and the unfree splits the community and creates chasms between its members, there can be no true people, there can be no more "God's people." So, the criticism and demands are directed toward every individual on whom other individuals depend, everyone who has a hand in shaping the destinies of others, and that means they are directed toward everyone of us. When Isaiah speaks of justice, he is not thinking of institutions but of you and me, because without you and me, the most glorious institution becomes a lie.

Finally, the criticism and demands apply to Israel's relationship to other nations. They warn Israel not to consent to the making of treaties, not to rely on this or that so-called world-power, but to "keep calm" (Isa. 7:4; 30:15), to make our own people a true people, faithful to its divine King, and then we will have nothing to be afraid of. "The head of Damascus," Isaiah said to Ahaz in the highway of the fuller's field, "is Rezin, and the head of Samaria, Pekah," meaning "but you know who is the Head of Jerusalem—if you want to know." But "If ye will not have faith, surely ye shall not endure (cf. Isa. 7:9). There has been much talk in this connection of "Utopian" politics which would relate Isaiah's failure to that of Plato, who wrote the Utopian *Republic*. What Isaiah said to Ahaz is accepted as a sublimely "religious" but politically valueless utterance, meaning one which lends itself to solemn quotation but is not applicable to reality. Yet the only political chance for a small people hemmed in between world powers is the metapolitical chance to which Isaiah pointed. He proclaimed a truth which could not, indeed, be tested in history up to that time, but only because no one ever thought of testing it. Nations can be led to peace only by a people which has made peace a reality within itself. The realization of the spirit has a magnetic effect on mankind which despairs of the spirit. That is the meaning which Isaiah's teachings have for us. When the mountain of the Lord's house is "established" on the reality of true community life, then, and only then, the nations will "flow" toward it (Isa. 2:2), there to learn peace in place of war.

CHURCH

Isaiah too failed, as was predicted when he was called to give God's message. The people and the king opposed him, and even the king's successor, who attached himself to Isaiah, was found wanting in the decisive hour, when he flirted with the idea of joining the Babylonian rebel against Assyria. But this failure is quite different from Plato's. Our very existence as Jews testifies to this difference. We live by that encounter in the highway of the fuller's field, we live by virtue of the fact that there were people who were deadly serious about this *ha-Melekh* in relation to all of their social and political reality. They are the cause of our survival until this new opportunity to translate the spirit into the reality we have a presentiment of. We may yet experience an era of history which refutes "history." The prophet fails in one hour in history, but not so far as the future of his people is concerned. For his people preserve his message as something which will be realized at another hour, under other conditions, and in other forms.

The prophet's spirit does not, like Plato's, believe that he possesses an abstract and general, a timeless concept of truth. He always receives only one message for one situation. That is exactly why after thousands of years, his words still address the changing situations in history. He does not confront man with a generally valid image of perfection, with a Pantopia or a Utopia. Neither has he the choice between his native land and some other country which might be "more suitable to him." In his work of realization, he is bound to the *topos,* to this place, to this people, because it is the people who must make the *begin-*

ning. But when the prophet feels like one who finds himself surrounded by wild beasts, he cannot withdraw to the role of the silent spectator, as Plato did. He must speak his message. The message will be misunderstood, misinterpreted, misused, it will even confirm and harden the people in their faithlessness. But its sting will rankle within them for all time.

False Prophets

When Hananiah took the yoke from off the prophet Jeremiah's neck, broke it, and announced to the people that within two years God would break the yoke of Nebuchadnezzar from off the necks of all the nations, Jeremiah went his way in silence. Not until God sent him to Hananiah with a message, did Jeremiah go to him and say what he had to say.

I am always deeply moved when I come to this passage, and always learn from it anew. Of all the prophets, Jeremiah is the only one who knew he was elected to his office at the very hour of his birth—in accordance with the gravity of the historical juncture and the decisions it dictated. He felt that the hand of God had touched his mouth and with that touch had enabled him to speak the words of God. It was God himself who told him that he was "set over the nations and over the kingdoms" and that the judgment of God which would be realized in history would be communicated to him. And even more: It was in response to God's command that Jeremiah had laid the bar, which Hananiah broke, on his own neck as a sign that in this historical juncture it was God's will that the nations be subject to Nebuchadnezzar, his strange "servant." Yet, in spite of all this, he was silent when the bar was broken and went his way. He went in order to listen for God's word. Why did he go? Obviously, because in spite of everything there were still things he did not know. Hananiah had spoken like a man who "knows it all." Jeremiah had heard him speak like a man who "knows it all," but there were still things Jeremiah himself did not know. God had, indeed, spoken to him only an hour before. But this was another hour. History is a dynamic process, and history means that one hour is never like the one that has gone before. God operates in history, and God is not a machine which, once it has been wound up, keeps on running until it runs down. He is a living God. Even the word God speaks at a certain hour, the word one obeys by laying a yoke on one's neck, must not be hung up like a placard. God has truth, but he does not have a system. He expresses his truth through his will, but his will is not a program. At this hour, God wills this or that for mankind, but he has endowed mankind with a will of its own, and even with sufficient power to carry it out. So, mankind can change its will from one hour to the next, and God, who is deeply concerned about mankind and its will, and the possible changes it may undergo, can, when that will changes, change his plan for mankind. That means that historical reality can have been changed. One must not rely on one's knowledge. One must go one's way and listen all over again. There were things Jeremiah did not know, and knew that he did not know. Socrates has told something similar about himself. But Jeremiah differed from Socrates in that he realized that from time to time he could learn something new. Socrates too—so he tells us—occasionally heard the voice of Daimonion, but it always told him only what he was not to do. The voice which instructed Jeremiah told him what he was to do and say. If one hears Hananiah's voice, and cannot hear the voice of God, perhaps because "the still small voice" (I Kings 19:12) can be drowned out by that of the Hananiahs, it is best to go one's way and to listen.

Hananiah "knew it all." He did not know the truth, because he "knew it all." What does this mean? He said that God had spoken and that he would break the yoke of the king of Babylon. How did he know it? He did not say that God had spoken to him. He, the false prophet, did not lie. Hananiah was no liar.

He told what truth he knew. But the unfortunate thing was that he did not know any truth and could not know any because he never understood what it meant to go one's way and listen. He has very aptly been called a caricature of Isaiah. What is more, he parrots Isaiah. The prophet Isaiah proclaimed God's will to break the yoke of Asshur from off the necks of His people (Isa. 10:27). From this Hananiah concluded that God had promised to break the yoke of Babylon, for the situation seemed the same. But the situation was *not* the same. When Isaiah transmitted the will of God, Israel was assigned a historical task, not a religious obligation in the ordinary sense of the word, but a task concerned with domestic and foreign politics and comprehending the entire life of the people. Hezekiah's generation had been expected to assume and fulfil this task, and it had looked as though it would. But it did not. Josiah's generation, which did assume it, was no longer able to accomplish it because the historical conditions had changed. The failure to accomplish it led to a situation because of which and for which Jeremiah required the people to accept *destiny* and to fulfil the deepest meaning of this destiny by turning wholly to God, i.e., by taking on themselves the yoke of Babylon and preparing the new freedom, the true freedom in the midst of servitude. Later, after the catastrophe had occurred, after the exile had begun, Jeremiah made a promise in accordance with altered conditions and a changing generation. He promised that the yoke of Babylon would be broken from off their neck; so altered, Hananiah's prophecy had come true. But Hananiah knew nothing of all this. As far as he was concerned, God was a man faithful to his principles, who had tied himself down by the promise he had given Isaiah. He had promised to protect "this city," and so the false prophets have him say—at a completely different historical juncture—that he would give Israel true peace "in this place." Hananiah did not know that there was such a thing as a different historical juncture. He did not know that there was such a thing as guilt, guilt which means the neglect of the task of the hour. And so he did not know that something which had existed was no longer. Neither did he know that there is a turning through which we are granted a possibility which only a moment ago did not exist. He did not know that history is a dynamic process. All he knew was the revolving wheel, not the scales and the pointer on the scales which trembles like a human heart.

Hananiah was a forthright patriot, and he was convinced that being patriotic meant being as he was. He was convinced that Jeremiah had no love whatsoever for his country, for if he had, how could he have expected his people to bend their necks to the yoke? But Jeremiah had a concrete concern for what was taking place. "Wherefore should this city become desolate?" Hananiah had no such concern. Instead, he had his patriotism which does not allow such concerns to come up. What he called his fatherland was a political concept. Jeremiah's fatherland was a land inhabited by human beings, a settlement that was alive and mortal. His God did not wish it to perish. He wished to preserve it by putting those human beings under the yoke.

Hananiah considered himself a great politician, for he thought that in an hour of danger he had succeeded in strengthening the people's resistance. But what he actually strengthened was an illusion, which when it collapsed would cause the collapse of the people's strength. Jeremiah, on the other hand, wanted to protect Israel from just that. The only way to salvation is by the steep and stony path over the recognition of reality. The feet of those who take it bleed, and there is always the threat of dizziness, but it is the one and only way.

The true prophets are the true politicians of reality, for they proclaim their political tidings from the viewpoint of the complete historical reality, which it is given them to see. The false prophets, the politicians who foster illusions, use the power of their wishful thinking to tear a scrap out of historical reality and sew it into their quilt of motley illusions. When they are out to influence through suggestion, they display the gay colors; and when they are asked for the material of truth, they point to the scrap, torn out of reality.

As early as the days of Hezekiah, the false prophets with their illusion-politics prevented the persons concerned from growing fully aware of the great task, from resolving to take it upon themselves and educating the people to its accomplishment. They popularized only the promise contained in Isaiah's tidings, passing over the conditions under which it would be valid, for every prophecy of salvation is conditional. The false prophets perverted the conditional promise to an Israel which would accomplish its task into an unconditional promise of security for all time. When this illusion became dominant and everything happened as it did, they blocked the way—which was still open—to the people's acceptance of their destiny and their changing it by that very acceptance. They blocked the way by adapting old, and manufacturing new and dazzling illusions, by pretending the existence of a path where there was none, and clouding over the one and only open way. That was the stubborn situation which Jeremiah came up against with his powerless word. How poor is the one reality in the face of the thousand dreams!

False prophets are not godless. They adore the god "Success." They themselves are in constant need of success and achieve it promising it to the people. But they do honestly want success for the people. The craving for success governs their hearts and determines what rises from them. That is what Jeremiah called "the deceit of their own heart." They do not deceive; they are deceived, and can breathe only in the air of deceit.

The true prophets know the little bloated idol which goes by the name of "Success" through and through. They know that ten successes that are nothing but successes can lead to defeat, while on the contrary ten failures can add up to a victory, provided the spirit stands firm. When true prophets address the people, they are usually unsuccessful; everything in the people which craves for success opposes them. But the moment they are thrown into the pit, whatever spirit is still alive in Israel bursts into flame, and the turning begins in secret which, in the midst of the deepest distress, will lead to renewal.

The false prophet feeds on dreams, and acts as if dreams were reality. The true prophet lives by the true word he hears, and must endure having it treated as though it only held true for some "ideological" sphere, "morals" or "religion," but not for the real life of the people.

We have no Jeremiah at this juncture. Neither have we a Micaiah, the son of Imlah (I Kings 22). But at every street corner you are likely to run into Hananiah, or standing slightly to the right, his colleague Zedekiah, the son of Chenaanah, with horns of iron or cardboard on his temples, and empty air issuing from his mouth. Brilliant or insignificant—he is always the same. Look him straight in the eye, as though to say, "I know you!" His glance will not waver. But perhaps the next time he dreams his dream, he will remember how you looked at him, and be startled out of his fantasies. And the next time he tells his dream as if it were the word of God, perhaps he will trip over a phrase and pause. No more than an instant, but these instants of incipient reflection are important.

Biblical Leadership

I DO NOT imagine that you will expect me to give you any so-called character sketches of biblical leaders. That would be an impossible undertaking, for the Bible does not concern itself with character, nor with individuality, and one cannot draw from it any description of characters or individualities. The Bible depicts something else, namely, persons in situations. The Bible is not concerned with the difference between these persons; but the difference between the situations in which the person, the creaturely person, the appointed person, stands his test or fails, is all-important to it.

But neither can it be my task to delve beneath the biblical account to a picture more trustworthy historically, to historical data out of which I could piece together a historically useful picture. This too is impossible. It is not that the biblical figures are unhistorical. I believe that we are standing at the beginning of a new era in biblical studies; whereas the past era was concerned with proving that the Bible did not contain history, the coming era will succeed in demonstrating its historicity. By this I do not mean that the Bible depicts men and women and events as they were in actual history; rather do I mean that its descriptions and narratives are the organic, legitimate ways of giving an account of what existed and what happened. I have nothing against calling these narratives myths and sagas, so long as we remember that myths and sagas are essentially memories which are actually conveyed from person to person. But what kind of memory is it which manifests itself in these accounts? I say again: memory; not imagination. It is an organic memory molding its material. We know of it today, because occasionally, though indeed in unlikely and indeed in incredible ways, the existence of great poets with such organic memories still extends into our time. If we want to distinguish between narrators, between a great narrator and one who is simply very talented, the best way is to consider how each of them handles the events of his own life. The great narrator allows the events to drop into him as they happen, careless, trusting, with faith. And memory does its part: what has thus been dropped into it, it molds organically, unarbitrarily, unfancifully into a valid account and narrative; a whole on which admittedly a great deal of conscious work has then to be done, but the distinguishing mark was put upon it by the unarbitrarily shaping memory. The other narrator registers, he makes an inventory in what he also calls the memory, but which is really something quite different; he preserves the events while they are happening in order to be able to draw them forth unaltered when he needs them. Well, he will certainly draw them forth from the preservative after a fashion unaltered, and fit for use after a fashion, and then he may do with them what he can.

I said that the great poets show us in their way how the nascence of myths and sagas takes place. Each myth, even the myth we usually call the most fantastic of all, is creation around a memory core, around the kernel of the organically shaping memory. It is not that people to whom something like the exodus from Egypt has happened subsequently improvise events, allowing their fancy to add elements which they do not remember and to "embroider" on what happened; what happened continues to function, the event itself is still active and at work in their souls, but these souls, this community soul, is so made that its memory is formative, myth-creating, and the task before the biblical writers is then to work on the product of this memory. Nowhere is there any point where arbitrariness is observable or interference by alien elements; there is in it no juggling.

This being the case, we cannot disentangle the historical from the biblical. The power of the biblical writing, which springs from this shaping memory, is so great, the elemental nature of this memory so mighty, that it is quite impossible to extract any so-called historical matter from the Bible. The historical matter thus obtained would be unreal, amorphous, without significance. But it is also impossible to distil "the historical matter" from the Bible for another reason. In contrast to the sacred historiography of the other nations, there exists in the case of Israel no evidence from profane parallels by which one might correct the sacred documents; there is no historiography of another tendency than that which resides in this shaping memory; and this shaping memory stands under a law. It is this law which I shall try to elucidate by the examples with which I deal today.

In order to bring out still more clearly and exactly what I have in mind, I shall ask you to recall one of the nations with whom Israel came into historical contact and dispute; I do so for the purpose of considering the aspect under which this nation must have regarded one of the biblical leaders. Let us try to imagine how Abraham must have been regarded by one of the nations against whose kings he fought, according to Gen. 14, a chapter whose fundamental historical character seems to me beyond doubt. Undoubtedly Abraham was a historical figure to this nation in the same sense in which we usually speak about history today. But he was no longer Abraham. That which is important for us about Abraham, that which makes him a biblical character, a "Father," that which is the reason why the Bible tells us about Abraham, that is no longer embraced under this aspect, the significance of the figure has vanished. Or, take for instance the Egyptians and Moses, and imagine how an Egyptian historian would have described Moses and his cause.

Nothing essential would have been left; it would be a skeleton taking the place of the living person.

All we can do therefore, is to refer to the Bible, to that which is characteristic of the biblical leader as the Bible, without arbitrariness, tells of him and thinks of him, under the law of *its* conception of history, *its* living of history, which is unlike everything which we are accustomed to call history. But from this law, from this biblical way of regarding leader and leadership, different from all other ways in which leader and leadership have been regarded, from this have we—from this has Judaism—arisen.

As I now wish to investigate the question of the essence of biblical leadership, I must exclude from the inquiry all those figures who are not *biblical* leaders in the strict sense of the term: and this means, characteristically enough, I must exclude all those figures who appear as continuators, all those who are not called, elected, appointed anew, as the Bible says, directly by God, but who enter upon a task already begun without such personal call—whether it is a disciple to whom the person who is not permitted to finish the task hands over his office, breathing as it were toward his disciple the spirit that breathes upon him; or whether it is a son who succeeds an elected, originally anointed king, without receiving any other anointing than the already customary official one, which is thus no longer the anointing that comes upon a person and turns him into another man.

Thus I do not consider figures like Joshua and Solomon because the Bible has such figures in common with history—they are figures of universal history. Joshua is a great army leader, a great conqueror, but a historical figure like any other, only with special religious affiliations added, which, however, do not characterize his person. Solomon is an Oriental king, only a very wise one; he does his task, he builds the Temple, but we are not shown that this task colors and determines him. What has happened here is simply that the completion of a task, the completion of a task already intended and already begun, has been taken over by a disciple or a successor. The task of Moses, which he had already begun but was not allowed to finish, was taken over by Joshua; the task of David, which he was not allowed to finish, was taken over by Solomon. In this connection I recall the words that David and God exchanged in the second book of Samuel on the proposed building of the Temple and the prohibition against David's carrying it out: "It is not for you," says God, reproving David as he had reproved Moses when he told Moses that it was not for him to bring into their land the people whom he had led out of Egypt. The work is taken away from him, and taken away from him, moreover, in view of his special inner and outer situations; another man has nothing more to do than to bring the work to its conclusion.

Only the elected, only those who begin, are then comprised under the biblical aspect of leadership. A new beginning may also occur within a sequence of generations, as for instance within those which we call the generations of the patriarchs; this is clearly seen in the case of Jacob, with whom something new begins, as the particular way in which revelation comes to him indicates.

I would like first to attempt a negative characterization of the essential features of biblical leadership. It goes beyond both nature and history. To the men who wrote the Bible, nature, as well as history, is of God; and that in such a way that the biblical cosmogony relates each separately; in the first chapter the creation of the world is described as the coming of nature into being; and then in the second chapter this same creation of the world is described as the rise of history. Both are of God, but then the biblical event goes beyond them, God goes beyond them, not in the sense that they—nature and history—come to be ignored by God, but in the sense that time and again God's hand thrusts through them and interferes with what is happening—it so chooses, so sends, and so commands, as it does not seem to accord with the laws of nature and history to send, to choose, and to command.

I shall here show only by two particularly clear examples what I mean by this. First of all, it is the weak and the humble who are chosen. By nature it is the strong, those who can force their cause through, who are able and therefore chosen to perform the historical deeds. But in the Bible it is often precisely the younger sons who are chosen—from Abel, through Jacob, Joseph and Moses, to David; and this choosing is accompanied by a rejection, often a very emphatic rejection, of the older sons; or else those who are chosen were born out of wedlock, or of humble origin. And if it happens that a strong man like Samson appears, a man who has not all these limitations, then his strength is not his own, it is only loaned, not given, and he trifles it away, squanders it, in the way in which we are told, to get it back only in order to die.

A different but no less telling expression of what is meant by this peculiar election against nature is represented by the battle and victory of Gideon. The Bible makes him do the strangest thing any commander ever did. He has an army of ten thousand men, and he reduces its numbers again and again, till only three hundred men remain with him; and with these three hundred he gives battle and conquers.

It is always the same story. The purpose of God is fulfilled, as the Bible itself says in one place, not by might, nor by power, but "by my spirit."

It is "against nature" that in one way or another the leaders are mostly the weak and the humble. The way in which they carry out their leadership is "contrary to history." It is the moment of success which determines the selection of events which seem important to history. "World history" is the history of successes; the heroes who have not succeeded but who cannot be excluded from it on account of their very conspicuous heroism serve only as a foil, as it were. True, the conquered have also their place in "world history"; but if we scrutinize how it treats the conquerors and the conquered, what is of importance to history becomes abundantly clear. Granted that one takes Croesus together with Cyrus, that Herodotus has a use for him; nevertheless, in the heart of history only the conquerors have value. It murmurs a low dirge over the overpowered heroes, but its paean for those who stand firm, who force their cause through, for those who are crowned with success, rings out loud. This is current history, the history which we are accustomed to identify with what happens, with the real happenings in the world, in spite of the fact that this history is based only on the particular principle of picking and choosing, on the selection made by the historian, on the so-called historical consciousness.

The Bible knows nothing of this intrinsic value of success. On the contrary, when it announces a successful deed, it is duty-bound to announce in complete detail the failure involved in the success. When we consider the history of Moses we see how much failure is mingled in the one great successful action, so much so that when we set the individual events which make up his history side by side, we see that his life consists of one failure after another, through which runs the thread of his success. True, Moses brought the people out of Egypt; but each stage of this leadership is a failure. Whenever he comes to deal with this people, he is defeated by them, let God ever so often interfere and punish them. And the real history of this leadership is not the history of the exodus, but the history of the wandering in the desert. The personal history of Moses' own life, too, does not point back to his youth and to what grew out of it; it points beyond, to death, to the death of the unsuccessful man, whose work, it is true, survives him, but only in new defeats, new disappointments, and continual new failures—and yet his work survives also in a hope which is beyond all these failures.

Or let us consider the life of David. So far as we are told of it, it consists essentially of two great stories of flight. Before his accession to the throne there are the manifold accounts of his flight from Saul, and then follows an interruption which is not trifling in terms of length and its value for profane history, but which in the account appears paltry enough, and after this there is the flight from Absalom, painted for us in detail. And even where the Bible recounts David's triumph, as for instance with the entry of the Ark into Jerusalem, this triumph is clearly described as a disgrace in a worldly sense; this is very unlike the language of "world history." What Michal, his wife, says to David of his triumph, how he ought to have felt ashamed of himself behaving as he did in front of his people—that is the language of profane history, i.e. of history *par excellence*. To history such a royal appearance is not permitted, and, rightly so, seeing that history is what it is.

And, finally, this glorification of failure culminates in the long line of prophets whose existence is failure through and through. They live in failure; it is for them to fight and not to conquer. It is the fundamental experience of biblical leadership, of the leadership described by one of them, a nameless prophet whose words are preserved in the second part of the Book of Isaiah where he speaks in the first person of himself as "the servant of the Lord," and says of God:

> "He hath made my mouth like a sharp sword,
> In the shadow of His hand hath He hid me;
> And He hath made me a polished shaft,—
> In his quiver hath He concealed me!" (Isa. 49:2).

This existence in the shadow, in the quiver, is the final word of the leaders in the biblical world; this enclosure in failure, in obscurity, even when one stands in the blaze of public life, in the presence of the whole national life. The truth is hidden in obscurity and yet does its work; though indeed in a way far different from that which is known and lauded as effective by world history.

Biblical leadership falls into five basic types, not according to differences in the personality and character of the leader—I have already said that personality and character do not come into consideration—but according to the difference in the successive situations, the great stages in the history of the people which the Bible describes, the stages in the dialogue between God and the people. For what the Bible understands by history is a dialogue in which man, in which the people, is spoken to and fails to answer, yet where the people in the midst of its failure continually rises up and tries to answer. It is the history of God's disappointments, but this history of disappointments constitutes a way, a way that leads from disappointment to disappointment and beyond all disappointments; it is the way of the people, the way of man, yes, the way of God through mankind. I said that there are five basic types in accordance with the successive stages of the situations in the dialogue: first, the Patriarch; second, the Leader in the original sense of one who leads the wandering; third, the so-called Judge; fourth, the King, but of course not the king who is a successor, a member of a dynasty, but the founder of the dynasty, called the first anointed; fifth, the Prophet. All these constitute different forms of leadership in accordance with the different situations.

First the Patriarch. This is a current conception which is not quite correct. No rulership is here exercised, and, when we understand the conception in its accurate sense, we cannot here speak of any leadership, for there is as yet no people to lead. The conception indicates a way along which the people are to be led beginning with these men. They are Fathers. It is for them to beget a people. It is the peculiar point in biblical history where God, as it were, narrows down his original plan for the whole of mankind and causes a people to be begotten that is called to do its appointed work toward the completion of the creation, the coming of the kingdom. The fathers of this people are the men of whom I speak. They are Fathers, nothing else. Patriarch expresses too much. They are the real fathers, they are those from whom this tribe, this people, proceeds; and when God speaks to them, when God blesses them, the same thing is always involved: conception and birth, the beginning of a people. And the great story which stands in the middle of the story of the patriarchs—the birth and offering of Isaac—makes exactly this point, in a paradoxical manner. Kierkegaard has presented this paradox very beautifully in the first part of his book *Fear and Trembling.* This paradoxical story of the second in the line of the patriarchs, of his being born and very nearly being killed, shows what is at stake: a begetting, but the begetting of a people standing at the disposal of God; a begetting, but a begetting commanded by God.

We have a people, and the people is in bondage. A man receives the charge to lead it out. That is he whom I have described as the Leader in the original meaning of the word. It is he who serves in a human way as a tool for the act which God pronounces, "I bore you on eagles' wings, and brought you unto myself" (Exod. 19:4). I have already spoken of his life. But in the middle of his life the event takes place in which Moses, after the passage through the Red Sea, intones the song in which the people joins, and which is the proclamation of a King. The words with which the song ends proclaim it: "King shall the Lord be for ever and ever" (Exod. 15:18). The people has here chosen God himself for its King, and that means that it has made a vital and experienced truth out of the tradition of a divine kingdom which was common to all Semitic peoples but which never had been taken quite seriously. The Hebrew leaders are so much in earnest about it, that after the land has been conquered they undertake to do what is "contrary to history": they try to build up a society without a ruling power save only that of God. It is that experiment in primitive theocracy of which the Book of Judges tells, and which degenerates into anarchy, as is shown by the examples given in its last part.

The so-called Judge constitutes the third type of leadership. This type is to be understood as the attempt made by a leading group among the people that are dominated by the desire to make actual the proclamation of God as king, and try to induce the people to follow them. This attempt miscarries time and again. Time and again the people, to use the biblical phrase, falls away from God. But we can also express this in the language of history: time and again the people fall apart; it is one and the same thing whichever language we use. The attempt to establish a society under no other dominion than God's—this too can be expressed in the language of history, or if one likes, in the language of sociology: the attempt to establish a society on pure voluntarism fails over and over again. The people falls away. This is always succeeded by an invasion by one of the neighboring peoples, and Israel, from a historical point of view fallen apart and disunited, does not stand firm. But in its conquered state it again makes itself subject to the will of God, resolves anew to accept God's dominion, and again a divine mission occurs; there is always a leader whom the spirit lays hold of as it laid hold of Moses. This leader, whose mission it is to free the people, is "the Judge," or more correctly, "he who makes right"; he makes this right exist in the actual world for the people, which after its return to God now again has right on its side, by defeating the enemy. This is the rhythm of the Book of Judges; it might almost be called a tragic rhythm, were it not that the word tragic is so foreign to the spirit of biblical language.

But in this Book of Judges there is also something being prepared. The experience of failure, of the inability to bring about this intended, naïve, primitive theocracy becomes ever deeper, ever stronger grows the demand for a human kingdom. Judges itself is in its greater part written from an anti-monarchical standpoint. The Kings of the peoples file before one in a way determined by this point of view, which reaches its height in that ironic fable of Jotham's (Judg. 9). But in its final chapters the Book of Judges has to acknowledge the disappointment of the theocratic hope, because the people is as it is, because men are as they are. And so kingship is demanded under Samuel. And it is granted by God. I said before, the way leads through the disappointments. Thus the demand of the people is as it were laid hold of and consecrated from above; for by the anointing of the King a man is transformed into the bearer of a charge laid upon him. But this is no longer—as was the case with the Judge—a single charge the completion of which brings his leadership to an end; it is a governor's charge which goes beyond individual acts, indeed beyond the life of individual men. Anointing may also imply the beginning of a dynasty, when the king is not rejected by God, as Saul was.

The kingdom is a new stage in the dialogue, a new stage of attempt and failure, only in this stage the account lays the burden of the failure on the king and not any longer, as in the Book of Judges, on the whole people. It is no longer those who are led but the leader himself who fails, who cannot stand the test of the charge, who does not make the anointing come true in his own person—a crucial problem in religious history. The history of the great religions, and in general all great history, is bound up with the problem: How do human beings stand the test of what is here called anointing?

The history of the kings is the history of the failure of him who has been anointed to realize the promise of his anointing. The rise of messianism, the belief in the anointed king who realizes the promise of his anointing, is to be understood only in this context.

But now in the situation of the failure of kings the new and last type of leader in biblical history arises, the leader who above all other types is "contrary to history," the Prophet, he who is appointed to oppose the king, and even more, history. When God says to Jeremiah, "I have made thee . . . a brazen wall against the whole land" (Jer. 1:18), it is really so; the prophet stands not only against the ruler but against the people itself. The prophet is the man who has been set up against his own natural instincts that bind him to the community, and who likewise sets himself up against the will of the people to live on as they have always lived, which, naturally, for the people is identical with the will to live. It goes without saying that not only the rulers but also the people treat the prophet as their enemy in the way in which, as a matter of history, it falls to the lot of such men to be treated. These experiences of suffering which thus come upon the prophet join together to form that image of the servant of the Lord, of his suffering and dying for the sake of God's purpose.

When the Bible then tries to look beyond these manifestations of leadership to one which no longer stands amidst disintegration and failure, when the idea of the messianic leader is conceived, it means nothing else by it than that at last the answer shall be given: from out of mankind itself the word shall come, the word that is spoken with the whole being of man, the word that answers God's word. It is an earthly consummation which is awaited, a consummation in and with mankind. But this precisely is the consummation toward which God's hand pushes through that which he has created, through nature and through history. This is what the messianic belief means, the belief in the real leader, in the setting right of the dialogue, in God's disappointment being at an end. And when a fragment of an apocryphal gospel has God say to Jesus: "In all the prophets have I awaited thee, that thou wouldst come and I rest in thee, for thou art My rest," this is the late elaboration of a truly Jewish conception.

The biblical question of leadership is concerned with something greater than moral perfection. The biblical leaders are the foreshadowings of the dialogical man, of the man who commits his whole being to God's dialogue with the world, and who stands firm throughout this dialogue. The life of those people to whom I have referred is absorbed in this dialogue, whether the dialogue comes about through an intervention, as in Abraham's talk with God about Sodom, or Moses' after the sin of the golden calf; or whether it comes about through a resistance they offer against that which comes upon them and tries to overpower them; but their resistance ends in submission, which we find documented from Moses to Jeremiah; or whether the dialogue comes about through the struggle for a purpose and a task, as we know from that dialogue which took place between David and God; whatever the way, man enters into the dialogue again and again; imperfect entry, but yet one which is not refused, an entry which is determined to persevere in the dialogical world. All that happens is here experienced as dialogue, what befalls man is taken as a sign, what man tries to do and what miscarries is taken as an attempt and a failure to answer, as a stammering attempt to respond as well as one can.

Because this is so, biblical leadership always means a process of being-led. These men are leaders insofar as they allow themselves to be led, that is, insofar as they accept that which is offered them, insofar as they take upon themselves the responsibility for that which is entrusted to them, insofar as they make real that which has been laid upon them from outside of themselves, make it real with the free will of their own being, in the "autonomy" of their person.

So long as we remember this, we can make the lives of these leaders clear. Almost always what we see is the taking of a man out of the community. God lifts the man out of the community, cuts him off from his natural ties; from Abraham to Jeremiah he must go forth out of the land in which he has taken root, away to the place where he has to proclaim the name of God; it is the same story, whether it is a wandering over the earth like Abraham's, or a becoming utterly alone in the midst of the people like the prophets'. They are drawn out of their natural community;

they fight with it, they experience in this community the inner contradiction of human existence. All this is intensified to the utmost precisely in the prophets. The great suffering of the prophets, preserved for us by Jeremiah himself in a small number of (in the highest sense of the word) autobiographical sayings is the ultimate expression of this condition.

But this ever widening gulf between leader and community, the ever greater failure of the leader, the leader's ever greater incompatibility with "history"—this means, from the biblical standpoint, the gradual overcoming of history. What we are accustomed to call history is from the biblical standpoint only the façade of reality. It is the great failure, the refusal to enter into the dialogue, not the failure in the dialogue, as exemplified by biblical man. This great refusal is sanctioned with the imposing sanction provided by so-called history. The biblical point of view repudiates with ever increasing strength this two-dimensional reality, most strongly in the prophets; it proclaims that the way, the real way, from the Creation to the Kingdom is trod not on the surface of success, but in the deep of failure. The real work, from the biblical point of view, is the late-recorded, the unrecorded, the anonymous work. The real work is done in the shadow, in the quiver. Official leadership fails more and more, leadership devolves more and more upon the secret. The way leads through the work which history does not write down, and which history cannot write down, work which is not ascribed to him who did it, but which possibly at some time in a distant generation will emerge as having been done, without the name of the doer—the secret working of the secret leadership. And when the biblical writer turns his eyes toward the final, messianic overcoming of history, he sees how the outer history becomes engulfed, or rather how both the outer history and the inner history fuse, how the secret which the leadership had become rises up out of the darkness and illumines the surface of history, how the meaning of biblical history is consummated in the whole reality.

LEARNING AND EDUCATION

Teaching and Deed

[ADDRESS DELIVERED AT THE LEHRHAUS IN FRANKFORT ON THE MAIN * IN 1934]

AMONG ALL peoples, two kinds and lines of propagation exist side by side; for quite as continuous as the biological line and parallel to it, is, in the words of the philosopher Rudolf Pannwitz, the line of "the propagation of values." Just as organic life is transmitted from parents to children and guarantees the survival of the community, so the transmission and reception, the new begetting and new birth of the spirit, goes on uninterruptedly. The life of the spirit of a people is renewed whenever a teaching generation transmits it to a learning generation which, in turn, growing into teachers, transmits the spirit through the lips of new teachers to the ears of new pupils; yet this process of education involves the person as a whole, just as in physical propagation.

In Judaism, this cycle of propagation involves another and peculiar factor. In Israel of old the propagation of values itself assumed an organic character and penetrated the natural life of the people. It is true that it does not imitate biological reproduction in guaranteeing the survival of the community as such; it only guarantees its survival as Israel. But can we drown out the voice which tells us that if our life as Israel were to come to an end we

---

* The Jewish house of study (*Freies Jüdisches Lehrhaus*) was established in Frankfort on the Main in the year 1920 under the leadership of Franz Rosenzweig. It aimed at a renascence of Jewish learning and thinking. Soon the Lehrhaus became the intellectual center of the Frankfort Jewish community, exerting a strong influence on Jewish cultural life in Germany. The events of the year 1933 brought about an expansion of the program and an intensification of the Lehrhaus movement, which was then headed by Martin Buber.—*Ed.*

could not go on living as one of the nations? We, and we only, once received both life and the teachings at once, and the selfsame hour became a nation and a religious community. Since then, the transmission of life and that of the teachings have been bound together, and we consider the spiritual transmission as vital as bodily propagation.

The talmudic sages say: "He who teaches the tradition to his fellow man is regarded as though he had formed and made him, and brought him into the world. As it is said (Jer. 15:19): 'And if thou bring forth the precious out of the vile, thou shalt be as My mouth.'" In this quotation from the Bible, God summons the prophet, who has just begged for help to wreak vengeance on his foes, to the turning, to the conquest of his own hatred and repugnance, and promises him that if he turns he shall be allowed adequately to fulfil a divine action. And the "forming" and the "making" of the child in the womb (Jer. 1:5; Ps. 139:15), is counted among such divine action. The influence of the teacher upon the pupil, of the right teacher upon the right pupil, is not merely compared to, but even set on a par with, divine works which are linked with the human, maternal act of giving birth. The inner turning of the prophet is an actual rebirth, and the educator, who brings the precious ore in the soul of his pupil to light and frees it from dross, affords him a second birth, birth into a loftier life. Spirit begets and gives birth; spirit is begotten and born; spirit becomes body.

Even today, in spite of all deterioration, the spiritual life of Jewry is not merely a superstructure, a nonobligatory transfiguration, an object of pride which imposes no duties. Rather, it is a binding and obligatory power, but one which attains to earthly, bodily reality only through that which it binds to the obligations of Jewish spiritual life. So profoundly is the spirit here merged with the physical life that even the survival of the community in time can be guaranteed only by both operating together.

But if we are serious about the simile of generation, we must realize that in spiritual as well as in physical propagation it is not the same thing that is passed on, but something which acquires newness in the very act of transmission. For tradition does not consist in letting contents and forms pass on, finished and inflexible, from generation to generation. The values live on in the host who receives them by becoming part of his very flesh, for they choose and assume his body as the new form which suits the function of the new generation. A child does not represent the sum total of his parents; it is something that has never been before, something quite unpredictable. Similarly, a generation can only receive the teachings in the sense that it renews them. We do not take unless we also give. In the living tradition it is not possible to draw a line between preserving and producing. The work of embodiment takes place spontaneously; and that person is honest and faithful who utters words he has never heard as though they had come to him; for it is thus—and not as if he had "created" them—that such words live within him. Everyone is convinced that he is doing no more than further advancing that which has advanced him to this point, and he may, nonetheless, be the originator of a new movement.

That this holds for Jewry is due to the intensity which time and again characterizes the encounters between generations, involving mutual and radical interactions and bringing forth changes in values as though they were not changes at all. In these recurring encounters between a generation which has reached its full development and one which is still developing, the ultimate aim is not to transmit a separable something. What matters is that time and again an older generation, staking its entire existence on that act, comes to a younger with the desire to teach, waken, and shape it; then the holy spark leaps across the gap. Transmitted content and form are subordinate to the tradition of existence as such and become valid only because of it. The total, living, Jewish human being is the transmitting agent; total, living, Jewish humanity is transmitted. Tradition is concentrated in the existence of the Jew himself. He lives it, and it is he who approaches the new generation and influences it by producing the blend of the old and the new. Israel is inherent in these human beings; they are Israel. Israel is renewed, not by what they say but by the totality of their existence.

We have already indicated that in our case teaching is inseparably bound up with doing. Here, if anywhere, it is impossible to teach or to learn without living. The teachings must not be treated as a collection of knowable material; they resist such treatment. Either the teachings live in the life of a responsible human being, or they are not alive at all. The teachings do not center in themselves; they do not exist for their own sake. They refer to, they are directed toward the deed. In this connection the concept of "deed" does not, of course, connote "activism," but life that realizes the teachings in the changing potentialities of every hour.

Among all the peoples in the world, Israel is probably the only one in which wisdom that does not lead directly to the unity of knowledge and deed is meaningless. This becomes most evident when we compare the biblical concept of *hokhmah* with the Greek concept of *sophia.* The latter specifies a closed realm of thought, knowledge for its own sake. It is totally alien to the *hokhmah,* which regards such a delimitation of an independent spiritual sphere, governed by its own laws, as the misconstruction of meaning, the violation of continuity, the severance of thought from reality.

The supreme command of *hokhmah* is the unity of teaching and life, for only through this unity can we recognize and avow the all-embracing unity of God. In the light of our doctrine, He who gives life and gives that life meaning is wronged by a teaching which is satisfied with and delights in itself, which rears structures however monumental above life, and yet does not succeed in wresting even a shred of realization out of all the outer and inner obstacles we must struggle with in every precarious hour of our lives. For our God makes only one demand upon us. He does not expect a humanly unattainable completeness and perfection, but only the willingness to do as much as we possibly can at every single instant.

Man is a creature able to make spirit independent of physical life, and his great danger is that he may tolerate and even sanction existence on two different levels: one, up above and fervently adored, the habitation of the spirit; and one down below, the dwelling of urges and petty concerns, equipped with a fairly good conscience acquired in hours of meditation in the upper story.

The teachings do not rely on the hope that he who knows them will also observe them. Socratic man believes that all virtue is cognition, and that all that is needed to do what is right is to know what is right. This does not hold for Mosaic man who is informed with the profound experience that cognition is never enough, that the deepest part of him must be seized by the teachings, that for realization to take place his elemental totality must submit to the spirit as clay to the potter.

Here dualism is fought with the utmost vigor. "One who studies with a different intent than to act," says the Talmud, "it would have been more fitting for him never to have been created."* It is bad to have teaching without the deed, worse when the teaching is one of action. Living in the detached spirit is evil, and worse when the spirit is one of ethos. Again and again, from the Sayings of the Fathers down to the definitive formulation of hasidism, the simple man who acts is given preference over the scholar whose knowledge is not expressed in deeds. "He whose deeds exceed his wisdom, his wisdom shall endure; but he whose wisdom exceeds his deeds, his wisdom shall not endure." And in the same vein: "He whose wisdom exceeds his deeds—what does he resemble? A tree with many boughs and few roots. A wind, springing up, uproots it, and overturns it. But he whose deeds exceed his wisdom—what does he resemble? A tree with few boughs but many

* Palestinian Talmud, Shabbat 3b.

roots. Though all the winds in the world come and blow at it, it cannot be budged." What counts is not the extent of spiritual possessions, not the thoroughness of knowledge, nor the keenness of thought, but to know what one knows and to believe what one believes so directly that it can be translated into the life one lives.

I repeat that in Judaism the true value of the deed has nothing to do with "activism." Nothing is more remote from Judaism than the glorification of self-confident virtue. But Judaism knows that *true* autonomy is one with true theonomy: God wants man to fulfil his commands as a human being, and with the quality peculiar to human beings. The law is not thrust upon man; it rests deep within him, to waken when the call comes. The word which thundered down from Sinai was echoed by the word that is "in thy mouth and in thy heart" (Deut. 30:14). Again and again, man tries to evade the two notes that are one chord; he denies his heart and rejects the call. But it has been promised that a time will come when the Torah will be manifest as the Scripture present in the hearts of all living men, and the word will fulfil itself in the harmony of heaven and earth. In Jewry, the way which leads to that promised time, the way of man's contribution to ultimate fulfilment, is trodden whenever one generation encounters the next, whenever the generation which has reached its full development transmits the teachings to the generation which is still in the process of developing, so that the teachings spontaneously waken to new life in the new generation.

We live in an age when deeds tend to assert their superiority over the teachings. The present generation universally believes more and more unreservedly that it can get along without the teachings and rely on a mode of action which—in its own opinion—is correct. In an address I delivered years ago at a Zionist congress, in memory of our teacher Ahad Haam, I drew attention to the fact that "it is not only the official state politics which are freeing themselves of spiritual teachings—that has, on occasion, happened before—but the internal popular movements, and national groupings are also stressing their independence from spiritual teachings, and even regard independence as a warrant of success. And," I went on to say, "they are not entirely mistaken. The conduct of life without the teachings is successful: something is achieved. But the something thus achieved is quite different and at times the very caricature of what one is striving for at the bottom of one's heart, where the true goal is divined. And what then? As long as the goal was a pure goal, yearning and hope were dominant. But if in the course of being achieved the goal is distorted, what then?"

The implied warning I intended for Jewry passed them by almost unnoticed—as was to be expected. Although we are less able to get along without the teachings than any other community, a widespread assimilation of the errors of the other nations has been rampant among us for a long time. It is not my office to discuss what may happen to other nations because of their denial of the spirit. But I know that we, who believe that there can be no teaching apart from doing, will be destroyed when our doing becomes independent of the teachings.

A Jewish house of study—that is a declaration of war upon all those who imagine they can be Jews and live a Jewish life outside of the teachings, who think by cutting off the propagation of values to accomplish something salutary for Jewry. A truly Jewish communal life cannot develop in Palestine if the continuity of Judaism is interrupted. Let me reiterate that such continuity does not imply the preservation of the old, but the ceaseless begetting and giving birth to the same single spirit, and its continuous integration into life. Do not let us delude ourselves: once we are content to perpetuate biological substance and a "civilization" springing from it, we shall not be able to maintain even such a civilization. For the land and the language in themselves will not support our body and soul on earth—only land and language when linked to the holy origin and the holy destination. Moreover, in this crisis of humanity in which we stand at the most exposed point, the Diaspora cannot preserve its vital connection, which has so long defied history's attempt at severance, without recognizing and renewing the power the teachings possess, a power strong enough to overcome all corroding forces. For all that which is merely social, merely national, merely religious, and therefore lacking the fiery breath of the teachings, is involved in the abysmal problematic of the hour and does not suffice to ward off decay. Only the teachings truly rejuvenated can liberate us from limitations and bind us to the unconditional, so that spiritualized and spirited, united within the circle of the eternal union, we may recognize one another and ourselves and, empowered by the fathomless laws of history, hold out against the powers moving on the surface of history.

Concerning the words of Isaac, the patriarch: "The voice is the voice of Jacob, but the hands are the hands of Esau" (Gen. 27:22), the Midrash tells this story: Delegates of the other nations were once dispatched to a Greek sage to ask him how the Jews could be subjugated. This is what he said to them: "Go and walk past their houses of prayer and of study... So long as the voice of Jacob rings from their houses of prayer and study, they will not be surrendered into the hands of Esau. But if not, the hands are Esau's and you will overcome them." *

The teachings cannot be severed from the deed, but neither can the deeds be severed from the teachings! Our tradition assigned quite as much importance to the one danger as to the other. The Talmud tells us that at a gathering of sages the question arose as to which was greater, deeds or teachings. And one of them, who seemed to share our point of view, said that deeds were greater. But Rabbi Akiba said: "The teachings are greater!" And all agreed, saying: "The teachings are greater, for the teachings beget the deed." † This sounds like a contradiction of the assertions of the importance of action. But after we have more deeply

* Gen. Rabbah on 27:22.

† Kiddushin 40b.

pondered these assertions, we comprehend that the teachings are central and that they are the gate through which we must pass to enter life. It is true that simple souls can live the true life without learning, provided they are linked to God. But this is possible only because the teachings which represent just such a link to God have, although they are unaware of it, become the very foundation of their existence. To do the right thing in the right way, the deed must spring from the bond with Him who commands us. Our link with Him is the beginning, and the function of the teachings is to make us aware of our bond and make it fruitful.

Again we are confronted with the concepts of continuity and spontaneity, the bond of transmission and begetting. The teachings themselves are the way. Their full content is not comprehended in any book, in any code, in any formulation. Nothing that has ever existed is broad enough to show what they are. In order that they may live and bring forth life, generations must continue to meet, and the teachings assume the form of a human link, awakening and activating our common bond with our Father. The spark that leaps from him who teaches to him who learns rekindles a spark of that fire which lifted the mountain of revelation "to the very heart of heaven."

Why We Should Study Jewish Sources

[FROM A SYLLABUS FOR THE SCHOOL FOR JEWISH YOUTH OF BERLIN, 1932]

I HAVE BEEN asked why our young people should be charged to study and examine historical Jewish values. There are many possible answers to this question, but as far as I can see only one is relevant. And so I shall here limit myself to discussing this one answer.

We Jews are a community based on memory. A common memory has kept us together and enabled us to survive. This does not mean that we based our life on any one particular past, even on the loftiest of pasts; it simply means that one generation passed on to the next a memory which gained in scope—for new destiny and new emotional life were constantly accruing to it—and which realized itself in a way we can call organic. This expanding memory was more than a spiritual motif; it was a power which sustained, fed, and quickened Jewish existence itself. I might even say that these memories realized themselves biologically, for in their strength the Jewish substance was renewed.

To avoid misunderstandings, we should realize two things. First, that we are not dealing here with that awareness of history which is common to all nations. Such awareness is one form of expression of the spiritual life of every nation. But the spiritual life of the Jews is part and parcel of their memory. The universal awareness of history is a reflection of history, an image which grows richer in contours and colors in eras of uncertainty, and fires the current generation with enthusiasm, while it may pale—though without losing its vitality—in years of security, when it may even be opposed as something "romantic" and out of tune with the times. But in our case the characteristic potency of our Jewish collective memory is the very origin of our own characteristic history. For the core of this history does not consist of a sequence of objective events, but of a sequence of essential attitudes toward such events, and these attitudes are the product of collective memory.

Secondly—and this is a corollary to what has gone before—here it is not a question of sentimentally looking back or longing for the return of the past but of the factual connection between generations. Sons and grandsons have the memory of their fathers and forebears in their bones. But such remembering does not, of course, begin in and develop mystically out of itself; it is jogged by a force that wakens and reveals. This force is the passion to hand down which kindled each of our sons the moment he became a father. He had to "remind" others of what he was reminded of, only that he added to it the experiences of his own life-span. There was never an *am ha-aretz* so hopeless that he could not teach his children what had happened. The Passover Seder is the most striking proof of this. Every man who set up a home knew how to conduct the Seder, and indeed with fervor.

Much has disappeared from Jewry in the past one hundred and fifty years, but nothing is so ominous as the disappearance of the collective memory and the passion for handing down. All attempts to replace this vital force with substitute morals or forms have been inadequate and will prove more and more so. But more misleading than these attempts was the notion that it might be possible to dispense with this force altogether, to make a fresh and "unburdened" start—best of all in Palestine. Why cling to a community based on memory when it is possible to live as a nation among other nations! But we cannot become a nation like other nations. For the magnetism of Palestine itself, and even its power to call forth sacrifice, are due to nothing but organic memory. And from the generation which is just now growing up—let alone from future generations—the Yishuv (Palestinian community) will discover that it cannot establish a new continuity unless the age-old bond of memory is revived in a new form. As for the Diaspora—it will disintegrate if the connection between the generations is not restored, if the organic bond with "Israel" is not made real again, if the words of the Passover Haggadah: "*We,* all of us, have gone forth out of Egypt," are not rescued from being a mere phrase, and reinstated in their authenticity.

But how can all this be done? What the fathers no longer hand down the sons must get as best they can—they must study it. In times gone by, all we really had to learn was the Oral Law. Everything else we needed to know was handed down and remembered without any particular effort. Today what was once matter of course—our language, the Scriptures, our history—must become curriculum of the most crucial importance. The passion to hand down can be replaced only by the passion to study, the passion of the fathers only by that of the sons, who must work unremittingly to regain the approach to the ancestral treasure, and thus re-establish the bond of memory that joins the community together. Whether there are many such sons or few, they constitute a beginning.

On National Education

1.

THERE ARE two basic approaches to education and the task of the educator. According to the first, "to educate" means to draw out of the child that which is in him; not to bring the child anything from the outside, but merely to overcome the disturbing influences, to set aside the obstacles which hinder his free development —to allow the child to "become himself."

According to the second approach, education means shaping the child into a form which the educator must first visualize, so that it may serve as a directive for his work. He does not rely on the child's natural endowment but sets up an opposing pattern which determines how such endowment is to be handled.

The first approach may be compared to that of the gardener who fertilizes and waters the soil, prunes and props the young plant, and removes the rank weeds from around it. But after he has done all this, if the weather is propitious, he trusts to the natural growth of that which is inherent in the seed.

The second approach is that of the sculptor. Like Michelangelo, he sometimes sees the shape hidden in the crude marble, but it is the image which exists in his soul which guides him in working on the block, and which he wishes to realize in the material at his disposal.

In the first case, education indicates the care given to a soul in the making, in order that the natural process of growth may reach its culmination; in the second, it means influencing a soul to develop in accordance with what the educator who exerts the influence considers to be right. Whoever employs the gardener's method is apt to believe that—fundamentally—man is good, but also that the individual is predetermined by his innate endowment. The educator with the sculptor's outlook tends to regard man as a creature with divers potentialities, but plastic and educable, and, therefore, not rigidly bound inside a pale of possibilities. The first kind of education is more humble, but also more passive; the second shows greater initiative, but carries with it graver responsibilities. The dangers of the first are *laissez aller* and excessive indulgence, those of the second, restraint and compulsion. The gardener educator has not enough confidence; the sculptor too much.

One might think that both these forms of education are individualistic, that the first gives full scope to the individualism of the pupils, in that it does not set a common ideal against their personal differences, while the second gives free rein to the individualism of the educator, whose theory apparently empowers him to shape everyone in his own image. But this second supposition, at any rate, does not correspond to the truth. If every teacher could confront his pupils with a particular pattern he wished them to strive toward, the result would be anarchy rather than individualism.

Yet even the most distinguished educator cannot create a true and truly valid ideal. An ideal whose source is the fancy cannot be realized in the flesh-and-blood objects of education. The patterns familiar to us from the history of culture are never personal or arbitrary. Every period of genuine and vigorous culture produces such a pattern, one which is the basis of community life as well as the goal of education: from the *polites* pattern of classical Greek antiquity to the "gentleman" of the great era in English history. Just as certain general concepts are recognized as valid by all thinking persons, so these ideals are accepted by everybody as the supreme and authoritative patterns for the life of the individual, although they remain valid only for limited periods of civilization. Often this civilization embraces only a single nation, but sometimes it is more comprehensive. Then we have an ideal common to a number of nations, like that of the Christian knight during the Middle Ages, especially from the tenth to the thirteenth century. Neither the will nor the imagination of an individual, even of a genius, produces these patterns. They express the deepest life of an entire epoch, and its character and desires at the same time. Educators regard them as the goal of their work; but they are so little thought out and so tightly linked with the realities of the epoch, that the collective social environment and even nature itself: landscape, air, and light, seem to assist these educators to reaching their goal.

Even more: During eras of true civilization, the gardener and sculptor types of education are to a certain degree synthesized. Everything, the remembered past and the present life, works in a common direction to such an extent that from early childhood on there is a great, universal, elementary wish to resemble the commonly accepted pattern, making it unnecessary for educators to superimpose their personal ideals on their pupils. All they need do is give them access to the proper subject matter and see to it that they have the right kind of practice. For the rest, they may be fairly confident that the individual will develop along the desired lines.

The period after the French Revolution, when Europe's cultural productivity began to decline along with the disintegration of her cultural tradition, marked the end of the rise of those ideal patterns which simply express the reality of a culture and the character and life of the epoch through the character and conduct of the individual. At that moment, the individualistic gardener type of education got the upper hand, as was quite natural in an era such as ours, with its accumulation of cultural material and lack of cultural independence.

From that time on, the task of education was no longer determined by the pattern of a true ideal. The goal of education was to produce a person of culture [*Bildung*], i.e., one who had acquired a so-called "universal culture" [*allgemeine Bildung*]. But what should and what should not be included in such a universal culture? In eras dominated by ideal types, the choice of educational material and especially of material used for teaching purposes was governed by the prevailing pattern. The choice fell on whatever was likely to develop a human being in accordance with that pattern. Now, however, the selection of subject matter is decided by convention or by a number of conventions: a humanistic convention based on old cultural traditions, a realistic convention closely connected with the progress in technics, and one which is a mixture of both, due in part to honest perplexity and in part to the wish to avoid choosing at all.

Even social thinking, in all its various manifestations, has failed to set a new homogeneous goal for education. The fact that our modern class society does not admit of such a homogeneous goal is only partly responsible. The far more cogent cause is that up to now thinking along social lines has been directed solely to a task, toward striving and planning, and has no connection with the original forces. So, it is concerned with the "whither" and not the "whence" of man. But all true education must also be linked to the origin, to the "whence," must be bound up with history and tradition. Up to now there have been only a very few scattered indications that social thinking is undergoing a change in this direction, and they are unfortunately scarcely visible in the trends of the day. But we may at least hope that with change in the sense we have implied, Western education will strike out in a new direction.

But quite independent of all this, the first half of the nineteenth century produced significant attempts to create new ideal patterns as the goals of education. These patterns no longer emerged from a growing civilization which was producing a type of human being in which such patterns were embodied; they sprang from the historical situation of a community and the will to overcome such a situation through decisive action. What I have in mind are the movements in behalf of national liberation.

In the final analysis, these movements derive from the French Revolution, which not only proclaimed the *droits de l'homme,* the right to political freedom for all men, but—either directly or indirectly—also awakened the consciousness of the *droits de la nation,* the right of every nation to an independent existence. Those nations which, in the course of history, had lost their liberty and along with it their inner freedom, their spiritual independence, rebelled in movements that combined the striving for national rebirth with the fight for liberation. The spiritual leaders of such a movement realized the necessity for rearing a type of human being able and willing to carry on the fight until the end was achieved, until his nation was free. The new ideal of this epoch, the pattern which did not spring from a civilization but from a situation and a purpose, was the man equal to shouldering the problems of his nation, to achieving national revival. Fichte in Germany, Mickiewicz in Poland, and Mazzini in Italy, for instance, were all protagonists of national education. It is evident that the human type they wished to realize was not arbitrary but legitimate, called to a spiritual-historical task in a spiritual-historical reality. The nation was not considered as an end in itself. In all such movements the nation as a whole is assigned an inner task which goes beyond its factual existence. It is not enough for the nation to be what it is. It is to become what it is called on to become, and to be something not only for itself but for the world. The norm imposed on a nation refers, in the last analysis, to its relationship to the world. In these cases, national education is subordinated to a supernational standard. Among the national movements in Europe, Polish messianism was the most supernational in character. If Mickiewicz, the leader of this movement, pointed so emphatically to a kinship with Judaism and its prophets, it was because the prophets of Israel, more than anyone else in the history of the human spirit, express the truth that a people does not exist for its own sake, that its historic mission is to act upon its fellow nations in accordance with the task it assumed, that of "being a blessing." The nation's own destiny depends on whether it devotes itself to this task. National egoism may seem to result in success, but in the end it must lead to catastrophe. The leaders of great national movements have taken this prophetic law to heart and made it the basic law of national education.

But it must be particularly stressed that here the ideal pattern is not that of the type of man who represents a certain civilization, but one who is expected to meet certain historical situations. It is the type of the generation or generations who are destined to perform a unique historical feat, the feat of liberating a nation. The first type of man had meaning and justification as long as the civilization he represented was in its prime. The meaning and justification of the new type can persist only until its task has been accomplished. The culture type does not depend on individual historical events; the situation type, on the other hand, loses all content as soon as the situation which has produced it has been met, i.e., when the nation has won its independence. National education is true creative education as long as it strives toward a certain ideal pattern of a human being, the pattern of the liberator. But when liberation has been effected, the ideal pattern fades and national education ceases to be true creative education. So, if education wishes to remain faithful to its task and not decay into nationalistic convention, it must set itself a new and greater purpose. The educators cannot think up this purpose. They can, however, derive it from the supernational norm of their own national movement, a norm which must now be developed and expressed particularly in education. For the real destiny of a nation is not decided in the act of national liberation, but only after that liberation. It is then that the choice must be made between creativity and convention, between a generous world-receptive human attitude, or an inflexible, narrow and sterile egoism.

I have already suggested that "universal culture," arising from the collapse of the real pattern of European civilization, does not constitute a valid goal for education. If the gardener-educator takes it as his guide, he will produce no complete piece of work. The terrains of a-national "universal culture" are inhabited by no living humanism. But great national movements contain the germ of a new, national humanism. Education can develop this germ, provided it accepts as its authority the supernational norm of its own national movement. A curious phenomenon will occur, its forcefulness depending on the extent to which education follows that rule: the ideal pattern, which had apparently disintegrated, will re-emerge, but in an altered form, in the new form of the liberated man of a national humanism. Here I should like to add that I am convinced such change and renewal will bring with it that change and renewal in the social concept of which I have spoken: the change and renewal of the social concept that springs from man's union with the forces of history and tradition, that means, with the very powers whose effects beget national movements.

If, however, national education fails to discover the supernational task of the nation and derive from it the goal for its activities, if it is only concerned with the nation as such, if, for instance, it concentrates solely on producing the pure Chinese—then, as I have already indicated, it falls into a new convention, the nationalistic convention which is perhaps the most sterile and pernicious of all. The Chinese sage represents a true ideal pattern, but the pure synthetic Chinese is nothing but a caricature. Education can derive a great goal from the human purpose inherent in the Chinese spirit, but the breeding of unadulterated Chinese leads into the field of zoology. The nationalistic convention replaces the maternal powers of the Origin by an abstract compulsion; it substitutes cramped collective egoism for fruitful intercourse with the world, and sets factory-made human goods, all stamped alike, in place of the free sons of a free nation. Nationalistic convention, which regards itself as the supreme triumph of national education, is its death.

2.

The Jewish people differ from all the other nations in that the supernational task was not imposed on its national life at a late period in its history, not in a movement for liberation, but during an early epoch. I consider even the tradition that this happened at the very beginning of its history reliable. In the earliest age authenticated by literature, the message and commandment of a just society was an integral part of this people's history. The early manifestation and the influence of this ideal can be recognized in the predictions of the prophets that unless Israel fulfilled the commandment to establish a just society during the era of its independence, it would have to go into exile and there learn what is unjust and what is just. But if afterward Israel should return to its own land and there begin to realize the kingdom of the just God in its own community life and in its foreign relations, international peace and the beginnings of true humanity would issue forth from the mountain of Zion. This peculiar heritage of the Jewish people had a substantial share in influencing the new type of man which emerged from its national movement. It could not well be a type concerned solely with national liberation, because here the supernational task was always the more powerful formative factor. From Moses Hess to A. D. Gordon, all the spiritual leaders of the movement have realized and formulated this task in theory, and even a political leader like Theodore Herzl could not ignore it. The panhuman, moral, social, eternal work of the nation has been proclaimed by all of them. But it also lay as an elemental creative force in the womb of life itself, and helped mold the new Jewish individual.

This new individual has not merely the limited duty of achieving liberation, like the members of other national movements. We were not intent merely on throwing off an alien yoke, but on transforming the entire life of the people, within and without. Even our main work, that of building up a Palestinian society, was, as a matter of course, distributed over several generations, and unfolded as a life process rather than as a series of isolated actions. The human ideal of national education is not that of an individual who is participating in a definite historically determined deed, but that of one who is taking part in a new and changed life. The goal is greater than mere liberation. It is a regeneration of the very being; it is an inner renewal, a rescue from physical and spiritual deterioration, the turning from a fragmentary, contradictory existence to a whole and unified way of life; it is purification and redemption.

No matter from what angle we view this goal, we are bound to come to the conclusion that it cannot be interpreted merely as a national idea, but only as one of a national humanism. The survival of the nation is nothing but a necessary premise. But it must survive not for the sake of surviving, of extending its span of life, but in order to fulfil its vocation, in order to realize a great Jewish human community. From time immemorial, all the really productive powers of the Jewish people have flowed into this national and yet supernational task. That is why every attempt to give a nationalistic turn to national education, every attempt to regard the nation as an end in itself rather than the element of a new humanism, and to substitute the pattern of a self-centered and reserved individual for that of one who is an independent and responsive being, is even more fatal in our national movement than in that of any other nation. National education is the way that leads to the fulfilment of Judaism; nationalistic education is the way that leads to de-Judaization under a Jewish banner. It is contrary to our character and our task. In our case, more than in any other, nationalistic education is antinational.

3.

Ideologies, programs, or political orientation are not the true response of a generation to the situation it finds itself in, of a generation which, at long last, wishes to respond to that situation. Such a response must express itself in life, in the language of active life, and in the break-through of this live answer it begets the new type of man. The halutz, the Palestinian pioneer, is the most striking example of the new Jewish type and the most distinct goal of national education. In him we see how the supernational task has been converted into a living urge, into a vital personal endeavor and creative power, even though the individual is frequently unaware of the supernational character of what he is doing.

We cannot understand the true halutz unless we learn to recognize him as a personification of the union of national and social elements. The social element is evinced by the very fact that he wants to participate in the rebirth of his people in the home of his people, and through his own labors. He wants to devote his entire self to physical labor, for he wishes to participate as a worker, and only as a worker—not as who directs the work of others. And this personal ambition is closely connected with his ambition in regard to his objective: the goal of both ambitions is the "working society in Palestine," i.e., the social synthesis of people, land, and labor. But here there is more in the connotation of the word "society" than society per se. It implies the will to realize the human community in a formal society, i.e., a union of persons living together, a union founded on the direct and just relations of all to all.

The halutz does not draw this will to realize this ideal out of himself, or out of his era, or out of the Western world; nor does he derive it from the occidental socialism of his century. Whether or not he knows it, whether or not he likes it, he is animated by the age-old Jewish longing to incorporate social truth in the life of individuals living with one another, the longing to translate the idea of a true community into reality. The new type is a result of the development of very early traits. What we call "Israel" is not merely the result of biological and historical development; it is the product of a decision made long ago, the decision in favor of a God of justice and against a god of instinctive egoism. It was a decision in favor of a God who leads his people into the Land in order to prepare it for its messianic work in the world, and against a god who dwells in various spots in the land of Canaan, lurking in brooks and trees, and whispering to all comers: "Take possession and enjoy!" It was a decision for the true God and against Baal. Nowhere else was the destiny of a people so bound up with its original choice and the attempts at realization of that choice. The unsuccessful function of the prophets was to remind the people of this ancient bond.

Hasidism was the one great attempt in the history of the Diaspora to make a reality of the original choice and to found a true and just community based on religious principles. This attempt failed for a number of reasons, among others because it did not aim for the independence, for the self-determination of the people; or, to state it differently, because its connections with Palestine were only sporadic and not influenced by the desire for national liberation. The political corruption which invaded the hasidic movement was the result of this deficiency. For in order to get the state to grant it religious self-determination, hasidism sacrificed the wholeness and purity of its life, and so its integrity was corroded. This tragi-comical end of a great social and religious venture was followed by a period of theorizing on the task of translating ideal into reality. But finally the Jewish national movement, either consciously or unconsciously, took up the age-old social message and, impelled by it, set up as the goal of national education the pattern of the new type of man, of the man who can translate ideas into life, who along with the national idea will satisfy the longing for a just communal life.

In the meantime, however, Judaism has had to face a grave crisis of faith, perhaps the most ominous development in the religious crisis of the man of today. In most instances, the halutz has become estranged from the much deteriorated structure of

Jewish religion. He even rebels against it. He takes over the ambition to realize the ideal of a society, but in a secular form, without the bond of faith. If he is at all aware of the religious bond, he usually rejects it, separates it from the social will and makes that will autonomous. But this means that at a certain point of his consciousness which is of basic importance for the national movement the new type of man has no connection with the earliest tradition of his people, i.e., with the original choice of Israel.

I say "of his consciousness," and not "of his existence." For we have seen that certain traditional forces influence the character and life of the halutz, even though he may be unaware of it. But in consciously severing himself from his earliest tradition, he is resisting these forces and working counter to them.

The relation to tradition is a vital problem in all national movements and in every kind of national education. The greatest virtue of a national movement and of national education is that the generations which are growing up are made conscious of the great spiritual values whose source is the origin of their people, and that these values are deliberately woven into the design of their lives. Such values may be compared to waters gathered in a vast basin and thence distributed through thousands of pipes to drench the thirsty fields. The most profound meaning of the concept "national *movement*" is that a people's truth and ethos which, as abstract qualities, are one might say enthroned high above life, are now becoming movement, life in motion. And so the destiny of a national movement depends on whether, and to what extent, it acknowledges the national tradition.

National movements can have three possible relationships to tradition. The first is positive: The adherents of the movement open their hearts to the tide of the elements, absorb and transform what they have absorbed in response to the demands of the hour. They allow the forces inherent in the beginnings to shape present-day life in accordance with present-day needs.

The second form of relationship is negative. The impact of the age-old tidings is warded off as neither credible, nor usable, nor timely.

The third approach I should call the fictitious. Those who follow it exalt the works and values of national tradition, regard them as the subject of pride and piety, and point to them with the mien of collectors and owners, as though they were coronation robes in a museum, not, of course, suitable apparel for a living sovereign. While they boast of their tradition, they do not believe in it. They teach it in school but not with the purpose of seriously integrating it into actual life. All that seems necessary to them is to "have" it. Unfortunately the relationship of our national movement and national education to tradition is mainly a mixture of the second and third forms.

No mere good intentions can work a thoroughgoing change in the status quo. The power to transform life must spring from life itself. Already the halutz and his communes, the kibbutzim, are beginning to feel that something is lacking in the structure of their existence. Somewhere in the life of the week there is a dead end; somewhere in the web of the work there is a hole. No one knows just what it is, and certainly no one will name it. There is silence on that score, silence and suffering. I am under the impression that this suffering will increase in the course of the next decade and penetrate consciousness until it breaks the silence.

I do not believe that it is important for the halutz, or the national type of which he is the best representative, to accept *en bloc* either a ready-made tradition, or one or another part of it. Any such acceptance would be purely arbitrary and would share the fate of all arbitrary actions: it would be wholly unfruitful. One project, in particular, which is bruited about in the country, seems to me quite hopeless: the project of reviving religious forms without their religious content. Forms in themselves are nothing. What value they have accrues to them only through that which has been expressed in them, what has pervaded them as the soul pervades the body. The secret of their origin is the secret of their effectiveness. Once they have grown empty, one cannot fill them with a new, timely content; they will not hold it. Once they have decayed, they cannot be resuscitated by infusion with a spirit other than their own. They will seem only as lifelike as dolls. All such attempts are dilettantish—devoid of reverence and vigor; they are unblessed. A Passover Seder which is held to celebrate the national liberation as such will always be lacking in the essential, and that essential can only be won when we feel that self-liberation only enfolds the redemption of man and the world through a redeeming power as the husk enfolds the kernel. The Feast of Weeks is of course a nature festival, a festival in honor of a season and its abundance, the festival of the farmer who time and again experiences the miracle that earth gives him so much more than he has given her. But one cannot do justice to this festival by explaining it as a nature symbol. One must also know that nature herself is a symbol, that man can attain to true life only by surrendering himself to the unknown, and that the reward, the manifold harvest, is called revelation. No matter how devotedly the Sabbath is kept, the rite will be threadbare if the joy in a day of rest for everybody is not filled with the divination of a cosmic mystery of work and rest which is reflected in that day. This mystery is figuratively expressed with a childlike ingenuousness: in the idea that the Creator of heaven and earth "draws breath" after his labors on that day just as much as the "son of thy handmaid." Thus the breath of relaxation which we draw merges with the breath of the world.

But what shall we do when a generation, like that of today, has become alienated from the religious content of the forms?

We must provide them with a truly national education, and this means that we must convey the primordial utterances of their people to their ears and their hearts. We must surmount the prejudice of this era which claims that those utterances can have interest for us only as literary history, as cultural history, religious history, etc., and that instruction should treat them only as the main literary creation of the nation, as the source for the study of its ancient culture and the oldest document of its religious beginnings. We must surmount the superstition of the era which seems to hold that the world of faith to which those utterances bear witness is the subject of our knowledge only and not a reality which makes life worth living. We must keep the younger generation free from the bias that says: "We know all about ourselves and the world, and that in any event these utterances can no longer exert an authoritative influence on our lives." This generation must be taught to despise the inflexible self-assurance which says: "I am well prepared. Nothing can happen to change me fundamentally and transform the world before my eyes. I know what I know; I am what I am; tomorrow can be no different than today." This generation must be made receptive for the Unforeseen which upsets all logical arrangements. Their ears and hearts must be opened to the voice of the mystery which speaks in those utterances. And we should not do all this with the purpose of preparing them to repeat the teachings and perform prescribed rites, but so that they may acquire the power to make the original choice, that—listening to the voice with that power—they may hear the message it has for their hour and their work; that they may learn to trust the voice, and through this trust, come to faith, to a faith of their own.

ISRAEL AND THE WORLD

The Jew in the World

[ADDRESS DELIVERED AT THE LEHRHAUS IN FRANKFORT ON THE MAIN IN 1934]

THE CONCEPT of the "Jew in the world" in its most serious sense did not arise until a certain quite definite juncture. This juncture did not—as one might suppose—coincide with the destruction of the Jewish state by Titus, but with the collapse of the Bar Kokhba rebellion. When Jerusalem ceased to be a Jewish city, when the Jew was no longer permitted to be at home in his own country—it was then that he was hurled into the abyss of the world. Ever since, he has represented to the world the insecure man. Within that general insecurity which marks human existence as a whole, there has since that time lived a species of man to whom destiny has denied even the small share of dubious security other beings possess. Whether or not it is aware of it, this people is always living on ground that may at any moment give way beneath its feet. Every symbiosis it enters upon is treacherous. Every alliance in its history contains an invisible terminating clause, every union with other civilizations is informed with a secret divisive force. It is this inescapable state of insecurity which we have in mind when we designate the Jewish Diaspora as *galut,* i.e., as exile.

What is the cause of this fate of insecurity? The Jewish group plainly cannot be fitted into any known scheme. It resists all historical categories and general concepts; it is unique. This uniqueness of Israel necessarily thwarts the nations' very natural desire for an explanation, and explanation always implies arrangement in categories. The existence of whatever cannot be cubbyholed and hence understood is alarming. This state of affairs provides a basis of truth for the observation that anti-Semitism is a kind of fear of ghosts. The wandering, roving, defenseless group which is different from any other and comparable to none seems to the nations among which it lives to have something spectral about it, because it does not fit into any other given group. It could not be otherwise. The Jewish people was, indeed, always a "sinister," homeless specter. This people, which resisted inclusion in any category, a resistance which the other peoples could never become quite accustomed to, was always the first victim of fanatical mass movements (the Crusades of the eleventh century, for instance). It was branded as the cause of mass misfortunes ("the Jew is responsible for the 'Black Death' "). No matter how hard it tried, it never quite succeeded in adjusting to its environment. (The Inquisition followed upon Marranism.)

When I say that the nations regard us as a specter—and this myth is symbolized in the form of the wandering Jew—we must distinguish between being and appearance. We ourselves know very well that we are not specters, but a living community, and so we must ask ourselves what our nonclassifiability really signifies. Is it due merely to a lack of vision and insight on the part of the nations? Is it that we can be fitted into a system, only they are not able to do it? Is this resistance of ours to classification merely a negative phenomenon, one that is temporary? Does it simply mean that we cannot be classified until—at some future time—we are?

We have only *one* way to apprehend the positive meaning of this negative phenomenon: the way of faith. From any viewpoint other than faith, our inability to fit into a category would be intolerable, as something counter to history and counter to nature. But from the viewpoint of faith, our inability to fit into a category is the foundation and meaning of our living avowal of the uniqueness of Israel. We would differentiate this uniqueness from the general uniqueness we attribute to every group and each individual. The uniqueness of Israel signifies something which in its nature, its history, and its vocation is so individual that it cannot be classified.

Moreover, Israel will not fit into the two categories most frequently invoked in attempts at classification: "nation" and "creed." One criterion serves to distinguish a nation from a creed. Nations experience history *as nations*. What individuals as such experience, is not history. In creeds, on the other hand, salient experiences are undergone by *individuals,* and, in their purest and sublime form, these experiences are what we call "revelation." When such individuals communicate their experiences to the masses, and their tidings cause groups to form, a creed comes into being. Thus, nations and creeds differ in the same way as history and revelation. Only in one instance do they coincide. Israel receives its decisive religious experience *as a people;* it is not the prophet alone but the community as such that is involved. The community of Israel experiences history and revelation as one phenomenon, history as revelation and revelation as history. In the hour of its experience of faith the group becomes a people. Only as a people can it hear what it is destined to hear. The unity of nationality and faith which constitutes the uniqueness of Israel is not only our destiny, in the empirical sense of the word: here humanity is touched by the divine.

Now, in order to understand our position in the world, we must realize that a twofold desire comes to the fore in the history of Diaspora Jewry: the insecure Jew strives for security, the Jewish community which cannot be classified strives to be classified. These two strivings are by no means on a par. Like all human longing for security, this search for security is in itself quite legitimate. Man cannot be condemned to spend his life in insecurity. So the striving toward security is unobjectionable, but the means taken to arrive at this desired end may well be questioned.

The striving for security is familiar to us from the history of the ancient Hebrew state which presaged the insecurity of the Diaspora in a rather curious way. Wedged between Egypt and Babylonia, the two great powers of the ancient Orient, this state attempted time and again to overcome its geographic and political insecurity by employing power politics. Driven by the hope of overcoming its insecurity, it veered and compromised now with the one side, now with the other. The actual political content of the prophets is a warning against such false security. The prophets knew and predicted that in spite of all its veering and compromising Israel must perish if it intends to exist only as a political structure. It can persist—and this is the paradox in their warning and the paradox of the reality of Jewish history—if it insists *on its vocation of uniqueness,* if it translates into reality the divine words spoken during the making of the Covenant. When the prophets say that there is no security for Israel save that in God, they are not referring to something unearthly, to something "religious" in the common sense of the word; they are referring to the realization of the true communal living to which Israel was summoned by the Covenant with God, and which it is called upon to sustain in history, in the way it alone is capable of. The prophets call upon a people which represents the *first real attempt at "community"* to enter world history as a prototype of that attempt. Israel's function is to encourage the nations to change their inner structure and their relations to one another. By maintaining such relations with the nations and being involved in the development of humanity, Israel may attain its unimperiled existence, its true security.

In the late Diaspora the need for security assumed the anomalous form of a need to be categorized. It was reasoned that if it was our nonclassification which made us seem mysterious to the others, then that characteristic must be removed. This too is presaged in our ancient history, in the wanting to be "like unto all the nations" in the crisis during Samuel's time. But then and ever since then, the inner strength of faith was and is the resisting factor. The need for inclusion does not assume actual historical shape (if only history in caricature) until a late period of the exile, until the Emancipation. The Jews, to be sure, are not primarily to blame for the inadequacy of the Emancipation, for the fact that they were accepted as individuals, but not as a community.

At the beginning of the Emancipation, the nations pondered the question whether this unclassifiable Israel could not, after all, be included in one of the usual categories, and so they asked whether the Jews were a nation or a religion. The discussions which preceded the Emancipation in France anticipate all the later differences of opinion connected with this problem. Among other statements, we find the following words of Portalis, the French minister of education, whom Napoleon had asked to report on the Jews in 1802. What he wrote was: "The Government could not but consider the eternal life of this people, which has been preserved up to the present through all the stupendous changes and all the misfortunes of the centuries, since . . . it enjoys the privilege of having God himself as its lawgiver."

These words might well have been the prelude to the legal recognition of our people as such. But not one of the nations perceived the great task of liberating and accepting the Jewish community as a community *sui generis,* and not a single Jew from out of his age-old awareness thought to exert such a claim upon the unaware nations. Jewry disintegrated into small particles to comply with the nations' demand. The urge to conform became a cramp. Israel lost its reality by becoming a "confession." Our era attempted to counteract this by nationalization. The attempt failed: the one thing that is essential, the element of uniqueness, was ignored.

There is no re-establishing of Israel, there is no security for it save one: it must assume the burden of its own uniqueness; it must assume the yoke of the kingdom of God.

Since this can be accomplished only in the rounded life of a community, we must reassemble, we must again root in the soil, we must govern ourselves. But these are mere *prerequisites!* Only when the community recognizes and realizes them as such in its own life, will they serve as the cornerstones of its salvation.

The Power of the Spirit

[ADDRESS DELIVERED AT THE LEHRHAUS IN FRANKFORT ON THE MAIN IN 1934]

COUNT HERMANN KEYSERLING described the situation prevailing in national life in modern times. The gist of what he had to say was that the type of person who influences by suggestion is crowding out the type of the guide. Correspondingly, the majority of mankind have become intellectually passive. This passivity originates in the revolt of the nonintellectual, of the "tellurian forces," as he calls them, though I myself should prefer the term "elemental." He went on to explain that the basis of our civilization is too narrow to accommodate more than a very limited number of human capacities and urges, that those tellurian forces are therefore neglected, and that this is the cause of the reaction which is expressing itself in a strong tendency to repaganize, to reinstate heathenism. Pagan antiquity, he asserts, was the last era in European civilization during which man accepted and approved himself for what he was, in his entirety. Why, asks Keyserling, should we not consciously strive toward a new integration of all our vital conscious forces? Why not try to achieve a new synthesis which would give adequate scope to all the vitality within us, just as antiquity did at the peak of its conception? He even goes so far as to say that the new culture might well be superior to that of antiquity, since our understanding of things and of the ways in which they are interrelated has become both more precise and more profound.

I have cited the ideas of a thoughtful contemporary because they serve to demonstrate two trends characteristically connected: true insight into present conditions, and—bound up with it—the setting up of a false goal and an incorrect description of the underlying cause of those conditions. One cannot actually strive toward a synthesis which in one's judgment characterized an era belonging to the past. Historical reality does not allow a renewal through thought. There is indeed such a thing as the power and influence of the spirit in and upon history, but it cannot be deliberate. Keyserling's plan of setting up a goal shows itself questionable the moment he applies the attribute "new" to the culture of the future. True, new things do arise, again and again, but they are certainly not those which were heralded as such. The great novelty never advertises itself as something new. Particularly suspect is the prediction of a new heathenism which we hear bruited abroad. Only those who mistake the meaning of the development of the history of the human spirit can believe that all we need to do to obtain building materials or a pattern for the "new" is to reach back into bygone eras of world history. This could not possibly lead to the reconquest of those pagan splendors which grew spontaneously in their own time, involuntarily, and never according to a set goal. The hand which reaches back will always seize on something negative: not the original stuff of paganism which cannot be recaptured, but only that part of it which has not yet become Christianity.

So, the examination into the power of the elemental in our own era gives rise to a question which is, as a matter of fact, the basic question of the hour: Is there *another* kind of power, that of the spirit, in present-day history? Is there a vital power which is superior to the elemental powers ruling the moment? Or has the meaning and the function of the spirit changed so much in the course of history that it can no longer lord it over the elemental powers, but must resign its supremacy? There were, of course, recurring junctures in history when the spirit was attacked by powers which swarmed up from below; but it not only mastered each successive revolt, but actually set on these powers the brand of its own power. Does the same still hold for our own era?

Confronted by this question, we must first of all clear up a fatal misunderstanding. In our use of the word, "spirit" does not indicate something which gradually developed in the history of mankind. Spirit is not a late bloom on the tree Man, but what constitutes man. The fact that man is a unit of substance which cannot be grasped if we regard it merely as a phenomenon of nature, the fact that there is a category of existence called Man, is based on the particular human consciousness. Spirit, then, is not just one human faculty among others. It is man's totality that has become consciousness, the totality which comprises and integrates all his capacities, powers, qualities, and urges. When a man thinks, he thinks with his entire body; spiritual man thinks even with his fingertips. Spiritual life is nothing but the existence of man, insofar as he possesses that true human conscious totality, which is not the result of development; it goes back to the origin of mankind, though it may unfold differently in different individuals. Nowadays the word spirit is used in a very different sense by persons who forget or scorn its great past in both the East and the West, and designate by it that part of human thinking which essentially regards all totality as something alien and hateful; the severed intellect. Severed from totality, yet greedy to govern all of man, for a number of centuries the intellect has been growing greedier and more independent and is attempting to reign from on high, but without the ability to flow freely into all organic vitality as the spirit it has dethroned can and does. The revolt of the "tellurian powers" is not directed against the spirit, the master from time immemorial, but toward the imposter, the spirit turned into a homunculus. Not this usurper, but only the human spirit in its totality can overcome elemental forces and elemental urges when occasion demands. They cannot be tamed like beasts of prey; they must be mastered as the artist masters and shapes the stuff he works with. Only the spirit in its totality can order and give true shape to the life of the individual and that of the species.

The relation of the spirit to the elemental forces and urges must not be interpreted from the point of view of pure thought. An attempt at interpretation must consider the influence of the spirit upon life. But—regardless of what it may call itself or be called at any given moment—the spirit which is not content in the area of thought and expresses itself in all of life becomes manifest as the power of *faith*. In the domain of the human soul, it appears as faithful courage and faithful love. Based on the power of faith, the spirit exerts its influence upon the world through its agents, courage and love. These constitute its power which may well govern the elemental forces because it has known them from the earliest times, and knows what is their due. Though in one historical era after another the spirit may seem dethroned and exiled, it does not lose its power. Again and again, unexpectedly and unpredictably, it causes what is intrinsic in the course of history through its agents, faithful courage and faithful love.

This fact results in something of fundamental importance, in opposition to the views I cited as my point of departure. In history there are not—as these views postulate—only two possible relationships of the spirit to the elemental forces: the one, demonstrated in classical antiquity, in which the sum total of the forces of man go to make up his existence and his attitude toward existence, and the other, in which the elemental forces can be overcome to the point of suppression. Actually there are three possible relationships. The first is the glorification of the elemental forces as such. We may call it the state of heathenism in the development of the peoples, though there never was a pure heathenism in history. The second is the conquest of the elemental forces, the most illustrious example being Christianity. The third however is the hallowing of the elemental forces: not their glorification or conquest but their sanctification and consequently their transformation. The most striking instance of this third relationship in the history of the Western world is Judaism.

Judaism has been misinterpreted from two utterly different standpoints. Christianity couples it with heathenism and claims that both are incapable of transcending the world and looking into a beyond that is over and above the world. Heathenism, on the other hand, and today this means "neo-heathenism," couples it with Christianity, arguing that it denies the great vital powers and has no sense of the secret of reality. Neither line of reasoning touches upon the essence of Judaism. This becomes clear when we compare the three forms which the power of the spirit assumes, in respect to their relationship to the elemental forces. Of course, this survey intends to draw sharp distinctions, and so the overlapping and fusion appearing in history cannot be given their full due. With regard to both heathenism and Christianity, our task will be to emphasize what is problematic in their relationship to the elemental forces, without identifying concrete historical patterns with such simplifications.

Heathenism glorifies elemental forces as such; they are considered sacred; they are declared holy, but not transformed. The spirit does not include them in the realm of the eternal, unconditioned holy which springs neither from nature nor from the mental processes of man. This glorification, this divine rank of theirs, cannot be maintained because the spirit which has empowered them cannot draw upon inexhaustible depths. The sacred quality flakes off like gilding from a picture, and all the regildings attempted in Hellenistic times prove failures. In the end, heathenism necessarily breaks apart into spirit alien to the world and world alien to the spirit. Classical antiquity is nothing but a splendid dream or transport of existence sacred by nature. Greek tragedy represents the gradual awakening from this dream or transport, and Greek philosophy the ever hopeless attempt to recapture that which is irrevocably slipping away. Keyserling is wrong in believing that in antiquity man accepted himself with all the facets of his being. Rather, his incomparable creative genius overcame the actual and ineluctable conflict within him. But when his creative ability slackened, this conflict loomed larger and gave rise to an era colored with despair. That was the hour in which Christianity grew and came to power, and set up a new relationship to the elemental forces.

Christianity—by which I do not mean the teachings of Jesus—accomplished the desanctification of the elemental. To realize this, we must distinguish between elemental forces and elemental urges. Elemental forces is the term I apply to those powers of nature which, both in prehistory and in history, built the kind, the species, and the destinies of man. The most frequently cited instances are the elemental forces of "blood" and "soil." By refusing to admit them into its sanctuary, Christianity brought about the negative effect of the desanctification of these forces. But at the same time Christianity accomplished the positive task of desanctifying the elemental urges. Elemental forces build human existence objectively; but elemental urges are those factors in human existence which enable human existence to develop subjectively, though in accordance with a common core which shapes a man partly like all other creatures and partly as a man and an individual endowed with his own peculiar traits. We know these urges under the names of hunger, sex, and the will to power. Christianity desanctifies these in a positive sense by rendering them subservient to an entirely different kind of holiness. The most notable expression of such subservience is in Paul's phrase about "the law of sin which is in my members," warring against the "law of my mind" and "working death in" him. The world of antiquity had split into a spirit alien to the world, and a world alien to the spirit. In Paul's dual law they dwell side by side. The spirit is holy, the world unholy. Even when Christianity includes natural life in its sacredness, as in the sacrament of marriage, the bodily life of man is not hallowed but merely made subservient to holiness. Although the ascetic ideal was not imposed on the people at large, still it was set up as the pattern of the adequate Christian and that pattern gave the Christianity of the Western world its definitive form. A fundamental dualism in existence resulted: spirit and world became subject to different laws: man can accomplish nothing by himself. All he can do is surrender to the other, to redemption which has come from the beyond and has assumed bodily shape in his earthly sphere. The corollary of this dualism in principle was a factual dualism between human life as it is intended to be and as it *is* lived, the great rift which was expressed only in the confessions of a few great devout men: up above, a miraculous dome—once more painted in golden colors—arching life, comforting and sating the gaze of man; and below, actual life, governed by the elemental which is at core unhallowed, even when it has been consecrated.

I must repeat that I have, of necessity, given a one-sided, simplified picture. Christianity contains another characteristic element, which does not originate in the disintegrating antiquity but in the tradition of biblical faith. But the whole Christian as well as the whole heathen spirit is a genuine spirit which establishes a binding relationship to the elemental forces. This situation has, however, suffered intrinsic change in the course of the last few centuries when spirit was often dethroned in favor of the usurper of the severed intellect, which presumes to master the elemental by despiritualizing being. It is this usurper who is the subject of the rebellion of the elemental forces, a revolt which frequently misunderstands itself and fights the spirit instead of the spurious authority of the severed intellect.

The only approach to understanding the importance of Judaism in the history of thought is to study it in connection with the "reality system" of the ancient peoples of the Orient, and by studying it as that system which is indirectly connected with the life structure of occidental peoples and directly attached to it. To differentiate it from all purely ideal systems, the term "reality" is here used to designate that basic unity of a great community which relates all the fields of social, family, and personal life, of politics, economics, and culture, to a single underlying principle which cannot be derived from any one of these fields, but which permeates and gives meaning to them all. This underlying principle does not entirely correspond to nationality, but transcends and gives nationality a basis and soul. One system, Judaism, separated off from the "reality systems" of Asia which are now either in the state of or approaching a state of dissolution, and—through its encystation in the West—has persisted past the flowering of the East, certainly not unharmed, but as yet uncorrupted. In this system spirit is nothing but that power which hallows the world. If anywhere, here this spirit is not independent and tyrannical, but is the connecting link, and existent only in the sense that it links, or rather, is the bond between this community of man and its origin, a bond with God which is not present simply as something firm and immutable grafted onto man. Rather, Jewish spirit is something which time and again wells up, streams, pours itself out, and settles. In short, man's bond with God *which is always taking place.* This spirit is in search of its own reality. That is why it takes possession of man for the sake of hallowing the world. The fact that the world was created is seriously accepted and recognized as its reality. For the world is a creation, not a reflection, not semblance, not play. The world is not something which must be overcome. It is created reality, but reality created to be hallowed. Everything created has a need to be hallowed and is capable of receiving it: all created corporeality, all created urges and elemental forces of the body. Hallowing enables the body to fulfil the meaning for which it was created. The meaning with which Creation informed man, informed the world, is fulfilled through the hallowing. Here then, the world is neither transfigured into something wholly spiritual nor overcome by the spirit. The spirit does not embrace a holy world, rejoicing in its holiness, nor does it float above an unholy world, clutching all holiness to itself: it produces holiness, and the world is made holy.

In the "reality system" of Judaism, the elemental forces are connected with the living faith in a union holy from time immemorial. Thus, blood and soil are hallowed in the promise made to Abraham, because they are bound up with the command to be "a blessing" (Gen. 12:2). "Seed" and "earth" are promised, but only in order that—in the race of man scattered through the confusion of languages and divided into "islands of the nations" (Gen. 10:5)—a new people may "keep the way of the Lord to do righteousness and justice" (Gen. 18:19) in his land, and so begin building humanity. In the Israel of the Bible, land and people are represented as elemental forces which are hallowed because of God's goal in creating them. They are neither declared holy nor removed from sanctity, but accepted by holiness and made holy as part of it. The elemental urges are hallowed: hunger, by the sacrament of sacrifice, later persisting in altered form in ritual slaughter and dietary laws, connects the partaking of animal flesh with an offering to God. The original meaning of the offering was that man owes himself to God, but may ransom himself by substituting an animal. Sex is hallowed by the sacrament of the circumcision covenant which survives in its original purity and not only confirms the act of begetting but converts it into a holy vocation; the will to power, by the sacrament of the anointing of kings (surviving only in the hope for a Messiah), obligating the exponent of power, as the lieutenant of God, to found a realm of justice (II Sam. 23:3f). Hallowing transforms the urges by confronting them with holiness and making them *responsible* toward what is holy. In post-biblical times this great concept became a teaching in the notion of the *yetzer ha-ra,* the so-called Evil Urge or, as we would say it, passion. Passion, too, is a creation of God, which he created in man as the power without which no work and no holy work can prosper, but through which it can prosper only if man who has the freedom of choice, determined to give that urge direction, lends it the full force of his will, even though this determination can be no more than the beginning of a movement which it is not in his power to complete. In the hallowing, the total man is accepted, confirmed, and fulfilled. This is the true integration of man.

It is not up to us to give a universal valid answer to the question concerning the power of the spirit in this phase of history. But it is up to us to give a specific answer, which is valid for us. It is our duty to reconsider the power of the spirit in Judaism, in our "reality system" which includes the elemental in one great bond with that which is holy: the holiness of God and the hallowing deriving from him and granted for his sake. Our living faith recognizes the rule of no spirit over the elemental forces and urges save this spirit which includes the elemental in holiness. If this spirit which is master of the elemental in its own domain is given a new shape, it will be able to resist even in areas where the barely tamed elemental forces and urges are supreme.

The Spirit of Israel and the World of Today

For many years now, Jews all over the world have been asking one another: "How is it all going to end? Are we completely in the hands of Evil? Will the power of wickedness continue to grow stronger? Or are we possibly entitled to hope, to hope with a trembling heart, that the spirit of Israel will prove victorious?"

When I am asked these questions, I respond with a query of my own: "What is it you have in mind when you speak of the spirit of Israel? Your own spirit? Or that spirit which we have betrayed and which we continue to betray day after day?" The reply to the question posed by these various Jews turns on their reply to my question. Everything, indeed, depends on their answer.

There is a Jewish tradition about seventy angels known as princes who are set in charge of the seventy nations of the world. Each of these princes supervises his own nation, acting as its spokesman before the throne of glory. When their respective nations are embattled, they too become involved against each other. The princes are the real victors and the real vanquished; and their wars, victories and defeats, their ascents and descents on the mighty ladder, are what historians characterize by the name of history. Each of them has a purpose and function of his own; and so long as the prince does his part, so long as he accomplishes his purpose and fufils his function, he is entrusted with power. But he is responsible to his Master, and is required to render an accounting to him. Therefore, when he becomes so intoxicated with power as to forget who he is and what his function is, arrogantly assuming himself to be the lord and master—then the hand of his Sovereign falls upon him: falling either in the form of lightning which flings him into the abyss of nothingness, or gradually as a steady rain, which carries him little by little down to the abyss of nothingness.

Now it is said that the Jewish people, too, have a prince appointed over them; but there are those who assert that the children of Israel refused to accept the yoke of any angel, rejecting all yokes except that of the Kingdom of God and all authority save that of the very Godhead.

And it is alone this latter belief—in the light of the world view and conception of history held by Jewish tradition as a whole—which, we see, has an inner connection with the totality of thought concerning the relationship between Israel and the Divinity. The source of the people of Israel is to be found not in that world of multiplicity where princes contend with one another, but rather in the world of the one truth which, indeed, reveals only a hint of its essence to human beings. But even that hint is adequate for man and nation to know that there is one truth above them; and that, furthermore, neither that people nor the prince of that people is the possessor of the truth, its sole possessor being the prince of princes and the Lord of the World.

The typical individual of our times is no longer capable of believing in God; but he finds it impossible to believe even in his own substance, that substance which has neither pediment nor basis; and so he holds fast to his faith in his expanded ego, his nation, as being the highest authority within his reach. And since he has no genuine and vital relation to the truth which is above all the nations, to the truth which requires the nations to fulfil it, he transforms his nation into an idol, he sets up the personality of his people as god; he makes the "prince" who is a mere ministering angel into a god. And since there is no level above that of the nations, since there is no court of appeal on high, the end must be that the nations and their princes wage war against each other using every means they can and without balking at anything until they encompass their own destruction.

Those secret forces, the princes, are nowadays nothing more than the various national ideologies, the various state myths used by the leaders and misleaders of the nations in order to fire their egoism with the illusions and deceits of an imaginary idealism. This is the hour when the princes forget who they are and what their function is, and vaunt their arrogance; each of them imagines that he is the supreme master. But the hand of their Master is over them.

But what of us Jews? We talk of the spirit of Israel and assume that we are not like unto all the nations because there is a spirit of Israel. But if the spirit of Israel is no more to us than the synthetic personality of our nation, no more than a fine justification for our collective egoism, no more than our prince transformed into an idol—after we had refused to accept any prince other than the Lord of the Universe!—then we are indeed like unto all the nations; and we are drinking together with them from the cup that inebriates. And when we grow drunk after their fashion, we become weaker than any other nation, and find ourselves entirely defenseless in their hands.

It is only if we do not really become like them, it is only if we refer by the term "spirit" not to ourselves but to the living truth, which is not in our possession, but by which we can be possessed, which is not dependent upon us, but we upon it, and which nonetheless needs us in order to become something that is of the lower realm, something concrete, something "historic"—it is then, and only then, that we have the ground of combat and victory beneath our feet.

But it may be that one of you is secretly asking me the question: "What then is this spirit of Israel of which you are speaking?"

It is the spirit of fulfilment. Fulfilment of what? Fulfilment of the simple truth, that man has been created for a purpose.

There is a purpose to creation; there is a purpose to the human race, one we have not made up ourselves, or agreed to among ourselves; we have not decided that henceforward this, that, or the other shall serve as the purpose of our existence. No. The purpose itself revealed its face to us and we have gazed upon it.

Again, this cannot be defined in terms of concepts; yet we can know and express the fact that unity, not division and separation, is the purpose of creation, and that the purpose is not an everlasting struggle to the death between sects or classes or nations. Our purpose is the great upbuilding of peace. And when the nations are all bound together in one association, to borrow a phrase from our sages, they atone for each other. In other words: the world of humanity is meant to become a single body; but it is as yet nothing more than a heap of limbs each of which is of the opinion that it constitutes an entire body. Furthermore, the human world is meant to become a single body through the actions of men themselves. We men are charged to perfect our own portion of the universe—the human world. There is one nation which once upon a time heard this charge so loudly and clearly that the charge penetrated to the very depths of its soul. That nation accepted the charge, not as an inchoate mass of individuals but as a nation. As a nation it accepted the truth which calls for its fulfilment by the human nation, the human race as a whole. And that is its spirit, the spirit of Israel.

The charge is not addressed to isolated individuals but to a nation. For only an entire nation, which comprehends peoples of all kinds, can demonstrate a life of unity and peace, of righteousness and justice to the human race, as a sort of example and beginning. A true humanity, that is, a nation composed of many nations, can only commence with a certain definite and true nation. The hearkening nation was charged to become a true nation. Only the fulfilment of this truth in the relations between the various sections of this people, between its sects and classes, is capable of serving as a commencement of an international fulfilment of the truth and of the development of a true fellowship of nations, a nation consisting of nations. Only nations each of which is a true nation living in the light of righteousness and justice are capable of entering into upright relations with one another. The people of Israel was charged to lead the way toward this realization.

From age to age the people of Israel has preserved its heritage, which is this charge. As long as it lived in its own land, it represented the charge to other nations. When it was exiled from its land, it introduced it to the other nations. The people of Israel proclaimed it in that confession to which it was faithful even unto martyrdom, and proclaimed it by its very indestructible existence: the existence of those who guard the heritage. But the Jewish nation did not meet the test. For untold generations the Jews observed the six hundred and thirteen injunctions of the Torah; but the charge which is higher than every formulation of individual precepts was not fulfilled. The life of the nation as such never became one of righteousness and justice. The people did not become a true nation taking the lead in the fufilment of the ideal. Only one great attempt was made to create, under the restricted and restrictive conditions of the exile, a concrete social life, the fraternal life of sons of the One God living together. That was the attempt of hasidism, and even it did not pierce to the vital, the essential problem, but crumbled away after a time. The local community, too, the sole social basis in the life of the Diaspora, lost more and more of the originality of its form and content. But how can the Community of Israel continue to live in truth when there are no longer any local communities that live in truth?

And now that we have once again achieved, though only for a section of our people, a chance to live in our country and an authority of our own which, restricted though it is, would be nonetheless adequate for the formation of a just society, what have we done? Important social experiments, to be sure, have been made.

Independent forms of social association have been born, particularly different varieties of communal settlements which will yet prove of the utmost importance in the development of the new human society. But, to what extent has the communal settlement influenced the Jewish community in Palestine? How much weight does it carry in the emerging social form of that community? And has it reached the level of genuine fraternity itself? Can it be that there is no perfect brotherhood in the world without fatherhood or motherhood? Can it be that there is no living truth between one man and another without the common acceptance of that truth from on high which does not depend upon us but upon which we depend? It is waiting to be accepted even at this very moment; but there is none to accept it. To be sure, one must not forget that saying which Jewish tradition puts in the mouth of God: "If only they were to forsake me, and observe my teachings!" * Yet though the teacher desires nothing more than the fulfilment of his teaching, no teaching can be adequately fulfilled until and unless it leads to the feet of the teacher.

Age after age the Jewish people believed in the messianic tidings. They believed them and proclaimed them, and occasionally even rose to the summons of false Messiahs and hastened to join them. But they did not realize what is incumbent upon the individual and the nation: the commencement. Of course it lies in the power of heaven to introduce the Kingdom of God; the preparation of the world in readiness for that kingdom, the commencement of a fulfilment of the truth calls for men and a nation consisting of men. And now, after a proclamation without fulfilment, there has come some measure of fulfilment without proclamation; but then what is the proclamation of a Kingdom without a King?

The spirit of Israel is the spirit of realization. But where does it exist? For if it has not existence, it has no force at this hour. Not

* Palestinian Talmud, Hagigah 76c.

only do we have no realization of the truth to any adequate extent, but faith in the truth is growing steadily weaker even among ourselves. Day by day an increasing number of us are saying: "The period of humanism is past! You cannot swim against the current! Those messianic tidings, the charge of righteousness and justice, was nothing but an expression of our weakness! So come, let us be strong!" Their only wish is to join the wolf pack. If we are not acceptable in the pack, it is enough to live on its fringes, in its neighborhood. And if we cannot be the head, it is also quite enough to be the tail. Of all the many kinds of assimilation in the course of our history, this is the most terrifying, the most dangerous, this nationalist assimiliation. That which we lose on account of it we shall perhaps never acquire again.

If we consider all the reasons for anti-Semitism advanced by the Christian nations, we find that they are all superficial and transitory. But if we go deeper, we find that there is one deep and unconscious reason that is true for all periods of the exile. It is, that there has entered and become dispersed among them a people carrying a charge from heaven which is written in a book which became sacred for them too when they became Christians. It is unique in human history, strange and awesome, that heaven should make a specific demand in reference to human behavior, and that the demand should be recorded in a book, and that the book should be the heritage of a people which is dispersed among all the nations with this, its holy book, which is holy for all the nations as well. The demand stands above and remote from the nations, a comprehensive demand, differing entirely from the quality characteristic of their own lives; it hovers high over them as the demand which their God makes of them. And the nations refuse to submit to it. To be sure, they wish to retain the God they have received, but at the same time they would reject his demand. In so doing they rely upon the teachings of Saul, a

Jew from Tarsus, who asserted that it was impossible to fulfil the Torah and that it was necessary to cast off its yoke by submission to another Jew, Jesus of Nazareth, who had died during Saul's lifetime and was the Messiah, who had indeed fulfilled the Torah and abolished it at the same time; and who demanded nothing of his true believers save faith. Such was the argument of the nations who went in the footsteps of Saul, and a large part of their theology has been nothing but a detailed interpretation of the utterance of Saul, the apostle to the Gentiles.

Yet against all their opposition to the Torah stood that unfortunate Jewish people, bearing the book which was its own book and at the same time part of the holy book of the nations. That is the real reason for their hatred. Their theologians argue that God rejected this people, who no longer have any heritage because that heritage has now passed over to Christianity. But the Jewish people continued to exist, book in hand; and even though they were burned at the stake, the words of the book were still on their lips. That is the perennial source of anti-Semitism. In this sense there is an essential truth in the verse of the medieval Hebrew poet, Yannai, "Hated we are, for thee we love, O Holy!" For that reason there was only one way to abolish the hatred: realizing the truth. If we as a people had fufilled this requirement and had refuted the words of Saul of Tarsus by our actions, and if we had actually shown the nations by our actions the way to a better life upon the earth, a life of friendship within and without—then we would have ceased to be contradictory and terrifying to them, and we would have become what we truly are, their older brother. The Western peoples accepted the Gospel, some willingly and some under duress; but with it came the Torah of Israel, which comprehends three things: first, the history of creation, which develops into the history not of the nations but of Israel; second, the revelation of God, which was first of all his revelation to the Jewish people; and third, the messianic prophecy, whose center and focal point is the effort of the people of Israel for the redemption of humanity. And it is the books of the Gospel which relate the life of Jesus, the Jew in whom they see the redeemer himself as he lived among his people; and there he states expressly that he came only for the lost sheep of the House of Israel. This was too heavy a burden for the nations to accept in full as their own faith. So they rose against it time and again. Saul of Tarsus, to be sure, maintained the unity of the Hebrew Scriptures and the Gospel. But a mere twenty years after his death a man was born who undertook to separate them.

That was Marcion the Gnostic, who regarded himself as the disciple of Saul. At the time when the emperor Hadrian quenched the Bar Kokhba revolt in a sea of blood, transformed Jerusalem into a Roman colony, and set up a temple to Jupiter on the site of the Second Temple, Marcion came to Rome from Asia Minor, bringing with him his own Gospel as a kind of spiritual contribution to the destruction of Israel. In his Gospel he not only separated the Old from the New Testament and the history of Christianity from the history of Israel, but he also drew a line of demarcation between the Deities: on the one side the God of Israel, who is also the creator of this imperfect world and is himself imperfect, being only a just God, and not a good God; on the other side, the "strange," unknown God who has no concern with this world, yet takes pity on it and redeems it. The logical conclusion was the Gnostic transvaluation: there is no value to this material world, and no thought ought to be given to *its* correction.

Yet there is another conclusion which Marcion never expressed and which quite possibly he did not even realize. If such is the case, then the world is in the hands of the worldly powers without any check or limitation. Jesus told his followers to render unto Caesar the things that are Caesar's and to God the things that are God's. From the context we learn that he meant them to pay to Caesar the tax Caesar required and not to rebel against Caesar; but they were to give the whole reality of life to

God. Marcion rendered this world unto Caesar and the other world unto God. In the teachings of Marcion the nations of the world are absolved of the demands of heaven by an extreme dualism: the life of the redeemed soul on the one hand, and that of existing society on the other. In the former there is not justice but there is lovingkindness, while in the latter there is not even true justice.

The Church did not follow in Marcion's footsteps; for it knew that if its traditional link with the creation of the world and the revelation of Divinity were to be broken, the entire basis of its influence upon the order of this world would be undermined. Protestantism, while approximating more closely the doctrines of Marcion, did not accept them either. But in the year 1920 the Protestant theologian Adolf von Harnack, who was not in the least an anti-Semite but a representative of a broad liberalism and as such thought that the greater part of Scripture, with the exception of the Prophets and the Psalms, hindered the inner development of Christianity, wrote in his book on Marcion: "Any retention of the Old Testament as a canonical document in the Protestanism of the nineteenth century and later is an outcome of religious and ecclesiastical paralysis." Three years after the death of Harnack in 1930, his idea, the idea of Marcion, was put into action; not however by spiritual means but by means of violence and terror. The state of which Harnack was a citizen placed before the Church one of two alternatives: either to exclude Judaism and the spirit of Israel entirely from its midst, and thereby to renounce any influence over the affairs of this world, the affairs of the state and society; or else to be overthrown together with Judaism. The gift of Marcion had passed from Hadrian into other hands.

Meanwhile those hands have been severed. But we do not know into whose hands Marcion's gift will pass, we do not today know when Christianity will again be faced with the alternative of renunciation, which is an inner death, and external overthrowal, which is actually the prospect of returning to life in the darkness of the catacombs. But this we do know: that the extrusion of the Jewish element from Christianity means an extrusion of the divine demand and concrete messianism; its separation from the divine truth calling for fulfilment.

But what of us Jews?

We have no right to make use, as we have been accustomed to do, of the term "spirit of Israel" as a kind of epithet descriptive of the "prince" of our nation, one of the many warring princes on high, one of the conflicting national forces. We must not use this term as a kind of metaphorical mask for our own egoism. The true spirit of Israel is the divine demand implanted in our hearts. We should not take pride in ourselves because of it but should submit to it, for we have betrayed it. Our first step at the present time is to give a full account of our souls without concealing anything; without deceiving ourselves about anything; to make an inventory of the real, omitting fictitious values.

We are entitled to ask as did the people in the desert, whether we have the Lord in our midst or not, as long as we ask with the proper intention. In that case the meaning of the question becomes: Is there true devotion to God in our midst, or is there not? And true devotion to God in turn means: our will to fulfil his truth. That again means: to aid in accomplishing his purpose in creating man, in the establishment of a human people whose king he is. And how is it given us to fulfil this truth if not by building the social pattern of our own people in Palestine all the way, from the pattern of family, neighborhood and settlement to that of the whole community? For it is no real community if it is not composed of real families and real neighborhoods and real settlements, and it is not a real nation if it does not maintain its truthfulness in true relations as well, the relationships of a fruitful and creative peace with its neighbors. For the true nation, all of whose members live in peace, also exerts its influence in behalf of peace, and lives in peace with other nations as well. We must realize the truth by living a life of truth, both inwardly and outwardly, like that people which at the very commencement of its world-journey, at the Red Sea, made the Lord of the world their king in a song of redemption. The erection of the kingdom of righteousness with the material of our own being is the presentation of the truth.

If we seriously proceed to this realization within our own restricted circle, we shall also be entitled to proclaim our position in fundamental terms. We shall then be entitled to set up the spirit of Israel against the overt and covert Marcionism of the other nations. We shall be entitled to set up against the dualism of free soul on the one hand and action without responsibility on the other, the active aspiration to a life of unity, a life of responsible work in the service of unity. If we are able to point, as it were, to the evolving pattern of a true people, then we shall be entitled to impart to the despairing mankind the doctrine of a nation composed of many nations, which is the doctrine of the Kingdom of God.

NATIONALISM AND ZION

The Gods of the Nations and God

1.

Nachman Krochmal (1785–1840), the originator of the philosophy of Jewish history, followed Giambattista Vico (1668–1744), who inaugurated the modern philosophy of history, in many things, among others in dividing world history into the history of the nations and that of Iṣrael on the premise that they are governed by different laws.

Vico derives the principle of division from the twofold nature of Divine Providence which manifested itself to the nations by creating them, so that the course of their history is predetermined by their given talents and faculties. In the case of Israel, Divine Providence granted revelation as well, so that the singular course of its history is to be understood from the viewpoint of divine intervention.

Krochmal, on the other hand, does not base his theory on God, but on man. Every nation has a guiding spiritual characteristic, to which all its other faculties are subordinated, its genius, which it acknowledges as its "prince" or its "god." That national spirit unfolds, matures, and withers. That which limits the national spirit gives it its transitory nature. But this does not hold for Israel. Israel reveres whole, undivided spiritual being, and, because of this, persists and arises after every downfall to begin as a new force. The nations make idols of their supreme faculties, and are thus rendered subject to the judgment of history. Israel knows only one God, the Eternal, and thus knows the secret of rebirth.

In other words: Every nation elevates its own self to the absolute, and worships itself as such. Israel experiences the absolute as that which Israel itself is not and which it can never become, and reveres it as such. Or to put it differently: The nations can experience the absolute only because of what they are; Israel can experience the absolute only, when, and because that absolute faces it.

To continue: To be limited to one's self is to be condemned to die; to live for what is limitless is to be freed from death. The idolization of a people is closely bound up with its death. When the national spirit decays and disintegrates, and the nation turns its face to nothingness instead of to existence which participates in the whole and manifests the absolute, it is on the verge of death.

Reverence for the absolute without the use of an intermediate agency is the principle of Israel's everlasting life. This separates its history from that of the nations. They complete the course they have been assigned in time, but Israel is granted a new start with rejuvenated strength—on condition that the connection of its faith with the absolute shall persist unimpaired. Thus, in the history of Israel, there is an element which does not merely supplement, but also rectifies the history of the nations.

Krochmal has taken a great idea from the treasure of Jewish tradition and outlined it conceptually, but he has not drawn from it all the possible far-reaching conclusions for the understanding of our history and task. Besides, he fails necessarily to work out a distinction indispensable for clarifying the interpretation of history itself.

In the case of some peoples, such as the Chinese, the Jews, and the Greeks, lonely thinkers thought of the absolute as such, in its utmost metaphysical purity; but the actual life of the people was not influenced by those thoughts. Reverence for the absolute can become the life-principle of a people only when the people itself puts it into practice as a people, and not in the sphere of abstract thought, but in actual life. Reverence of the absolute by a people does not mean metaphysical ideation, but religious event.

Krochmal did not make this distinction because to him, as an intellectual, the intellectual act seemed enough; but it is not enough. If it were, we might imagine the people at Sinai replaced by a contemplative Moses, who could subsequently transmit the results of his contemplations in the Scriptures. But such a concept is a wholly inadequate basis for dividing world history into two parts. The reason why Israel, unlike the other nations, did not elevate itself to the absolute is because, at the very outset of its history, it, *as a people,* experienced the Divine. Because Krochmal did not recognize the focal significance of this distinction, the only philosopher of history on a grand scale whom we have produced failed to see the most profound historical problem of our people.

The decisive question for Krochmal is to what extent the people has avowed and served the absolute in various epochs; but he does not inquire—though, according to his underlying thesis, he should—whether, at various times, this absolute really retained its identity and was kept at a distance from all tendencies toward the absolutization of a national characteristic, in the manner of the other nations. But he who accepts Krochmal's premise of "the nations and the God of Israel" * and then proceeds to such an inquiry and examination will see the real dilemma of Jewish existence. On the one hand, it was our task not to let our own nature limit us in our relations to the absolute, lest we replace the divinity facing us with a God bearing our national character; on the other, it was our duty to maintain the organic and national character of this relationship, and not to let the living Divine in our midst evaporate into a lofty idea.

We can detect this dilemma even on the peaks of our classical philosophy of religion. But in our time too there is a secularized sequel in the struggle between nationalism which denies the

* Krochmal used this phrase (see II Sam. 7:23) as a heading for the chapter in his book "Guide for the Perplexed of This Age," in which he sets forth his main idea.

spirit of the people and assimilation which denies the body of the people. The overcoming of this dilemma is probably the most difficult task ever imposed on a human community; but we live by and for this task It is true that reverence for the absolute, without the use of an intermediate agency, is the principle of the eternal life of Israel. To this day, however, we have not yet learned to revere the absolute by our very existence. What has kept us alive until now is the task itself—not its fulfilment, the task which burns in our blood like a fire, and will not die down.

Krochmal repeatedly tells us that it is our vocation to teach the nations, teach them to worship the absolute in itself, and not the absolutized faculties of the nations. And it is true: we do have to teach this. But how can we teach what we ourselves have not yet learned? A people has only one means to point to God, and that is through life lived in accordance with his will. Up to now, our existence has only sufficed to shake the thrones of idols, not to erect a throne to God. It is that fact which makes our existence among the nations so mysterious. We pretend to teach the absolute, but what we actually do is say, No, to the other nations, or rather we ourselves are such a negation and nothing more. That is why we have become a nightmare to the nations. That is why every nation is bound to desire to get rid of us at the time it is in the act of setting itself up as the absolute, not only internally—as from time immemorial—but in the order of reality. That is why today we are not permitted to soar over the abyss and point the way to salvation, but are dragged to the bottom of the whirlpool of common wretchedness.

2.

If every nation in its absolutized national faculty has its "prince," then from the standpoint of world history an important question arises, and the more the nations have to do with one another on a continental scale, the more important it grows. It is the question whether and to what extent these princes—mythologically speaking—recognize and tolerate a "prince of princes" (Dan. 8:25) who is over and above them; in plain terms: whether and to what extent the nations recognize and tolerate a common and unquestionably superior authority. This is the point of view from which we must regard Christianity as a problem of world history.

Christianity came upon the nations of the West out of a spiritual world in which elements salvaged from the great disintegrating religions of Asia Minor and floating unattached, as it were, combined with the religious traditions and experiences of the Jewish people. This synthesis so completely transformed Jewish teachings that they could reach and penetrate the nations as a gospel; the religious task of the people was, however, eliminated in the process. Even when entire nations were converted *in toto* to Christianity all at once, not the nations as such but only individuals were received into the redeemed world which was the antechamber to a hereafter utterly removed from anything that had to do with nationality. This obviated the task set the people of Israel, which was to make the world into the Kingdom of God. This was replaced by the Christian transfiguration of historical power-tendencies and acts, the concept of a holy empire; though these refer time and again to the task of Israel, in reality the religious slogans concealed a declaration of the autonomy of the "princes."

But this autonomy was bounded by the authority the Church exerted over the nations. The boundary was not rigidly defined. Popes strove to extend it, emperors to narrow it down, but in spite of their maneuvers, there was still an authority which could moderate and make peace which was above the self-glorification and will to dominate of the nations, and the rule of the "princes" was transcended by a spiritual power actual enough not to allow them to become "gods."

Even when the Church began to disintegrate, and the established churches within the province of the Reformation tried to come to terms with the territorial rulers, so to speak as a matter of principle, this influence of Christianity, whose vital powers were still unimpaired, did not disappear. It can be detected in the inhibitions inhering in national life even more readily than in the written tenets of international law whose source was Christianity. Though moral laws held only for man as an individual, not as the member of a nation, and nations as such led their lives apart from the moral law of Christianity, the fury of enmity was repeatedly and effectively opposed by something nameless, something indefinable which indubitably came from Christendom. The "princes" might time and again behave like "gods," but time and again the hour came when they had to bend their heads before God.

If we look at our own era from this viewpoint, we may regard it as a crisis in Christianity, for a fundamental change has begun to take place. It is no mere accident that it is this era in which technics have reached so high a level of development, that geographical distance between nations is no longer an important obstacle to conflicts between any of them and that such conflicts, moreover, can be waged with instruments capable of annihilating vast masses of the population on both sides. In the very era which made such technical development possible, Christianity itself as well as its secular derivatives have ceased to be effective as a political supernational authority. The tragi-comic history of the so-called League of Nations proved unambiguously that such an authority no longer exists. Something without precedent is taking place in this era: Some of the national egoisms which have been held in check by Christianity as by a common and supreme truth have freed themselves not only from Christianity, but from all inhibitions whatsoever. In their eyes, truth is nothing more than the function of the nation and the "prince" proclaims himself God.

Almost half a century before the League of Nations was

founded, and two decades after the publication of Krochmal's book, a man who experienced the full intensity of the crisis in Christianity modernized the theory of the "princes" of the nations. He was Dostoevsky. In his novel *The Possessed,* which presents so many of the phenomena of his time in a spiritual atmosphere rather resembling that of our own age, he expresses this theory in a curious manner. It is not voiced by the demonic hero of the novel, to whom he ascribes it, but by a man who was once his pupil and is now battling against the disintegration of character in his former teacher and trying to persuade him to purify and perfect himself. To this end, he confronts his teacher with the theory he once held. Every nation has its goal in its particular god. That god is the "synthetic personality" of the nation which believes in him as in "the only true God." The nation believes that "it can be victorious and subjugate all other gods and nations, only with the help of *its* god." It believes that "*it alone* has the truth, *it* alone, unconditionally and *exclusively.*" This faith constitutes the strength and the historical magnitude of a nation. "A nation which loses this faith is no longer a nation."

What is stated above represents a thorough reshaping of what Krochmal taught concerning the nations from the point of view of the pagan aspect of universal history. But now something very odd ensues. The speaker leans way over to the other side—the author, who is putting his own words into his character's mouth, must certainly have been aware of this; perhaps he did not realize their far-reaching implications. "Since there is only one truth," says the former pupil, "only one people can have the one true God."

There is only *one* truth! Dostoevsky who drew this statement from the depths of time opposed it, as it were, to everything that would come after it, and with it he testified in behalf of God and against the "princes." (Obviously, the words are a profession of his own belief and at the same time of his own inner conflict.)

But his conclusion that only one nation can have the true God—not avow, not invoke, but "have"—instantly lays his testimony open to question. And when, immediately after, he proclaims the Russian nation as the only nation which does have the only true God (this too was stated at the outset of the conversation, and also that the Russian nation "will come to redeem the world and to renew it in the name of the new God")—it becomes fearfully clear that the speaker, and perhaps the author who has created him as well, is "straddling the fence." It is entirely consistent that when this man is asked straight out whether he himself believes in God, he first stammers that he believes in Russia then that he believes in the body of Christ, and finally says that he will believe in God.

The sublime cruelty of the author who, it must be admitted, does not spare himself, comes out in this desperate confession of a man who like a juggler had only just bandied about the inflexible concept of the one true God and the supple concept of many gods. (It *is* jugglery, for if God exists, then "gods" are nothing but metaphors, but if gods exist, then God is only a metaphor.) Dostoevsky was certainly a devout Christian, but I have known many such who believed in the "Son," without being able to have true faith in the Father. To be sure, in one of Dostoevsky's drafts for this novel there is a still more general formulation. The hero asks: "Is it possible for civilized men to believe?"

Yet in this part of the novel, there is a passage in which Dostoevsky comes closer to Krochmal than in his general statements, so close that it is next to impossible to bridge the gap between this section and the statement that the Russian nation is the one and only nation In it he gives examples of what he means when he speaks of the gods of the nations. "The Greeks deified nature, and they have left the world their religion, that is, philosophy and art. Rome deified the state, and it left the state to modern nations." This exactly corresponds to Krochmal's concept of the princes as the dominant "spiritual faculties" of nations elevated to the absolute, and might have been taken verbatim from his book.

But paralleling the characterizations of the Greeks and the Romans is a preceding statement concerning the Jews. "The Jews lived solely to await the advent of the true God, and they transmitted the true God to the world." This can be interpreted in only one way: While the Greeks, the Romans, and other nations absolutized faculties which were not absolute in themselves, and thereby transmitted them to men, the Jews had in mind the absolute itself, the "true God," and what they transmitted to mankind is the true God. That is precisely what Krochmal contends, except that Dostoevsky is, of course, speaking only of the Christian God. Nevertheless, it seems incredible that Dostoevsky can propound Krochmal's thesis at all, or in such a way. Against his will, as it were, the Jewish side of world history comes to the fore.

The crisis in Christianity originates in the fact that while we Jews transmitted the true God to the world, we transmitted him only in theory, and not through our life as a people. Viewed in the light of this explanation, the apparent incongruities in Dostoevsky disappear. He testifies in our behalf, but does not want to testify; he is not aware that he is doing it, and draws no conclusions.

3.

But the various points discussed do not exhaust what is of interest to us in this chapter of Dostoevsky's novel. It contains a curious passage—like a streak of clear blue in a stormy sky shot with lightning. The hero reproaches his former pupil with "debasing God into a mere attribute." "On the contrary," says the other, "I am elevating the nation to a God." This reply is meaningless unless we take it to refer to "the one true God." For the moment, this only sharpens the contradiction between the speaker's avowal of the "one truth" and his glorification of the national "gods," a contradiction which we might be tempted to ascribe to the imperfect composition of this novel, the least finished of all Dostoevsky's great novels. But it soon becomes evident that this passage is the expression of an attempt to overcome the contradiction. What he is saying is that due to the recognition of the existence of the gods of nations and their rivalry, the nation is lifted nearer to God. Thus all this must be interpreted as being a way the nations possess to the true God.

The "gods" can be nothing but broken and partial reflections, extremely diverse, and in their very diversity, historically necessary, reflections of the true God. If the way to him really leads through the gods, an hour must come when the reflections pale, and all that remains is the one light reflected in them. From the point of view of Dostoevsky's premises, that would be one of the two sides of world history. Contrary to the will or knowledge of the author, the other side is represented in the statement about the Jews who "have transmitted the true God to the world." On this side of history, there are not and cannot be any reflections, so long as the people remains true to its vocation. Dostoevsky tries to fit the Jews into a homogeneous universal history, but they do not let themselves be categorized. In spite of all their unfaithfulness, they stay on the other side of history.

To get down to the roots of this problem, we must go back to a time long before Krochmal.

Our realization that there are two sides to the history of the world begins with Amos, who repudiates the presumption (Amos 9:7) that from the standpoint of the history of the peoples, we should be on the side of world history which is opposite to that of the nations. For other nations, even those hostile to us, are also acquainted with a divine deed of liberation, such as our history reveals. The true God we avow is the liberator of the nations. But they do not know him; every nation calls its national god who determined its migrations and territorial conquests by the name of an idol, and ascribes to him the actions of idols. What distinguishes and separates Israel from them is the fact that (Amos 3:2) it was "known" by its God, and knew him in the course of this contact. Not the Red Sea but Sinai alone belongs to the other side of world history.

Amos teaches that all the nations in that they exist in history are concerned with the true God, only that they do not know him. Isaiah supplements the message by saying that they do not know him *as yet,* but that they will know him, for he himself will teach them his ways (Isa. 2:3). The only advantage we have over them is that we already know him. But this "already" is what imposes on us the task of preceding them "in the light of the Lord" (Isa. 2:5 concluding the prophecy), so that our mountain may be ready as the goal for the pilgrimage of all. The two sides have fused into one united world of God.

Micah, who seems to have been a disciple of Isaiah's, does not agree with this explanation. He replaces the summons to precede the nations by a weighty message (Mic. 4:5), in which national particularism breaks through national universalism. For he says that even when all the nations have gathered on the holy mountain, each will walk, as before, "in the name of its god," while we shall walk "in the name of the Lord our God." Even "in the end of days," the two sides of universal history will be separate "for ever."

What the nations call their gods—Amos implied—are poor images of the true God, poor images with false names. The day will come—so had Isaiah predicted—when the nations will assemble on the "mountain of the Lord's house," as the Sinai of the nations, and receive the Torah from him himself, from the God so poorly imaged and falsely named, when he will make peace among them and lead them on to the great peace of all mankind. But though all the nations are taught to walk in the ways of the Lord, though they are to receive the Torah and be led to peace, the images and names will persist. According to Micah, there is no redemption for the nations.

The verse from Micah, which Krochmal mistakenly used as a motto for his chapter, "The Nations and the God of Israel," is the beginning of the descent to Daniel's teaching of the "princes" and everything which attaches to it. According to Daniel, the nations are not conducted through history by the true God himself, but each is conducted by its own special deputy of God. Toward the end of this development, the deeds God performs in behalf of the nations are obscured, and he is visible at best as the Creator, but no longer as the Lord of the history of the peoples. The nations act on their own; even the princes are now only "the dominant spiritual faculties of the nation" (Krochmal), "synthetic national personalities" (Dostoevsky). Thus they are the powers that have grown up within the nations to rule their lives. And no nation knows of any other way to redemption, says Dostoevsky, save to conquer with its "god," and to subjugate all other gods and nations.

This gives us a more rounded view of the problem of our task in world history. All we need do is to go back past Daniel's teaching about the princes, even past Micah's teaching of the everlasting idol worship of the nations, until we reach the great line of thought which leads from Amos to Isaiah. If the gods of the nations are only partial and imperfect reflections of the true God, then it is precisely by way of these reflections that the nations must find him. They "flow" to the "mountain of the Lord's house," but not away from what they are. Each comes as what it is, but its character, which previously seemed a solid and independent entity, now exists only in relation to that which is seen through it as through clear glass. That which previously appeared to be absolute has been revealed as relative to the one great absolute.

But if this is so, what is the meaning of the task Krochmal assigns to us: to teach the nations the "unconditional faith"? It means two things which necessarily belong together, i.e., without the other each would have a false and even fatal effect. The first is: to prove that everything which is falsely accepted as the absolute is only relative; the second: to point out the true absolute in order to demonstrate the difference between it and all that is relative.

The nature of the first task places it in the field of the intellect: investigation, analysis, criticism. The nature of the second task removes it from the realm of the intellect, because the mind can never grasp the absolute sufficiently to show the difference between it and all that is relative to it. It is, at any rate, impossible to *point out* the true absolute as "the absolute" in itself, i.e., in intelligible terms. The true absolute can be pointed out only as God; i.e., though to our thinking it is the absolute, it is so only in terms of a personality, or, paradoxically expressed, in terms of the absolute personality who addresses us, addresses you and me, in person, and does not say to you and me: "I am God," but "I am your God." And even if this "you" is not said at the outset, it soon follows, as in "Walk before me . . ." (Gen. 17:1)

In one form or another, such a command always ensues. There is no revelation without commandment. Even when He who addresses us talks to us about himself, he is really talking about us. What he says of himself does not refer to his own being, but gives the reasons for and the elucidation of his demands on us. In that he addresses us, he distinguishes within human life between what is proper and what is not proper for man. Without ceasing to be the absolute, i.e., a power which cannot be identified with any attribute accessible to human understanding, he distinguishes between truth and lies, righteousness and unrighteousness. He challenges us to make such distinctions within the sphere of our life, just as he, in the sphere of nature, distinguished between the light and darkness he created. Our own life is, therefore, the only sphere in which we can point him out, and then only through this life of ours.

But the secret of the *nation* is that only in and through the nation can this distinction be converted into fullness of life. Though something of righteousness may become evident in the life of the individual, righteousness itself can only become wholly visible in the structures of the life of a people. These structures enable righteousness to be realized, functioning internally within the various groups of the people, and externally in the people's relations to other nations; to function in abundance and diversity and with regard to all possible social, political, and historical situations. Only life can demonstrate the absolute, and it must be the life of the people as a whole.

The speaker in Dostoevsky's novel declares that his teaching is lifting the nation toward God, and says: "The people—that is the body of God." This is Christian mysticism, but we too may say that only the people can—as it were—represent God, so to speak, corporeally, representing in its own life what God had in mind in creating man "in his image." The *tzelem,* the image of God, in which man was created as an individual, or rather as man and woman, is an outline which can be filled in only by the people. For the *tzelem* will be revealed to the eyes of mankind only through a multitude of individuals, varied in character and intention, yet living in harmony with one another, a human circle around a divine center.

The people as a people has the natural prerequisites for such a work; its members have enough in common to be able to use their relations to one another as a point of departure for realizing the idea of a community of mankind which is to lead a life pleasing to God, and thus point to God himself. The thought of the individual can shake the thrones which intellectual patterns have usurped, thrones which each nation in turn claimed were the throne of the world; but nothing save the life of the people can erect the throne for the true king. As I have indicated, each part of this twofold task depends on the other and cannot without it achieve the welfare of mankind.

If the false thrones were not shaken, the attempt to set up the true throne—assuming that such an attempt is made—would not be recognized for what it is. It would be regarded as a challenge to the nations and, as such, fought and thwarted. And if no visible effort has been made toward erecting the true throne, naked and undisguised national egoisms will occupy the thrones when they will have been cleared of those dominant intellectual patterns. Then, not the character of the idea of the people, but merely its technical efficiency will be proclaimed as absolute. If Israel has a historical task by dint of the historical fact that it was accepted for the service of the true God, it can be nothing less than this entire twofold task.

In the era after we entered the history of the Western nations with the coming of "equal rights" for the individual, our thinking played a major role in rendering relative the fictitious absolutes. Ideologies, ideals, and ideas, were subjected first to sociological, and then to psychological analysis and criticism. Marx saw through them, and stamped them as mere auxiliary constructs in the process of production and the class struggle arising from it. Freud unmasked them as sublimations of the sexual libido and configurations of the forces intent on suppressing it.

In these brilliant investigations, however, the vehemence of methods operating with uninhibited verve "reduced" the true, independent, spiritual element of the ideas as well. No distinctions and no boundaries were drawn within the ideal substance; instead it was abandoned out of hand, until its independent character became unrecognizable. The real residue left over from the process of criticism was the dynamics of a society based on economics, on the one hand, and, on the other, that of the individual determined by his instincts, both manifestations of a monistic central human system. But man cannot be converted into a monistic system until he renounces his actual totality, until every fingerprint of the absolute itself is blurred, or, in terms of religion: until the image of God is effaced. Man is not the image, but he is created *in* the image of God, and if the image is wiped out, man no longer exists as man.

In the course of the last century, the Jew in his capacity of critic has not by his shattering of the idols made room for God, but has set out to rob God himself of any place on earth. Instead of teaching the nations to serve truth rather than fiction, Jewish criticism has done its share in helping them stamp the idea of truth itself as illicit fiction. It is no mere accident that the analytic criticism of Jewish thought has taken this turn. Marx and Freud did not realize how dependent they were on the dominant spiritual trend of modern Jewry, which cannot grasp the actual existence of the absolute, let alone imagine the paradox of an absolute personality. Here it is not only a question of "civilized man" about whom Dostoevsky's hero expresses the doubt that he can believe at all. Here an organic bond, the bond which constituted the other side of world history, has been cut.

And the second half of the task, that which can be accomplished only by the life of the people itself? After so many centuries of historical compulsion, centuries in which we were not allowed to set up our own national order, history granted us a respite as it were, during which on our own tract of earth, small but ours, we had our own relatively independent say on how we wanted to live with one another and with our neighbors. And what happened during the respite? Much—and little. Generations who discovered within themselves and expended undreamed of working power and efficiency set the tablets of social justice up over their work. But the islands they created are swept by the waves of a life that knows no tablets, a life without a common spirit, without a common order.

We do not yet know which will prove stronger, the waves or the island-earth. And those tablets themselves—fundamental as they are, it is profoundly significant that they were not graven in response to a commandment. Here too, the absolute is regarded as an anachronism, a reactionary concept with the odor of unfree thinking about it. We need only compare our national writings, which furnished the theoretical foundations for the settlement of Palestine, with Krochmal's book. For even those thinkers who do not want us to be like "unto all the nations" have altered the spirit of the absolute spirit which Israel avows and serves, into a "spirit of Israel" which hardly differs in kind from the "spirits" of other nations—in other words, a "prince" among "princes." We have hoped that the settlement would become the center of the Jewish people; but what is the center of this "center"?

Nationalism

[ADDRESS DELIVERED DURING THE TWELFTH ZIONIST CONGRESS AT KARLSBAD, SEPTEMBER 5, 1921]

I AM ADDRESSING you at a very troubled moment in this congress and do not know how much attention you will be able to give me at this point. Nevertheless, I have decided not to postpone what I have to say. A consciousness of my responsibility urges me to speak before the confusion increases. What I am going to deal with is the unambiguous demarcation of a kind, a degenerate kind, of nationalism, which of late has begun to spread even in Judaism.

An unambiguous demarcation. I need not retract anything I have ever said against a-national Jewry, against those Jews for whom—when it comes to public life—the concept of Judaism has less reality than the concept of nation. But now we must draw a new, no less ambiguous line of demarcation within our own national movement.

We have passed from the difficult period of the World War into a period which outwardly seems more tolerable, but on closer examination proves still more difficult, a period of inner confusion. It is characteristic of this period that truth and lies, right and wrong are mingled in its various spiritual and political movements in an almost unprecedented fashion.

In the face of this monstrous and monstrously growing phenomenon, it is no longer enough to draw the usual distinctions according to general, currently accepted concepts. For in every such concept, the true and the false are now so intertwined, so tangled and meshed, that to apply them as heretofore, as though they were still homogeneous, would only give rise to greater error. If we are to pass out of confusion into new clarity, we must draw distinctions *within* each individual concept.

It is a well-known fact that, *sociologically* speaking, modern nationalism goes back to the French Revolution. The effects of the French Revolution were such that the old state systems which had weighed so heavily on the peoples of Europe were shaken and the subject nations were able to emerge from under the yoke. But as they emerged and grew aware of themselves, these nations became conscious of their own political insufficiencies, of their lack of independence, territorial unity, and outward solidarity. They strove to correct these insufficiencies, but their efforts did not lead them to the creation of new forms. They did not try to establish themselves *as peoples,* that is, as a new organic order growing out of the natural forms of the life of the people. All they wanted was to become just such states, just such powerful, mechanized, and centralized state apparatuses as those which had existed in the past. They looked back into past history rather than forward into a future nationally motivated in its very structure.

We shall understand this more readily if we review the *psychological* origin of modern nationalism. European man became more and more isolated in the centuries between the Reformation and the Revolution. United Christendom did not merely break in two; it was rent by numberless cracks, and human beings no longer stood on the solid ground of connectedness. The individual was deprived of the security of a closed cosmic system. He grew more and more specialized and at the same time isolated, and found himself faced with the dizzy infinity of the new world-image. In his desire for shelter, he reached out for a community-structure which was just putting in an appearance, for nationality. The individual felt himself warmly and firmly received into a unit he thought indestructible because it was "natural," sprung from and bound to the soil.

He found protection in the naturally evolved shelter of the nation, compared to which the state seemed man-made, and even the Church no more than the bearer of a mandate. But since the strongest factor in this bond he had just discovered was awareness that it had evolved naturally, the horizon narrowed and—even worse—the fruitfulness of the national element was impaired. In the individual, the original feeling of allegiance to a people, alive in the depth of his soul long before modern national awareness, changed from a creative power to the challenging will-to-power of the individual as a member of the community. The group-egoism of the individual emerged in its modern form.

A great historian has asserted that power is evil. But this is not so. Power is intrinsically guiltless; it is the precondition for the actions of man. The problematic element is the will-to-power, greedy to seize and establish power, and not the effect of a power whose development was internal. A will-to-power, less concerned with being powerful than with being "more powerful than," becomes destructive. Not power but power hysteria is evil.

In the life of human beings, both as individuals and groups, self-assertion can be genuine as well as false, legitimate as well as illegitimate. A genuine person too likes to affirm himself in the face of the world, but in doing so he also affirms the power with which the world confronts him. This requires constant demarcation of one's own right from the rights of others, and such demarcation cannot be made according to rules valid once and for all. Only the secret of hourly acting with a continually repeated sense of responsibility holds the rules for such demarcations. This applies both to the attitude of the individual toward his own life, and to the nation he is a member of.

Modern nationalism is in constant danger of slipping into power hysteria, which disintegrates the responsibility to draw lines of demarcation.

The distinction between the two kinds of nationalism I am concerned with depends entirely on the right understanding of this responsibility and this danger. But to arrive at this understanding, we must first analyze the phenomenon of nationalism and its relation to peoples and nations. Or to be more exact, we must define what "people" means. What, in this relation, is a nation? What is the significance of nationalism in relation to both people and nation?

The word "people" tends, above all, to evoke the idea of blood relationship. But kinship is not the *sine qua non* for the *origin* of a people. A people need not necessarily be the fusion of kindred stems; it can be the fusion of unrelated stems just as well. But the concept "people" always implies unity of fate. It presupposes that in a great creative hour throngs of human beings were shaped into a new entity by a great molding fate they experienced in common. This new "coined form" [*gepraegte Form*], which in the course of subsequent events "develops as living substance," survives by dint of the kinship established from this moment on; it need not be exclusive, but must retain unquestioned preponderance even in eras where there are strong admixtures of other strains. The physical factor of this survival is the propagation of the species in more or less rigid endogamy; the spiritual factor is an organic, potential, common memory which becomes actual in each successive generation as the pattern for experience, as language, and as a way of life. The people constitutes a particular sort of community, because new individuals are born into it as members of its physical and spiritual oneness, and they are born into it naturally, not symbolically, as in the case of the Church. The people survives biologically, yet it cannot be fitted into a biological category. Here nation and history combine in a unique fashion.

A people becomes a nation to the degree that it grows aware that its existence differs from that of other peoples (a difference originally expressed in the sacral principle which determines endogamy), and acts on the basis of this awareness. So the term "nation" signifies the unit "people," from the point of view of conscious and active difference. Historically speaking, this consciousness is usually the result of some inner—social or political—transformation, through which the people comes to realize its own peculiar structure and actions, and sets them off from those of others. It is decisive activity and suffering, especially in an age of migrations and land conquests, which produces a *people.* A *nation* is produced when its acquired status undergoes a decisive inner change which is accepted as such in the people's self-consciousness. To give an example: the great shift which made ancient Rome a republic made it a nation, too. Not until Rome became a republic did it become a nation aware of its own peculiar strength, organization, and function, differentiating itself in these from the surrounding world. This dynamic state of nationhood can then reach its height in a peculiar formulation of its historic task. The French state-people, for instance, did not attain to complete national existence until in its great revolution it became a missionary for the idea of revolution.

At certain moments in national life a new phenomenon makes its appearance. We call it nationalism. Its function is to indicate disease. Bodily organs do not draw attention to themselves until they are attacked by disease. Similarly, nationalism is at bottom the awareness of some lack, some disease or ailment. The people feels a more and more urgent compulsion to fill this lack, to cure this disease or ailment. The contradiction between the immanent task of the nation and its outer and inner condition has developed or been elaborated and this contradiction affects the feeling of the people. What we term nationalism is their spiritual reaction to it. Being a people may be compared to having strong eyes in one's head; being a nation, to the awareness of vision and its function; being nationalistic, to suffering in connection with a disease of the eyes from the constant preoccupation with the fact of having eyes. A people is a phenomenon of life, a nation one of awareness, nationalism one of overemphasized awareness.

In a people, assertiveness is an *impulse* that fulfils itself creatively; in a nation it is an *idea* inextricably joined to a task; with nationalism, it becomes a *program.*

A nationalist development can have two possible consequences. Either a healthy reaction will set in that will overcome the danger heralded by nationalism, and also nationalism itself, which has now fulfilled its purpose; or nationalism will establish itself as *the* permanent principle; in other words, it will exceed its function, pass beyond its proper bounds, and—with overemphasized consciousness—displace the spontaneous life of the nation. Unless some force arises to oppose this process, it may well be the beginning of the downfall of the people, a downfall dyed in the colors of nationalism.

We have already said at the outset that original nationalism is the indication of a fundamental lack in the life of the nation, a lack of unity, freedom, and territorial security, and that it warns the nation to mend this situation. It is a demand upon the world for what it needs, a demand that the unwritten *droits de la nation* be applied to a people to enable it to realize its essence as a people and thus discharge its duty to mankind. Original nationalism inspires the people to struggle for what they lack to achieve this. But when nationalism transgresses its lawful limits, when it tries to do more than overcome a deficiency, it becomes guilty of what has been called *hybris* in the lives of historical personalities; it crosses the holy border and grows presumptuous. And now it no longer indicates disease, but is itself a grave and complicated disease. A people can win the rights for which it strove and yet fail to regain its health—because nationalism, turned false, eats at its marrow.

When this false nationalism, i.e., a nationalism which has exceeded the function it was destined to, and persists and acts beyond it, prevails not only in *one* people, but in an entire epoch of world history, it means that the life of mankind, pulsing in its stock of peoples, is very sick indeed. And that is the situation today. The motto which Alfred Mombert, a remarkable German Jewish poet, prefaced to the third part of his *Aeon* trilogy, takes on new significance. It is: *Finis populorum.*

Every reflective member of a people is in duty bound to distinguish between legitimate and arbitrary nationalism and—in the sequence of situations and decisions—to refresh this distinction day after day. This is, above all, an obligation imposed on the leaders of a nation and of national movements. Whether or not they probe deeply into their conscience and do this unremittingly, will determine not only the fate of a movement—which must inevitably disintegrate if it becomes an end in itself—but often that of the nation, its recovery or decline. Thus drawing this distinction is not a mere moral postulate which entails no other obligations, but a question of life or death for a people which is irreparably impaired when its spontaneity, fed on the primordial forces of natural, historical existence, is thrust aside and strangled by an apparatus activated by an exaggerated self-awareness.

But the criterion which must govern the drawing of this distinction is not implicit in nationalism itself. It can be found only in the knowledge that the nation has an obligation which is more than merely national. He who regards the nation as the supreme principle, as the ultimate reality, as the final judge, and does not recognize that over and above all the countless and varied peoples there is an authority named or unnamed to which communities as well as individuals must inwardly render an account of themselves, could not possibly know how to draw this distinction, even if he attempted to do so.

Peoples can be regarded either as elements or as ends in themselves and can regard themselves either as elements or as ends in themselves.

For him to whom peoples are elements, they are the basic substances which go to build mankind, and the only means to build up a more homogeneous mankind, with more form and more meaning. But such elements cannot be compared to chemical elements which can enter into solution and be separated out again. Spiritual elements must maintain themselves because they are threatened with the loss of themselves. But just because they are elements, they are not preserved for their own sake, but to be put to use. A people fully aware of its own character regards itself as an element without comparing itself to other elements. It does not feel superior to others, but considers its task incomparably sublime, not because this task is greater than another, but because it is creation and a mission. There is no scale of values for the function of peoples. One cannot be ranked above another. God wants to use what he created, as an aid in his work. In an hour of crisis, true nationalism expresses the true self-awareness of a people and translates it into action.

He, on the other hand, who regards the nation as an end in itself will refuse to admit that there is a greater structure, unless it be the world-wide supremacy of his own particular nation. He tries to grapple with the problem of the cracked and shattered present by undermining it instead of by transcending it. He does not meet responsibility face to face. He considers the nation its own judge and responsible to no one but itself. An interpretation such as this converts the nation into a moloch which gulps the best of the people's youth.

National ideology, the *spirit* of nationalism, is fruitful just so long as it does not make the nation an end in itself; just so long as it remembers its part in the building of a greater structure. The moment national ideology makes the nation an end in itself, it annuls its own right to live, it grows sterile.

In this day and age, when false nationalism is on the rise, we are witness to the beginning of the decline of the national ideology which flowered in the nineteenth and early twentieth centuries. It goes without saying that it is perfectly possible for this decline to go hand in hand with increasing success of nationalistic politics. But we live in the hour when nationalism is about to annul itself spiritually.

It is an hour of decision, of a decision which depends on whether a distinction will be drawn, and how sharply it will be drawn. We all play a part, we can all play a part in such a distinction and decision.

I need not discuss in detail the application of these ideas to Judaism and its cause.

Judaism is not merely being a nation. It is being a nation, but because of its own peculiar connection with the quality of being a community of faith, it is more than that. Since Jewry has a character of its own, and a life of its own, just like any other nation, it is entitled to claim the rights and privileges of a nation. But we must never forget that it is, nevertheless, a *res sui generis,* which, in one very vital respect, goes beyond the classification it is supposed to fit into.

A great event in their history molded the Jews into a people. It was when the Jewish tribes were freed from the bondage of Egypt. But it required a great inner transformation to make them into a nation. In the course of this inner change, the concept of the government of God took on a political form, final for the time being, that of the "anointed" kingdom, i.e., the kingdom as the representative of God.

From the very beginning of the Diaspora, the uniqueness of Judaism became apparent in a very special way. In other nations, the national powers in themselves vouch for the survival of the people. In Judaism, this guarantee is given by another power which, as I have said, makes the Jews more than a nation: the membership in a community of faith. From the French Revolution on, this inner bond grew more and more insecure. Jewish religion was uprooted, and this is at the core of the disease indicated by the rise of Jewish nationalism around the middle of the nineteenth century. Over and over this nationalism lapses into trends toward "secularization" and thus mistakes its purpose. For Israel cannot be healed, and its welfare cannot be achieved by severing the concepts of people and community of faith, but only by setting up a new order including both as organic and renewed parts.

A Jewish national community in Palestine, a desideratum toward which Jewish nationalism must logically strive, is a station in this healing process. We must not however forget that in the thousands of years of its exile Jewry yearned for the Land of Israel, not as a nation like others, but as Judaism (*res sui generis*), and with motives and intentions which cannot be derived wholly from the category "nation." That original yearning is back of all the disguises which modern national Judaism has borrowed from the modern nationalism of the West. To forget one's own peculiar character, and accept the slogans and paroles of a nationalism that has nothing to do with the category of faith, means national assimilation.

When Jewish nationalism holds aloof from such procedure, which is alien to it, it is legitimate, in an especially clear and lofty sense. It is the nationalism of a people without land of its own, a people which has lost its country. Now, in an hour rife with decision, it wants to offset the deficiency it realized with merciless clarity only when its faith became rootless; it wants to regain its natural holy life.

Here the question may arise as to what the idea of the election of Israel has to do with all this. This idea does not indicate a feeling of superiority, but a sense of destiny. It does not spring from a comparison with others, but from the concentrated devotion to a task, to the task which molded the people into a nation when they attempted to accomplish it in their earlier history. The prophets formulated that task and never ceased uttering their warning: If you boast of being chosen instead of living up to it, if you turn election into a static object instead of obeying it as a command, you will forfeit it!

And what part does Jewish nationalism play at the present time? We—and by that I mean the group of persons I have belonged to since my youth, that group which has tried and will continue to try to do its share in educating the people—we have summoned the people to turn, and not to conceit, to be healed, and not to self-righteousness. We have equipped Jewish nationalism with an armor we did not weld, with the awareness of a unique history, a unique situation, a unique obligation, which can be conceived only from the supernational standpoint and which—whenever it is taken seriously—must point to a supernational sphere.

In this way we hoped to save Jewish nationalism from the error of making an idol of the people. We have not succeeded. Jewish nationalism is largely concerned with being "like unto all the nations," with affirming itself in the face of the world without affirming the world's reciprocal power. It too has frequently yielded to the delusion of regarding the horizon visible from one's own station as the whole sky. It too is guilty of offending against the words of that table of laws that has been set up above all nations: that all sovereignty becomes false and vain when in the struggle for power it fails to remain subject to the Sovereign of the world, who is the Sovereign of my rival, and my enemy's Sovereign, as well as mine. It forgets to lift its gaze from the shoals of "healthy egoism" to the Lord who "brought the children of Israel out of the land of Egypt, and the Philistines from Caphtor, and Aram from Kir" (Amos 9:7).

Jewish nationalism bases its spurious ideology on a "formal" nationalistic theory which—in this critical hour—should be called to account. This theory is justified in denying that the acceptance of certain principles by a people should be a criterion for membership in that people. It is justified in suggesting that such a criterion must spring from formal common characteristics, such as language and civilization. But it is not justified in denying to those principles a central normative meaning, in denying that they involve the task—posed in time immemorial—to which the inner life of this people is bound, and together with the inner, the outer life as well.

I repeat: this task cannot be defined, but it can be sensed, pointed out, and presented. Those who stand for that religious "reform" which—most unfortunate among the misfortunes of the period of emancipation!—became a substitute for a reformation of Judaism which did not come, certainly did all they could to discredit that task by trying to cram it into a concept. But to deny the task its focal position on such grounds is equivalent to throwing out the child along with the bath water. The supernational task of the Jewish nation cannot be properly accomplished unless—under its aegis—natural life is reconquered. In that formal nationalism disclaims the nation's being based on and conditioned by this more than national task; in that it has grown overconscious and dares to disengage Judaism from its connection with the world and to isolate it; in that it proclaims the nation as an end in itself, instead of comprehending that it is an element, formal nationalism sanctions a group egoism which disclaims responsibility.

It is true that, in the face of these results, attempts have been made from within the nationalistic movement to limit this expanding group egoism from without, and to humanize it on the basis of abstract moral or social postulates rather than on that of the character of the people itself, but all such efforts are bound to be futile. A foundation on which the nation is regarded as an end in itself has no room for supernational ethical demands because it does not permit the nation to act from a sense of true supernational responsibility. If the depth of faith, which is decisive in limiting national action, is robbed of its content of faith, then inorganic ethics cannot fill the void, and the emptiness will persist until the day of the turning.

We, who call upon you, are weighed down with deep concern lest this turning may come too late. The nationalistic crisis in Judaism is in sharp, perhaps too sharp, relief in the pattern of the nationalistic crises of current world history. In our case, more clearly than in any other, the decision between life and death has assumed the form of deciding between legitimate and arbitrary nationalism.

The Land and Its Possessors

[FROM AN OPEN LETTER TO GANDHI, 1939 *]

A LAND which a sacred book describes to the children of that land is never merely in their hearts; a land can never become a mere symbol. It is in the hearts because it is in the world; it is a symbol because it is a reality. Zion is the prophetic image of a promise to mankind: but it would be a poor metaphor if Mount Zion did not actually exist. This land is called "holy"; but it is not the holiness of an idea, it is the holiness of a piece of earth. That which is merely an idea and nothing more cannot become holy; but a piece of earth can become holy.

Dispersion is bearable; it can even be purposeful, if there is somewhere an ingathering, a growing home center, a piece of earth where one is in the midst of an ingathering and not in dispersion, and whence the spirit of ingathering may work its way into all the places of the dispersion. When there is this, there is also a striving common life, the life of a community which dares to live today because it may hope to live tomorrow. But when this growing center, this ceaseless process of ingathering is lacking, dispersion becomes dismemberment. From this point of view, the question of our Jewish destiny is indissolubly bound up with the possibility of ingathering, and that is bound up with Palestine.

You ask: "Why should they not, like the other nations of the earth, make that country their National Home where they are

* From a reply to Mahatma Gandhi who in the course of an article (in *Harijan*) comparing the Jewish situation in Palestine with that of the Hindus in South Africa had questioned the validity of the Jewish claim to Palestine.—*Ed.*

born and where they earn their livelihood?" Because their destiny is different from that of all the other nations of the earth: it is a destiny, in truth and justice, no nation on earth would accept. Because their destiny is dispersion, not the dispersion of a fraction and the preservation of the main substance as in the case of other nations; it is dispersion without the living heart and center; and because every nation has a right to demand the possession of a living heart. It is different, because a hundred adopted homes without one that is original and natural make a nation sick and miserable. It is different, because although the well-being and the achievement of the individual may flourish on stepmotherly soil, the nation as such must languish. And just as you, Mahatma, wish not only that all Indians should be able to live and work, but also that Indian substance, Indian wisdom and Indian truth should prosper and be fruitful, we wish the same for the Jews. For you there is no need of the awareness that the Indian substance could not prosper without the Indian's attachment to the mother-soil and without his ingathering therein. But we know what is essential: we know it because it is denied us or was so at least up to the generation which has just begun to work at the redemption of the mother-soil.

But painfully urgent as it is, this is not all: for us, for the Jews who think as I do, it is indeed not the decisive factor. You say, Mahatma Gandhi, that to support the cry for a national home which "does not much appeal to you," a sanction is "sought in the Bible." No—that is not so. We do not open the Bible and seek sanction in it, rather the opposite is true: the promises of return, of re-establishment, which have nourished the yearning hope of hundreds of generations give those of today an elementary stimulus, recognized by few in its full meaning but effective in the lives of many who do not believe in the message of the Bible. Still this, too, is not the determining factor for us who, although we do not see divine revelation in every sentence of Holy Scripture, yet trust in the spirit which inspired those who uttered them. What is decisive for us is not the promise of the Land, but the demand, whose fulfilment is bound up with the land, with the existence of a free Jewish community in this country. For the Bible tells us, and our inmost knowledge testifies to it, that once more than three thousand years ago our entry into this land took place with the consciousness of a mission from above to set up a just way of life through the generations of our people, a way of life that cannot be realized by individuals in the sphere of their private existence, but only by a nation in the establishment of its society: communal ownership of the land,* regularly recurrent leveling of social distinctions,† guarantee of the independence of each individual,‡ mutual aid,** a general Sabbath embracing serf and beast as beings with an equal claim to rest,†† a sabbatical year in which the soil is allowed to rest and everybody is admitted to the free enjoyment of its fruits.‡‡ These are not practical laws thought out by wise men; they are measures which the leaders of the nation, apparently themselves taken by surprise and overpowered, have found to be the set task and condition for taking possession of the land. No other nation has ever been faced at the beginning of its career with such a mission. Here is something which there is no forgetting and from which there is no release. At that time we did not carry out that which was imposed upon us; we went into exile with our task unperformed; but the command remained with us, and it has become more urgent than ever. We need our own soil in order to fulfil it: we need the freedom to order our own life: no attempt can be made on foreign soil and under foreign statute. It cannot be that the soil and the freedom for fulfilment are de-

* Lev. 25:23
† Lev. 25:13
‡ Exod. 21:2
** Exod. 23:4f
†† Exod. 23:12
‡‡ Lev. 25:2-7

nied us. We are not covetous, Mahatma: our one desire is that at last we may be able to obey.

Now you may well ask whether I speak for the Jewish people when I say "we." No, I speak only for those who feel themselves entrusted with the commission of fulfilling the command of justice given to Israel in the Bible. Were it but a handful—these constitute the pith of the people, and the future of the people depends on them; for the ancient mission of the people lives in them as the cotyledon in the core of the fruit. In this connection, I must tell you that you are mistaken when you assume that in general the Jews of today believe in God and derive from their faith guidance for their conduct. Contemporary Jewry is in the throes of a serious religious crisis. It seems to me that the lack of faith of present-day humanity, its inability truly to believe in God, finds its concentrated expression in this crisis of Jewry; here all is darker, more fraught with danger, more fateful than anywhere else in the world. Nor is this crisis resolved here in Palestine; indeed we recognize its severity here even more than elsewhere among Jews. But at the same time we realize that here alone it can be resolved. There is no solution to be found in the lives of isolated and abandoned individuals, although one may hope that the spark of faith will be kindled in their great need. The true solution can only issue from the life of a community which begins to carry out the will of God, often without being aware of doing so, without believing that God exists and that this is his will. It may issue from the life of the community, if believing people support it who neither direct nor demand, neither urge nor preach, but who share the common life, who help, wait and are ready for the moment when it will be their turn to give the true answer to the inquirers. This is the innermost truth of the Jewish life in the Land; perhaps it may be of significance for the solution of this crisis of faith not only for Jewry but for all humanity. The contact of this people with this land is not only a matter of sacred ancient history: we sense here a secret still more hidden. You, Mahatma Gandhi, who know of the connection between tradition and future, should not associate yourself with those who pass over our cause without understanding or sympathy.

But you say—and I consider it to be the most significant of all the things you tell us—that Palestine belongs to the Arabs and that it is therefore "wrong and inhuman to impose the Jews on the Arabs."

Here I must add a personal note in order to make clear to you on what premises I desire to consider your thesis.

I belong to a group of people who from the time Britain conquered Palestine have not ceased to strive for the concluding of a genuine peace between Jew and Arab.

By a genuine peace we inferred and still infer that both peoples together should develop the land without the one imposing its will on the other. In view of the international usages of our generation, this appeared to us to be very difficult but not impossible. We were and still are well aware that in this unusual—yes, unprecedented case, it is a question of seeking new ways of understanding and cordial agreement between the nations. Here again we stood and still stand under the sway of a commandment.

We considered it a fundamental point that in this case two vital claims are opposed to each other, two claims of a different nature and a different origin which cannot objectively be pitted against one another and between which no objective decision can be made as to which is just, which unjust. We considered and still consider it our duty to understand and to honor the claim which is opposed to ours and to endeavor to reconcile both claims. We could not and cannot renounce the Jewish claim; something even higher than the life of our people is bound up with this land, namely its work, its divine mission. But we have been and still are convinced that it must be possible to find some compromise between this claim and the other; for we love this land and we believe in its future; since such love and such faith are surely present on the other side as well, a union in the common service of the land must be within the range of possibility. Where there is faith and love, a solution may be found even to what appears to be a tragic opposition.

In order to carry out a task of such extreme difficulty—in the recognition of which we have to overcome an internal resistance on the Jewish side too, as foolish as it is natural—we were in need of the support of well-meaning persons of all nations, and hoped to receive it. But now you come and settle the whole existential dilemma with the simple formula: "Palestine belongs to the Arabs."

What do you mean by saying that a land belongs to a population? Evidently you do not intend only to describe a state of affairs by your formula, but to declare a certain right. You obviously mean to say that a people, being settled on the land, has so absolute a claim to that land that whoever settles on it without the permission of this people has committed a robbery. But by what means did the Arabs attain to the right of ownership in Palestine? Surely by conquest and in fact a conquest with intent to settle. You therefore admit that as a result their settlement gives them exclusive right of possession; whereas the subsequent conquests of the Mamelukes and the Turks which were conquests with a view to domination, not to settlement, do not constitute such a right in your opinion, but leave the earlier conquerors in rightful ownership. Thus settlement by conquest justifies for you a right of ownership of Palestine; whereas a settlement such as the Jewish—the methods of which, it is true, though not always doing full justice to Arab ways of life, were even in the most objectionable cases far removed from those of conquest—do not justify in your opinion any participation in this right of possession. These are the consequences which result from your axiomatic statement that a land belongs to its population. In an epoch when nations are migrating, you would first support the right of ownership of the nation that is threatened with dispossession or extermination; but were this once achieved, you would be compelled, not at once, but after a suitable number of generations had elapsed, to admit that the land "belongs" to the usurper. . . .

It seems to me that God does not give any one portion of the earth away, so that the owner may say as God says in the Bible: "For all the earth is Mine" (Exod. 19:5). The conquered land is, in my opinion, only lent even to the conqueror who has settled on it—and God waits to see what he will make of it.

I am told, however, I should not respect the cultivated soil and despise the desert. I am told, the desert is willing to wait for the work of her children: she no longer recognizes us, burdened with civilization, as her children. The desert inspires me with awe; but I do not believe in her absolute resistance, for I believe in the great marriage between man (*adam*) and earth (*adamah*). This land recognizes us, for it is fruitful through us: and precisely because it bears fruit for us, it recognizes us. Our settlers do not come here as do the colonists from the Occident to have natives do their work for them; they themselves set their shoulders to the plow and they spend their strength and their blood to make the land fruitful. But it is not only for ourselves that we desire its fertility. The Jewish farmers have begun to teach their brothers the Arab farmers to cultivate the land more intensively; we desire to teach them further: together with them we want to cultivate the land—to "serve" it, as the Hebrew has it. The more fertile this soil becomes, the more space there will be for us and for them. We have no desire to dispossess them: we want to live with them. We do not want to dominate them, we want to serve with them. . . .

"And If Not Now, When?"

[ADDRESS DELIVERED AT A CONVENTION OF JEWISH YOUTH REPRESENTATIVES IN ANTWERP IN 1932]

WE ARE living in an age of the depreciation of words. The intellect with its gift for language has been all too willing to put itself at the disposal of whatever trends prevail at the time. Instead of letting the word grow out of the thought in responsible silence, the intellect has manufactured words for every demand with almost mechanical skill. It is not only the intellectuals, who are now finding a suspicious reception for their disquisitions, who must suffer for this "treason." * What is worse is that their audience, above all the entire younger generation of our time, is deprived of the noblest happiness of youth: the happiness of believing in the spirit. It is easily understood that many of them now see nothing but "ideologies" in intellectual patterns, nothing but pompous robes for very obvious group interests; that they are no longer willing to believe there is a truth over and above parties, above those who wield and are greedy for power. They tell us, tell one another, and tell themselves, that they are tired of being fed on lofty illusions, that they want to go back to a "natural" foundation, to unconcealed instincts, that the life of the individual as well as that of every people must be built up on simple self-assertion.

No matter what others may do, we, my friends, should not choose this way. If we really are Jews, meaning the bearers of a tradition and a task, we know what has been transmitted to us.

* Cf. Julien Benda, *The Treason of the Intellectuals* (New York, 1928).

We know that there is a truth which is the seal of God, and we know that the task we have been entrusted with is to let this one truth set its stamp on all the various facets of our life. We cannot own this truth, for it belongs to God. We ourselves cannot use the seal, but we can be the divers wax which takes the seal. Every individual is wax of a different form and color, but all are potentially receptive to the stamp of truth, for all of us, created "in the image of God," are potentially able to become images of the divine. We do not own the truth. But this does not mean that we must depend either on vain ideologies or on mere instincts, for every one of us has the possibility of entering into a real relationship to truth. Such a relationship, however, cannot grow out of thinking alone, for the ability to think is only one part of us; but neither is feeling enough. We can attain to such a relationship only through the undivided whole of our life as we live it. The intellect can be redeemed from its last lapse into sin, from the desecration of the word, only if the word is backed and vouched for with the whole of one's life. The betrayal of the intellectuals cannot be atoned for by the intellect retreating into itself, but only by its proffering to reality true service in place of false. It must not serve the powers of the moment and what they call reality—not the short-lived semblance of truth. The intellect should serve the true great reality, whose function it is to embody the truth of God; it must serve. No matter how brilliant it may be, the human intellect which wishes to keep to a plane above the events of the day is not really alive. It can become fruitful, beget life and live, only when it enters into the events of the day without denying, but rather proving, its superior origin. Be true to the spirit, my friends, but be true to it on the plane of reality. Our first question must be: What is the truth? What has God commanded us to do? But our next must be: How can we accomplish it from where we are?

We shall accomplish nothing at all if we divide our world and our life into two domains: one in which God's command is paramount, the other governed exclusively by the laws of economics, politics, and the "simple self-assertion" of the group. Such dualism is far more ominous than the naturalism I spoke of before. Stopping one's ears so as not to hear the voice from above is breaking the connection between existence and the meaning of existence. But he who hears the voice and sets a limit to the area beyond which its rule shall not extend is not merely moving away from God, like the person who refuses to listen; he is standing up directly against him. The atheist does not know God, but the adherent of a form of ethics which ends where politics begin has the termerity to prescribe to God, whom he professes to know, how far his power may extend. The polytheists distribute life and the world among many powers. As far as they are concerned, Germany has one god and France another; there is a god of business, and a god of the state. Each of these domains has its own particular code of laws and is subject to no superior court. Western civilization professes one God and lives in polytheism. We Jews are connected to this civilization with thousands of strands, but if we share in its dualism of life and profession of faith, we shall forfeit our justification for living. If we were only one nation among others, we should long ago have perished from the earth. Paradoxically we exist only because we dared to be serious about the unity of God and his undivided, absolute sovereignty. If we give up God, he will give us up. And we do give him up when we profess him in synagogue and deny him when we come together for discussion, when we do his commands in our personal life, and set up other norms for the life of the group we belong to. What is wrong for the individual cannot be right for the community; for if it were, then God, the God of Sinai, would no longer be the Lord of peoples, but only of individuals. If we really are Jews, we believe that God gives his commands to men to observe throughout their whole life, and that whether or not life has a meaning depends on the fulfilment of those commands. And if we consult our deep inner knowledge about God's command to mankind, we shall not hesitate an instant to say that it is peace. There are many among us who think this command is intended for some more propitious future; for the present, we must participate in the universal war, in order to escape destruction. But it is only if we do participate in this war that we shall be destroyed; for as far as we are concerned, there is only one possible kind of destruction: God letting us slip out of his hand.

I frequently hear some among us saying: "We too want the spirit of Judaism to be fulfilled; we too want the Torah to issue forth from Zion, and we know that to realize this purpose the Torah must not be mere words, but actual life; we want God's word on Zion to become a reality. But this cannot happen until the world again has a Zion, and so first of all we want to build up Zion, and to build it—with every possible means." It may however be characteristic of Zion that it *cannot* be built with "every possible means," but only *bemishpat* (Isa. 1:27), only "with justice." It may be that God will refuse to receive his sanctuary from the hands of the devil. Suppose a man decided to steal and rob for six years, and, in the seventh, to build a temple with the fortune thus amassed; suppose he succeeded—would he really be rearing temple walls? Would he not rather be setting up a den of robbers (Jer. 7:11), or a robber's palace, on whose portals he dares to engrave the name of God? It is true that God does not build his own house. He wants us to build it with our human hands and our human strength, for "house" in this connection can mean only that at long last we may begin to live God's word on earth! But after we have laid the foundations of this house by his means, *bemishpat,* do you really imagine that God is not strong enough to let it be finished by those same means? If you do imagine that, stop talking about Judaism, Jewish spirit, and Jewish teachings! For Judaism is the teaching that there is really only One Power which, while at times it may permit the sham powers of the world to accomplish something in opposition to it, never permits such accomplishment to stand. But whatever is done in the service of that power, and done in such a way that not only the goal but the means to that goal are in accord with the spirit of justice, will survive, even though it may have to struggle for a time, and may seem in great peril, and weak compared to the effective sham powers.

I should like to bring a concept of the utmost importance home even to those who cannot or will not understand the language of religion, and, therefore, believe that I am discussing theology. I am speaking of the *reality of history*. In historical reality we do not set ourselves a righteous goal, choose whatever way to it an auspicious hour offers, and, following that way, reach the set goal. If the goal to be reached is like the goal which was set, then the nature of the way must be like the goal. A wrong way, i.e., a way in contradiction to the goal, must lead to a wrong goal. What is accomplished through lies can assume the mask of truth; what is accomplished through violence, can go in the guise of justice, and for a while the hoax may be successful. But soon people will realize that lies are lies at bottom, that in the final analysis, violence is violence, and both lies and violence will suffer the destiny history has in store for all that is false. I sometimes hear it said that a generation must sacrifice itself, "take the sin upon itself," so that coming generations may be free to live righteously. But it is self-delusion and folly to think that one can lead a dissolute life and raise one's children to be good and happy; they will usually turn out to be hypocrites or tormented.

History has much to teach us, but we must know how to receive her teaching. These temporary triumphs which are apt to catch our attention are nothing but the stage-setting for universal history. If we keep our eyes fixed on the foreground, the true victories, won in secret, sometimes look like defeats. True victories happen slowly and imperceptibly, but they have far-reaching effects. In the limelight, our faith that God is the Lord of history may sometimes appear ludicrous; but there is something secret in history which confirms our faith.

He who makes peace, our sages taught, is God's fellow worker. But addressing conciliatory words to others and occupying oneself with humane projects is not the way to make peace. We make peace, we help bring about world peace, if we make peace wherever we are destined and summoned to do so: in the active life of our own community and in that aspect of it which can actively help determine its relationship to another community. The prophecy of peace addressed to Israel is not valid only for the days of the coming of the Messiah. It holds for the day when the people will again be summoned to take part in shaping the destiny of its earliest home; it holds for today. "And if not now, when?" (Sayings of the Fathers I.14). Fulfilment in a Then is inextricably bound up with fulfilment in the Now.

Hebrew Humanism

1.

At the beginning of the century, when a circle of young people to which I belonged began to direct the attention of Jews in German-speaking countries to a rebirth of the Jewish people and of the Jew as an individual, we defined the goal of our efforts as a Jewish renascence. It was not by mere chance that we chose a historical concept which was not purely national. It is true that the beginnings of the Italian Renaissance were inspired by the idea of renewing the *populus Romanus,* of regenerating Italy. But there was something else behind the Renaissance. The nature of this "something" was demonstrated at the time by my teacher, the philosopher Wilhelm Dilthey, and with particular clarity ten years later by Konrad Burdach, the distinguished German philologist who followed our work with warm sympathy. They showed us that behind the Renaissance was the idea of affirming man and the community of man, and the belief that peoples as well as individuals could be reborn. We felt this to be the truth and it was in this sense in which I used the term renascence in my first essay on the subject. But its full meaning dawned on us only gradually in the course of the last four decades, when our own work brought us to realize the basic consequences deriving from our choice of this term. When in 1913 a group of my friends discussed the founding of a Jewish school of advanced studies—a project frustrated by World War I—it was this realization which led me to define the spirit required to direct a program of this kind as Hebrew humanism. And in 1929, when I spoke at the Zionist Congress and tried to summarize in one concept what I felt we lacked in our Palestinian system of education, I again used the term Hebrew humanism to express what I thought we needed. But, fearing that this might be interpreted as a plea for what—in Europe—is called a "humanistic Gymnasium," merely substituting Hebrew for Latin and Greek, I added, "Hebrew humanism in the truest sense of the term." These words were also intended to indicate that what I had in mind was not merely a pedagogical enterprise, but that whatever pedagogical elements it contained were inherent in the very goal of the movement for a Jewish rebirth—as I had, in the meantime, very clearly come to realize. I wished to point out the nature of this goal by saying humanism instead of "renascence" and Hebrew instead of "Jewish." When Adolf Hitler stepped into power in Germany, and I was faced with the task of strengthening the spirituality of our youth to bear up against his nonspirituality, I called the speech in which I developed my program, "Biblical Humanism," in order to make the first half of my concept still clearer. The title indicated that in this task of ours, the Bible, the great document of our own antiquity, must be assigned the decisive role which in European humanism was played by the writings of classical antiquity. Now that we Jews from Germany must contribute to the education of our people in Palestine who are striving for regeneration, now that we are called on to communicate what we envision such regeneration to be, I should like to define the second half of the concept, and so I shall not speak of humanism, but of humanity, *humanitas,* Hebrew *humanitas.* The adjective "Hebrew" is inserted to prevent the misunderstanding that I am concerned with some sort of vague humanity at large. By *humanitas* I mean the content of true humanism. I am using the word to imply that we are not merely striving for an intellectual movement, but for one which will encompass all of life's reality.

If we investigate the origin of the concept of *humanitas* on which humanism is based, we discover that it is primarily the belief in man as such, the belief that man is not merely a zoological species, but a unique creature: but this is true only if he really is human, i.e., if he translates into the reality of his life the one characteristic element which cannot be found anywhere else in the universe. "If you are a human being" is a phrase which occurs in Roman comedy, and in Greek comedy the same idea is stressed even more: "How delightful a thing a human being could be, if he were a human being." So it seems that there are many who are human, biologically speaking, but are inhuman in the real and profound sense of the concept—yet even they are not excluded from *humanitas*. But those who may be called true human beings are time and again in danger of slipping into inhumanity. We have a very characteristic saying on this subject by the younger Scipic which we paraphrase: "Just as we take our horses back to the trainer at the end of a campaign, so after every political victory we should again submit to the discipline of the philosopher, lest we lose touch with *humanitas*." But what if the human element threatens to pale and even disintegrate not only in the individual but in an entire epoch of world history? Then we must turn for help to an age when it existed in its full strength and purity, even though it had to struggle against inhumanity a thousand times—provided the existence of that age became manifest and that this manifestation was transmitted. I consider that to have been an important mainspring of early European humanism. There is, of course, another factor: we connect the individual instances of a new and freer humanity which we find in certain eras with that type of humanity which has been transmitted from antiquity, and regard them as an existential renewal of antiquity. Only both taken together: both the pattern in the writings of antiquity and the pattern of new life, lend us the power to struggle against the threatened downfall of humanity. The individual instances are not regarded as something new, but as a renewal of the old, as the living proof of the eternity of the old, even though it is obvious that here other conditions have produced another form.

In investigating certain of the roots of humanism, we must not, of course, lose sight of the fact that the human pattern of antiquity was transmitted in a special sense through language. We do not have merely reports or merely descriptions of the ideal man of antiquity. Human beings who strove toward this ideal preserved something of the essence of this humanity in the way in which they expressed themselves, and to receive and absorb their utterances with the right understanding gives one more direct access to that pattern of humanity than all the reports and descriptions. I am by no means referring to what such persons said about themselves. When a great man speaks, he need not tell us about his character in order to reveal it to us. Language itself takes care of that. No matter what he communicates to us, the language he uses for this purpose expresses him and provides us access to him. Even language per se, the characteristic branch of a language-group, the particular word order and word formation, the rhythmic flow of vowels and consonants, are the product of a special human pattern. Humanism comprehends this pattern via language and takes it for a model. This means that, as far as true humanistic understanding is concerned, literary tradition is not essentially a matter of aesthetic appreciation or of historical learning or of patriotic pride, although all these enter into it side by side with still other elements. Humanistic understanding sees literary tradition as the authority and the standard, for it shows us how to distinguish between what is human and what is inhuman; it bears witness to man and reveals him.

One more observation about the humanistic relationship to the human pattern of antiquity. We must at this point ask a question which is essential even though it is specifically modern. We must ask whether a human pattern which was evolved under an entirely different set of historical conditions can be valid for our own times; whether it can help realize humanity in an era which is utterly different in character. The answer is in the affirmative, provided we can separate the timeless elements in this pattern, the elements that are valid for all time, from those which were conditioned by its epoch. Thus true humanism involves a two-fold task in regard to the linguistic tradition of the antique ideal of man, the task of reception and of criticism. Neither has meaning or can persist without the other.

In the first place then, Hebrew humanism means the return to the linguistic tradition of our own classical antiquity, the return to the Bible; in the second place, it means reception of the Bible, not because of its literary, historical, and national values, important though these may be, but because of the normative value of the human patterns demonstrated in the Bible; thirdly, distinguishing between what is conditioned by the times and what is timeless, in order to make that reception achieve its purpose; and fourthly, setting the living human patterns thus obtained before the eyes of our time with its special conditions, tasks, and possibilities, for only in terms of special conditions can we translate the content we have received into reality.

2.

In his essay on the origin of humanism, Konrad Burdach elucidates his subject by quoting from Dante's *Convivio:* "The greatest desire Nature has implanted in every thing from its beginning is the desire to return to its origin." Burdach accordingly believes that the goal of humanism is "to return to the human origin, not by way of speculative thought, but by way of a *concrete transformation* of the whole of inner life." The Zionist movement was also moved by the drive to return to the origin of our nature through the concrete transformation of our life. By "return" neither Burdach nor the Zionist movement meant the restoration of bygone forms of life. So romantic an ideal is as alien to our humanism as it was to the earlier. In this connotation, return means re-establishing the original foundation to which we want to return with the material of a fundamentally different world of man, under set conditions of our contemporary existence as a people, with reference to the tasks the present situation imposes on us, and in accordance with the possibilities we are given here and now. As we consider these points, we may well speak of a similarity between European and Hebrew humanism. But on another point we must reach for a farther goal than European humanism. The concrete transformation of our whole inner life is not sufficient for us. We must strive for nothing less than the concrete transformation of our life as a whole. The process of transforming our inner lives must be expressed in the transformation of our outer life, of the life of the individual as well as that of the community. And the effect must be reciprocal: the change in the external arrangements of our life must be reflected in and renew our inner life time and again. Up to now, Zionist theory has not adequately realized the importance of this mutual influence. The power of external transformation has frequently been overestimated. Such overestimation cannot, of course, be counteracted by confronting it simply with faith in the power of the spirit. Only he who commends himself to both spirit and earth at the same time is in league with eternity.

Zionist thinking in its current forms has failed to grasp the principle that the transformation of life must spring from the return to the origin of our nature. It is true that every thoughtful Zionist realizes that our character is distorted in many ways, that we are out of joint, and expect the new life in our own land, the bond to the soil and to work, to set us straight and make us whole once more. But what a great many overlook is that the powers released by this renewed bond to the soil do not suffice to accomplish a true and complete transformation. Another factor, the factor of spiritual power, that same return to our origin, must accompany the material factor. But it cannot be achieved by any spiritual power save the primordial spirit of Israel, the spirit which made us such as we are, and to which we must continually account for the extent to which our character has remained steadfast in the face of our destiny. This spirit has not vanished. The way to it is still open; it is still possible for us to encounter it. The Book still lies before us, and the voice speaks forth from it as on the first day. But we must not dictate what it should and what it should not tell us. If we require it to confine itself to instructing us about our great literary productions, our glorious history, and our national pride, we shall only succeed in silencing it. For that is not what it has to tell us. What it does have to tell us, and what no other voice in the world can teach us with such simple power, is that there is truth and there are lies, and that human life cannot persist or have meaning save in the decision in behalf of truth and against lies; that there is right and wrong, and that the salvation of man depends on choosing what is right and rejecting what is wrong; and that it spells the destruction of our existence to divide our life up into areas where the discrimination between truth and lies, right and wrong holds, and others where it does not hold, so that in private life, for example, we feel obligated to be truthful, but can permit ourselves lies in public, or that we act justly in man-to-man relationships, but can and even should practice injustice in national relationships. The *humanitas* which speaks from this Book today, as it has always done, is the unity of human life under one divine direction which divides right from wrong and truth from lies as unconditionally as the words of the Creator divided light from darkness. It is true that we are not able to live in perfect justice, and in order to preserve the community of man, we are often compelled to accept wrongs in decisions concerning the community. But what matters is that in every hour of decision we are aware of our responsibility and summon our conscience to weigh exactly how much is necessary to preserve the community, and accept just so much and no more; that we do not interpret the demands of a will-to-power as a demand made by life itself; that we do not make a practice of setting aside a certain sphere in which God's command does not hold, but regard those actions as against his command, forced on us by the exigencies of the hour as painful sacrifices; that we do not salve, or let others salve, our conscience when we make decisions concerning public life, but struggle with destiny in fear and trembling lest it burden us with greater guilt than we are compelled to assume. This trembling of the magnetic needle which points the direction notwithstanding—this is biblical *humanitas.* The men in the Bible are sinners like ourselves, but there is one sin they do not commit, our arch-sin: they do not dare confine God to a circumscribed space or division of life, to "religion." They have not the insolence to draw boundaries around God's commandments and say to him: "Up to this point, you are sovereign, but beyond these bounds begins the sovereignty of science or society or the state." When they are forced to obey another power, every nerve in their body bears and suffers the load which is imposed upon them; they do not act light-heartedly nor toss their heads frivolously. He who has been reared in our Hebrew biblical humanism goes as far as he must in the hour of gravest responsibility, and not a step further. He resists patriotic bombast which clouds the gulf between the demand of life and the desire of the will-to-power. He resists the whisperings of false popularity which is the opposite of true service to the people. He is not taken in by the hoax of modern national egoism, according to which everything which can be of benefit to one's people must be true and right. He knows that a primordial decision has been made concerning right and wrong, between truth and lies, and that it confronts the existence of the people. He knows that, in the final analysis, the only thing that can help his people is what is true and right in the light of that age-old decision. But if, in an emergency, he cannot obey this recognition of "the final analysis," but responds to the nation's cry for help, he sins like the men in the Bible and, like them, prostrates himself before his Judge. That is the meaning in contemporary language of the return to the origins of our being. Let us hope that the language of tomorrow will be different, that to the best of our ability it will be the language of a positive realization of truth and right, in both the internal and external aspects of the structure of our entire community life.

3.

I am setting up Hebrew humanism in opposition to that Jewish nationalism which regards Israel as a nation like unto other nations and recognizes no task for Israel save that of preserving and asserting itself. But no nation in the world has this as its only task, for just as an individual who wishes merely to preserve and assert himself leads an unjustified and meaningless existence, so a nation with no other aim deserves to pass away.

By opposing Hebrew humanism to a nationalism which is nothing but empty self-assertion, I wish to indicate that, at this juncture, the Zionist movement must decide either for national egoism or national humanism. If it decides in favor of national egoism, it too will suffer the fate which will soon befall all shallow nationalism, i.e., nationalism which does not set the nation a true supernational task. If it decides in favor of Hebrew humanism, it will be strong and effective long after shallow nationalism has lost all meaning and justification, for it will have something to say and to bring to mankind.

Israel is not a nation like other nations, no matter how much its representatives have wished it during certain eras. Israel is a people like no other, for it is the only people in the world which, from its earliest beginnings, has been both a nation and a religious community. In the historical hour in which its tribes grew together to form a people, it became the carrier of a revelation. The covenant which the tribes made with one another and through which they became "Israel" takes the form of a common covenant with the God of Israel. The song of Deborah, that great document of our heroic age, expresses a fundamental reality by repeatedly alternating the name of this God with the name of Israel, like a refrain. Subsequently, when the people desire a dynasty so that they may be "like unto all the *nations*" (I Sam. 8:20), the Scriptures have the man who, a generation later, really did found a dynasty, speak words which sound as though they were uttered to counterbalance that desire: "And who is like Thy people Israel, a *nation* one in the earth" (I Sam. 7:23). And these words, regardless of what epoch they hail from, express the same profound reality as those earlier words of Deborah. Israel was and is a people and a religious community in one, and it is this unity which enabled it to survive in an exile no other nation had to suffer, an exile which lasted much longer than the period of its independence. He who severs this bond severs the life of Israel.

One defense against this recognition is to call it a "theological interpretation" and, in this way, debase it into a private affair concerning only such persons as have interest in so unfruitful a subject as theology. But this is nothing but shrewd polemics. For we are, in reality, dealing with a fundamental historical recognition without which Israel as a historical factor and fact could not be understood. An attempt has been made * to refute this allegedly "theological interpretation" by a "religious interpretation," the claim being made that it has nothing whatsoever to do with the Judaism of a series of eminent men, as the last of whom Rabbi Akiba is cited, the first being none other than Moses. Remarkable, to what lengths polemic enthusiasm will go! As a matter of fact, it is just as impossible to construct a historical Moses who did not realize the uniqueness of Israel as a historical Akiba who was not aware of it. Snatch from Rabbi Akiba his phrase about "special love" which God has for Israel (Sayings of the Fathers

* By David Ben-Gurion, first Prime Minister of Israel.—*Ed.*

III. 18), and you snatch the heart from his body. Try to delete the words: "Ye shall be Mine own treasure from among all peoples" (Exod. 19:5) from the account of the coming of Israel to the wilderness of Sinai, and the whole story collapses. If such comments as these about Moses have any foundation at all, I do not know on what hypotheses of Bible criticism they are based; they are certainly not supported by anything in the Scriptures.

There is still another popular device for evading the recognition of Israel's uniqueness. It is asserted that every great people regards itself as the chosen people; in other words, awareness of peculiarity is interpreted as a function of nationalism in general. Did not the National Socialists believe that Destiny had elected the German people to rule the entire world? According to this view, the very fact that we say, "Thou hast chosen us," would prove that we are like other nations. But the weak arguments which venture to put, "It shall be said unto them: Ye are the Children of the living God" (cf. Hos. 2:1) on a par with "The German essence will make the whole world well," are in opposition to the basic recognition we glean from history. The point is not whether we feel or do not feel that we are chosen. The point is that our role in history is actually unique. There is even more to it. The nature of our doctrine of election is entirely different from that of the theories of election of the other nations, even though these frequently depend on our doctrine. What they took over was never the essential part. Our doctrine is distinguished from their theories, in that our election is completely a demand. This is not the mythical shapes of a people's wishful dreams. This is not an unconditional promise of magnitude and might to a people. This is a stern demand, and the entire future existence of the people is made dependent on whether or not this demand is met. This is not a God speaking whom the people created in their own image, as their sublimation. He confronts the people and opposes them. He demands and judges. And he does so not only in the age of the prophets at a later stage of historical development, but from time immemorial; and no hypothesis of Bible criticism can ever deny this. What he demands he calls "truth" and "righteousness," and he does not demand these for certain isolated spheres of life, but for the whole life of man, for the whole life of the people. He wants the individual and the people to be "whole-hearted" with him. Israel is chosen to enable it to ascend from the biological law of power, which the nations glorify in their wishful thinking, to the sphere of truth and righteousness. God wishes man whom he has created to become man in the truest sense of the word, and wishes this to happen not only in sporadic instances, as it happens among other nations, but in the life of an entire people, thus providing an order of life for a future mankind, for all the peoples combined into one people. Israel was chosen to become a true people, and that means God's people.

Biblical man is man facing and recognizing such election and such a demand. He accepts it or rejects it. He fulfils it as best he can or he rebels against it. He violates it and then repents. He fends it off, and surrenders. But there is one thing he does not do: He does not pretend that it does not exist or that its claim is limited. And classical biblical man absorbs this demand for righteousness so wholly with his flesh and blood, that, from Abraham to Job, he dares to remind God of it. And God, who knows that human mind and spirit cannot grasp the ways of his justice, takes delight in the man who calls him to account, because that man has absorbed the demand for righteousness with his very flesh and blood. He calls Job his servant and Abraham his beloved. He tempted both; both called him to account, and both resisted temptation. That is Hebrew humanity.

4.

It remained for our time to separate the Jewish people and the Jewish religious community which were fused from earliest beginnings, and to establish each as an independent unit, a nation like unto other nations and a religion like unto other religions. Thanks to the unparalleled work in Palestine, the nation is on the rise. The religion, however, is on a steep downward fall, for it is no longer a power which determines all of life; it has been confined to the special sphere of ritual or sermons. But a Jewish nation cannot exist without religion any more than a Jewish religious community without nationality. Our only salvation is to become Israel again, to become a whole, the unique whole of a people and a religious community: a renewed people, a renewed religion, and the renewed unity of both.

According to the ideas current among Zionists today, all that is needed is to establish the conditions for a normal national life, and everything will come of itself. This is a fatal error. We do, of course, need the conditions of normal national life, but these are not enough—not enough for us, at any rate. We cannot enthrone "normalcy" in place of the eternal premise of our survival. If we want to be nothing but normal, we shall soon cease to be at all.

The great values we have produced issued from the marriage of a people and a faith. We cannot substitute a technical association of nation and religion for this original marriage, without incurring barrenness. The values of Israel cannot be reborn outside the sphere of this union and its uniqueness.

Objection will be made that this point is one that concerns intellectual and cultural problems, but not problems about actual, present-day life. No! Let us not forget we are as yet only striving to join the ranks of nations with a land and a law of their own. Tomorrow many little nations will be weighed and found wanting. But this will surely not be the fate of a people that brings great tidings to struggling mankind, and conveys them not only through the word, but through its own life, which realizes that word and represents such realization. We shall not, of course, be able to boast of possessing the Book, if we betray its demand for righteousness.

Israel and the Command of the Spirit

When I entered the Zionist movement more than sixty years ago, I very soon saw myself compelled to take sides in the conflict between the "political" and the "practical" tendencies within the movement. I decided without hesitation for the latter, and have remained faithful to it, manifold as have been its forms in the course of time. One can find in my writings from 1901 on, and in much stronger form after 1917, programmatic and concrete expressions of this trend.

What is at stake here is not usually understood with sufficient seriousness and depth. It is not basically a question of which activity was more urgent, the attainment of political concessions or the factual work of settlement. The "practical" tendency to create a reality first and then aspire to legal rights for it afterward did not stem from tactical considerations. It stemmed from the insight that the tremendous double work of completing the rebirth of the Jewish people and of its becoming a member of the world of the Near East could not be accomplished through a sudden, insufficiently-prepared mass settlement but only through the preparatory activity of generations in the Land.

We by no means sought a small center, as the Chovevei Zion formerly did; we wanted to establish a great productive Jewish community. But we recognized as the way to it a pioneering stage of work and peace, a selective organic principle of development that would take several generations. That meant, first, that an élite of workers who saw their future and that of their children in the building of just this land should realize this in as many generations as might be necessary until the core of a Jewish community able to serve as the base for a completed rebirth should be created, a community that would then be entitled to an autonomous government and could accordingly demand it from the world. Secondly, our principle of development meant that in cooperative living together with our neighbors, in helpful participation in their economic life, a relationship of solidarity should be made possible out of which a comprehensive working together of both peoples might then arise. This second meaning of the selective organic principle must be explained more exactly here because of its importance for our subject.

We had recognized early that a new, aspiring factor among the already existing peoples of the Near East could not establish itself and hold its ground as an enclave of the Western world; that a genuine, and not just a tactical, understanding with the surrounding peoples was therefore needed. It could by no means suffice to win the trust of the Arabs merely in order that they later should not oppose our desire for autonomy; not seeming, but real, objectively founded, comprehensive solidarity was meant. Only such solidarity could withstand the shocks coming from the outside for which one had to be ready. Thus it happened that more than forty years ago many of us recognized the incipient world crisis in which the Near East was to play an ever greater part as an essential element: an element in either a great construction or a great disintegration. If we were genuinely to enter into the life of the Near East, we could earn an important share in the decision between these alternatives.

The political side of this postulate was expressed by us wherever this matter was discussed, particularly by me in 1921 in the political committee of the Zionist Congress where, in opposition to what I stressed as the possibility of a federation of Arab states, I put forward the idea of a Near Eastern federation in which we should participate. But the indispensable presupposition of political activity in this direction was the creation of a common consciousness of solidarity.

In the age of the beginning world crisis, *halutziut* had realized a substantial part of the first postulate—the creation of the core of a community, without being able as yet to bring it to completion. The second postulate, in contrast, that of awakening a Jewish-Arab consciousness of solidarity, had been realized only fragmentarily, in sporadic, locally limited undertakings of good neighborliness; neither an organized work of this kind nor even a practical program of comprehensive co-operation had arisen.

In that hour our work of settlement, as well as the principle on which it was based—the principle of selective, organic development—found itself overrun by the consequences of the most frightful happening of modern history, the extermination of millions of Jews by Adolf Hitler. The harrassed, tormented masses crowded into Palestine. Unlike the halutzim for whom no sacrifice toward building the land of Jewish rebirth was too great, they saw in this land merely safety and security (even though the tradition of the Messianic promise still lived on in them). Who would have taken it on himself to obstruct this onrush of the homeless in the name of the continuation of the selective method! The masses came and with them came the necessity for political security. They came at a time when the first postulate had not yet found sufficient fulfillment and the second had not gone beyond isolated attempts. The first lack produced manifold difficulties, but the effects of the second were disastrous. Since a Jewish-Arab solidarity had not been instituted, either in the form of facts or even in an announced program of cooperation, the Arab peoples received the mass immigration as a threat and the Zionist movement as a "hireling of imperialism"—both wrongly, of course. Our *historical* reentry into our land took place through a false gateway.

But that hour in world history in which evil seemed to have become all powerful, able to extirpate everything odious to it with impunity, also exercised a harmful inner influence. The most pernicious of all false teachings, that according to which the way of history is determined by power alone, insinuated itself everywhere into the thinking of the peoples and their governments, while faith in the spirit was retained only as mere phraseology. What we experience today, the universal accumulation of the power of destruction in opposition to every command of the spirit, was only made possible through this inner disintegration, although since then it has been learned many times anew.

In a part of the Jewish people that was most cruelly afflicted through that victory of the subhuman over the human, the false teaching continued to prevail even when the subhuman was overthrown. And here, in Jewry, in an altogether special way, it meant the betrayal of faith. By means of the spirit this people had been preserved unbroken through the ages despite the most wretched of fates. By means of the spirit alone the Zionist movement established its position in Palestine and wrested for itself the first legal title of a political nature. Only if it preserved the spirit as its guide could it hope to bring forth something greater than just one more state among the states of the world. He who was here unfaithful to the spirit was also unfaithful to a great task.

How deep the evil had penetrated into a part of the people was first recognized by us when the fact could no longer be overlooked. Meanwhile, in opposition to the proposals for a binational state or a Jewish share in a Near Eastern federation, the unhappy partition of Palestine took place, the cleft between the two peoples was split wide asunder, the war raged.*

*I must add here a personal remark because on this point I can speak for most, to be sure, but not for all of my closest political friends. I am no radical pacifist; I do not believe that one must always answer violence with non-violence. I know what tragedy implies: when there is war, it must be fought.

Everything proceeded with frightening logical consistency and at the same time with frightening meaninglessness. It happened one day, however, that, outside of all regular conduct of the war, a band of armed Jews fell on an Arab village and destroyed it. Often in earlier times Arab hordes had committed outrages of this kind, and my soul bled with the sacrifice; but here it was a matter of our own, or my own crime, of the crime of Jews against the spirit. Even today I cannot think about this without feeling myself guilty. Our fighting faith in the spirit was too weak to prevent the outbreak and spread of false demonic teaching.

All this concerns the past, a never-to-be-forgotten past. But I must say a few words more about something that has remained present, something present in the most actual sense, in order that where I stand and where I do not stand may become clearer.

I have accepted as mine the State of Israel, the form of the new Jewish Community that has arisen from the war. I have nothing in common with those Jews who imagine that they may contest the factual shape which Jewish independence has taken. The command to serve the spirit is to be fulfilled by us today in this state, starting from it. But he who will truly serve the spirit must seek to make good all that was once missed: he must seek to free once again the blocked path to an understanding with the Arab peoples. Today it appears absurd to many—especially in the present intra-Arab situation—to think now about Israel's participation in a Near East federation. Tomorrow, with an alteration in certain world-political situations independent of us, this possibility may arise in a highly positive sense. Insofar as it depends on us, we must prepare the ground for it. There can be no peace between Jews and Arabs that is only a cessation of war; there can only be a peace of genuine cooperation. Today, under such manifoldly aggravated circumstances, the command of the spirit is still to prepare the way for the cooperation of peoples.

Israel's Mission and Zion

IT SEEMS TO ME that Ben-Gurion was justified in taking issue with the view expressed by Ezekiel Kaufmann that monotheism is the distinguishing feature which separates Israel from all other nations. He is not justified, however, in maintaining the thesis that the combination of religion and ethics distinguishes Israel from all other nations.

Monotheism, that religious view which holds that there is only one God, developed among a number of peoples, albeit in varying degrees of intensity and emphasis, and there is no need to assume that one people borrowed the idea from another. But the combination of religion and ethics is also to be found, for example, in the early teachings of India and Persia. What is peculiar to Israel is the demand that the people submit its entire life, including its social and political activity, to the will of God, as the true King. We have here not a combination of religion and ethics but a complete, all-pervading unity. That which distinguishes the monotheism of Judaism from all other monotheisms, is the all-embracing subservience to the divine Ruler, extending, without exception, over all areas of national life. It is the will of this God that the human world recognize his sovereignty freely and in deed. And of Israel He requires that it begin to give exemplary expression to His kingdom by subjecting its whole social life to His rule, which means the realization of justice and truth both in its internal and external national relationships, and in the private conduct of the individual in Israel, especially in his behavior as a member of society and as a citizen of the State.

This aspiration and the social order at which it aims, cannot be called a theocracy in the ordinary meaning of that term, which, as is well-known, originates in Josephus, and refers to the hegemony of the priesthood. Biblical theocracy appeared in two forms: the first was primitive rule, as described in the Book of Judges, according to which in those early days, in times of crisis, men, seized by the spirit, pronounced judgment in the name of God who alone is the Ruler; and the second, the historical form, whose essence found expression in the fact that the prophets anointed the kings to be God's representatives, and in the repeated demand of the prophets that the kings fulfill the obligation imposed upon them at the time of the anointing, the obligation to incorporate the divine ideals of justice and truth in the social and political life of the people. These prophets are men bereft of all political power and able only to protest: thus they stand before the rulers and protest in the name of their God and in His name they confront the rulers with the fateful choice.

True, other peoples of the ancient East also believed that the king was responsible for his deeds to "his father," the God who adopted him and gave him dominion. But this relationship of responsibility was expressed only in symbolical form. We know, for example, that in Babylon the high priest approached the king on New Year's day and slapped him, and immediately after this ritual everything returned to its former state and the king continued to act as before. In Biblical religion, however, you will find no symbolic rite performed with regard to the kings outside the solitary rite of anointing. Thus, "for his iniquities," for the iniquities of the king, called "the son of God" (II Sam. 7.4), God commands him to be chastised "with the rod of men," and this is actually carried out; and the prophets come as the messengers of Heaven and censure him for betraying his mission and prophesy that calamity will befall him and his people if he does not mend his ways and does not fulfill the obligations assumed in the act of being anointed. This mission they performed at the risk of their lives. This is the transcendent realism which distinguishes the faith of Israel: there is no room here for empty symbols.

What exactly was it that the prophets censured when they faced the rulers? It was the means that they used to arrive at their ultimate goal, concerning which the prophets did not differ—the glory of Israel. These means contradicted the ends, and one of the unexpressed principles of prophecy is that ends do not justify the means. And if the nature of the means is in contradiction to the nature of the end, they desecrate it, poison it and make of it a thing of horror.

Ben-Gurion is right in saying that youth in Israel is very much interested in certain parts of the Bible, especially in the stories about the conquest of the land, in the stories of the hero-kings and also in some words of the prophets. But on no account are the prophets to be regarded apart from their historic mission which sent them to those men who had seized the reins of power in order to summon them to stand in judgment before their God who made them king provisionally.

Ben-Gurion rightly sees in the Messianic vision the second corner-stone of living Judaism. But this also is in need of greater concreteness. It is not enough to set "the redemption of Israel" side by side with "the redemption of the human race." The Messianic message is unique in the demand God makes upon the nations of men to realize His kingdom and in this way to take part in the redemption of the world. The message is applied especially to Israel and demands of it that it make an exemplary beginning in the actual work of realization, that it be a nation which establishes justice and truth in its institutions and activities. Therefore, Isaiah not only calls upon the Gentiles to stream to Mount Zion and there receive the second Torah, the universal one; he supplements this by his summons to the House of Jacob to walk before them in the light of the Lord.

Just as the monotheism of Israel differed from the others in that, according to it, the people should live their whole lives as one great service to God, so did the tidings of redemption differ in Israel from all others in that they summoned the people to begin doing their part in putting this idea into actual practice. We do not have here only thoughts and visions but actual demands on whose fulfillment hangs the destiny of the people. These demands are not only directed to the generations to whom they were first presented but to all the generations, and especially to ours, the first generation after two thousand years that has the prerequisite for fulfilling its task, that is, the independence of a strong nucleus. This gives our generation at long last the power to determine for itself in no small measure its institutions, its modes of life and its relations to other nations.

Behind everything that Ben-Gurion has said on that point, there lies, it seems to me, the will to make the political factor supreme. He is one of the proponents of that kind of secularization which cultivates its "thoughts" and "visions" so diligently that it keeps men from hearing the voice of the living God. This secularization takes the form of an exaggerated "politization." This "politization" of life here strikes at the very spirit itself. The spirit with all its thoughts and visions descends and becomes a function of politics. This phenomenon, which is supreme in the whole world at present, has very old roots. Even some kings in Israel are said to have gone so far as to employ false prophets whose prophesying was merely a function of state policy.

Closely connected with all that I have been saying is the problem of Zionism in our day. Ben-Gurion has stated that this no longer has a real or positive content and that in the eyes of the Israeli generation, in whose name he speaks, it has become an ideological anachronism. Zionism, so his argument runs, means a longing for Zion, and since this longing has already attained its goal, there is no rhyme or reason for Zionism any more. But those who inscribed the name Zion on their banner, first calling themselves Lovers of Zion and thereafter Zionists, did not have in mind something which existed and needed only to be repossessed. I still recall what this circle of young Zionists to which I belonged some sixty years ago meant by the name. Had we been asked: "Are you striving for a country of Jews in Israel?", we would have answered: "We are striving for Zion and in order to establish Zion we desire independence for our people in our country." Even today there are many Zionists who share this feeling, not alone among the older ones; I myself know a number who came to the country and who continue to dream this dream which has as yet found no fulfillment, the dream of Zion. They hope with all their hearts that this country, as it is, is the first step in the direction of Zion. This quasi-Zionism which strives to have a country only, has attained its purpose. But the true Zionism, the love of Zion, the desire to establish something like "the city of a great king" (Ps.48.3), of "the king" (Is. 6.5), is a living and enduring thing. Come, let us awaken this Zionism in the hearts that have never felt it, in the Diaspora as well as here. For here in this country also we need a movement which strives for Zion, aspiring towards the emergence of the rebuilt Zion from the materials at our disposal. We need "Zionists of Zion," here and abroad.

What Ben-Gurion has said about the present Israeli generation is no doubt true of its majority. A remarkable and at the same time an understandable change has come over us as over the whole world in our day: after a generation which, though it had performed great things, was unable to confront the catastrophe, there came another generation which clings to the practical execution of great ideas—the execution that took place in our time whether on a large or small scale (and certainly what was done by us was by no means small). The members of this generation whether openly or secretly in their hearts, suspect ideas as ideas and put their trust only in tangible reality as such. Is it desirable to advocate such emphasis on the material, which threatens to swallow up the ideas that are still alive, or is it our duty to subdue this trend?

And now Ben-Gurion tells us that Zionist thought is dead but that the Messianic idea is alive and will live until the coming of the Messiah. And I answer him with the question: "In how many hearts of this generation in our country does the Messianic idea live in a form other than the narrow nationalistic form which is restricted to the Ingathering of the Exiles?" A Messianic idea without the yearning for the redemption of mankind and without the desire to take part in its realization, is no longer identical with the Messianic visions of the prophets of Israel, nor can that prophetic mission be identified with a Messianic ideal emptied of belief in the coming of the kingdom of God.

Sources

The Faith of Judaism [13]

First prepared in 1928 as a lecture for an institute of political science in Reichenhall, and later delivered at the Weltwirtschafliches Institut, in Kiel. *Kampf um Israel* (Berlin: Schocken Verlag, 1933), pp. 28-49. Translated by Greta Hort.

The Two Foci of the Jewish Soul [28]

An address delivered before an institute held by the four German-language Missions to Jews, at Stuttgart in March, 1930. *Kampf um Israel,* pp. 50-67. Translated by G. Hort.

The Prejudices of Youth [41]

From a speech delivered in Prague in 1937. *Worte an die Jugend* (Berlin: Buecherei des Schocken Verlages, 1938), pp. 74-86. Translated by Olga Marx.

The Love of God and the Idea of Deity [53]

Keneset, 5703 (1943). Translated by I. M. Lask.

Imitatio Dei [66]

Written in 1926. *Kampf um Israel,* pp. 68-83. Translated by G. Hort.

In the Midst of History [78]

Written in the summer of 1933. *Die Stunde und die Erkenntnis* (Berlin: Schocken Verlag, 1936), pp. 27-34. Translated by O. Marx.

What Are We to Do About the Ten Commandments? [85]

Literarische Welt, 1929. Translated by O. Marx.

The Man of Today and the Jewish Bible [89]

From a series of lectures delivered in 1926. *Die Schrift und ihre Verdeutschung* (Berlin: Schocken Verlag, 1936), pp. 13-31. Translated by O. Marx.

Plato and Isaiah [103]

From an introductory lecture delivered at the Hebrew University in Jerusalem and published by the University in 1938. Schocken printed a German version in a limited edition in 1938. *Ha-Ruah veha-Metziut* (Tel Aviv, 1942), pp. 10-21. Translated by O. Marx.

False Prophets [113]

Ha-Ruah veha-Metziut, pp. 64-69. Translated by O. Marx.

Biblical Leadership [119]

A lecture delivered in Munich in 1928. *Kampf um Israel,* pp. 84-106. Translated by G. Hort.

Teaching and Deed [137]

Address delivered at the Lehrhaus in Frankfort on the Main in 1934. *Die Stunde und die Erkenntnis,* pp. 61-73. Translated by O. Marx.

Why We Should Study Jewish Sources [146]

From a Syllabus for the School for Jewish Youth in Berlin, 1932. *Kampf um Israel,* pp. 136-140. Translated by O. Marx.

On National Education [149]

Ha-Ruah veha-Metziut, pp. 88-105.

The Jew in the World [167]

An address delivered at the Lehrhaus in Frankfort on the Main in 1934. *Die Stunde und die Erkenntnis,* pp. 41-48. Translated by O. Marx.

The Power of the Spirit [173]

An address delivered at the Lehrhaus in Frankfort on the Main in 1934. *Die Stunde und die Erkenntnis,* pp. 74-87. Translated by O. Marx.

The Spirit of Israel and the World of Today [183]

Public lecture delivered in Tel Aviv in 1939. *Ha-Ruah veha-Metziut,* pp. 22-33. Translated by I. M. Lask. Some textual changes have been introduced by the author, based upon a public lecture on the same subject in London in 1946.

The Gods of the Nations and God [197]

Keneset, 5701 (1941). Translated by O. Marx.

Nationalism [214]

Address delivered during the Twelfth Zionist Congress, at Karlsbad, September 5, 1921. *Kampf um Israel,* pp. 225-242. Translated by O. Marx.

The Land and Its Possessors [227]

From an open letter to Gandhi, 1939. *The Bond* (Jerusalem, 1939), pp. 1-22.

"And If Not Now, When?" [234]

Address delivered at a convention of Jewish Youth representatives, in Antwerp, 1932. (The theme of the convention was "Israel and World Peace.") *Kampf um Israel,* pp. 452-460. Translated by O. Marx.

Hebrew Humanism [240]

Ha-Ruah veha-Metziut, pp. 51-63. Translated by O. Marx.

Israel and the Command of the Spirit [253]

Address delivered before The American Friends of Ihud in New York, April 30, 1958. Reprinted, with the kind permission of the editor, from *Congress Weekly,* September 8, 1958. Translated by Maurice Friedman.

Israel's Mission and Zion [258]

Address delivered at the Jerusalem Ideological Conference in August 1957. Reprinted by permission of the Jewish Agency from *Forum,* Volume IV.